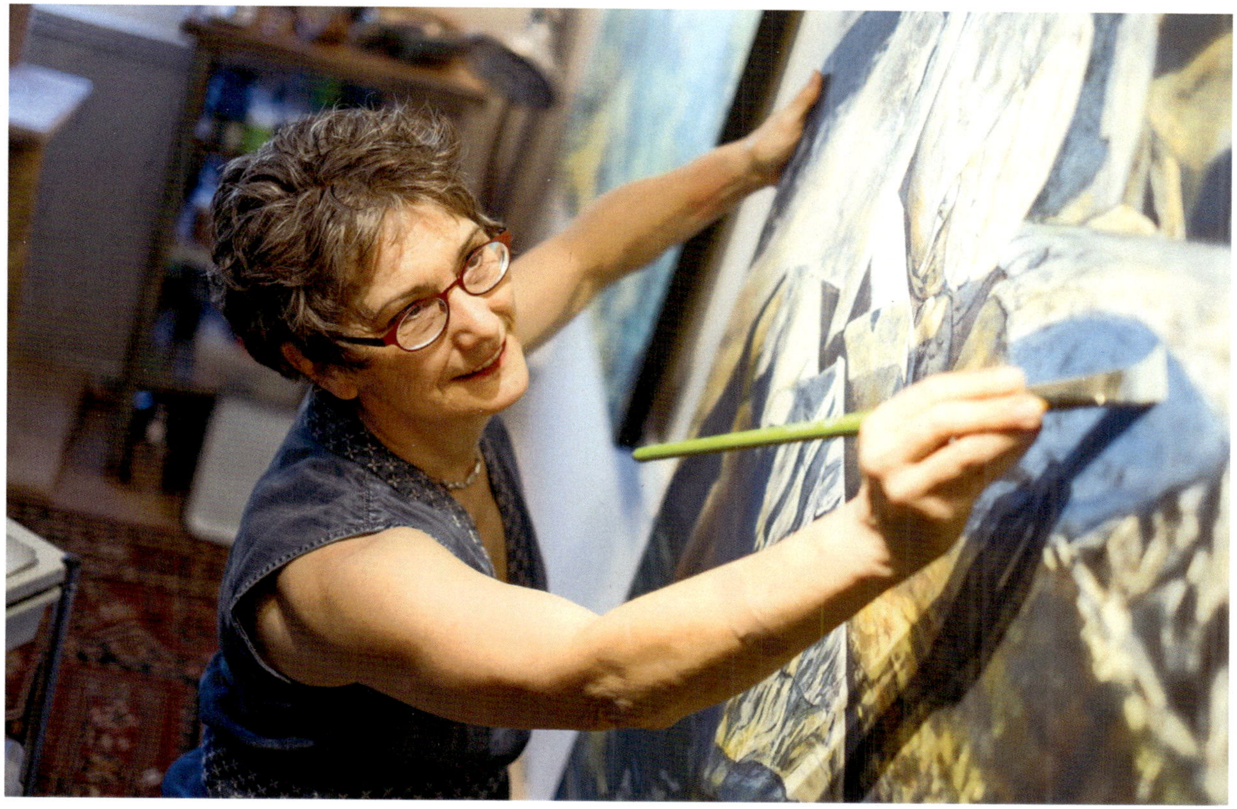

photo credit: Annabelle Schossig

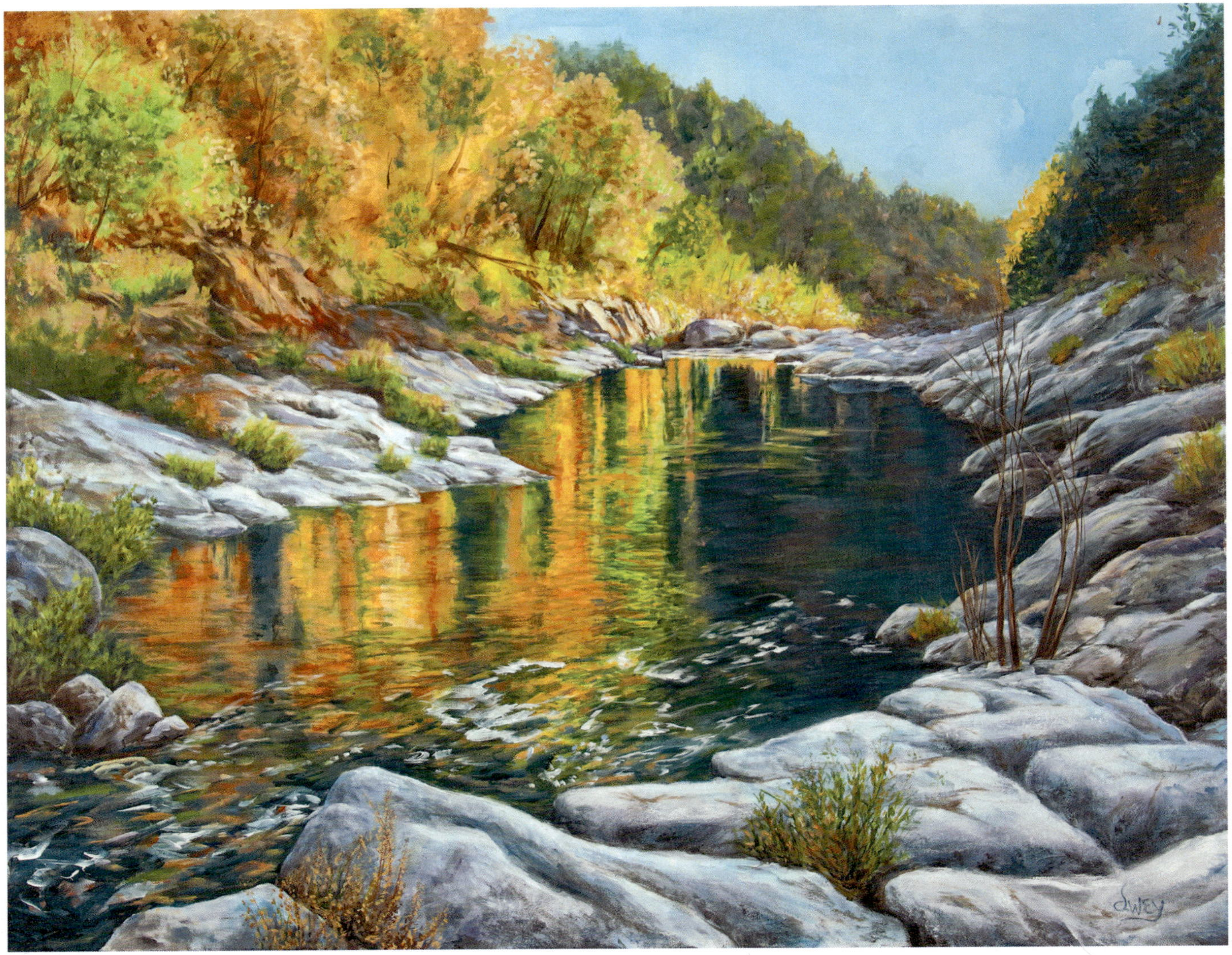

The River's Song III, #016, 48″ x 60″, acrylic on canvas, private collection

Denise Wey
A Retrospective

Twenty-Two Years of Painting the Yuba River

foreword by Iven Lourie

Denise Wey: A Retrospective
First Edition, First Printing 2020
Hardcover, Limited Edition ISBN: 978-1-945765-14-8
Trade Paperback ISBN: 978-1-945765-13-1
Printed in the U.S.A.

Grayscale photo of the artist by Ruth Chase

Cover design and interior layout by Gailyn Porter

Published by:
Artemis Books
P.O. Box 1108
Penn Valley, CA 95946
phone: (530) 277-5380
email: artemisbooks@gmail.com

DEDICATION

I feel that whatever I've managed to accomplish as a painter, it's really taken the village to produce this artist. I've received so much help in so many ways that I don't even dare to name them, lest I forget even one! From the encouragement and appreciation of my patrons, the troubleshooting of the final work with other artists, the numerous times friends have picked me up and dusted me off after I'd completely given up and wished to give away all of my brushes and also, lastly all of the help in all forms that my friends give to me unselfishly to see me succeed. This universe is full of angels!

So, here on these pages is the accomplishment of an artist who found her muse in the River of Life.

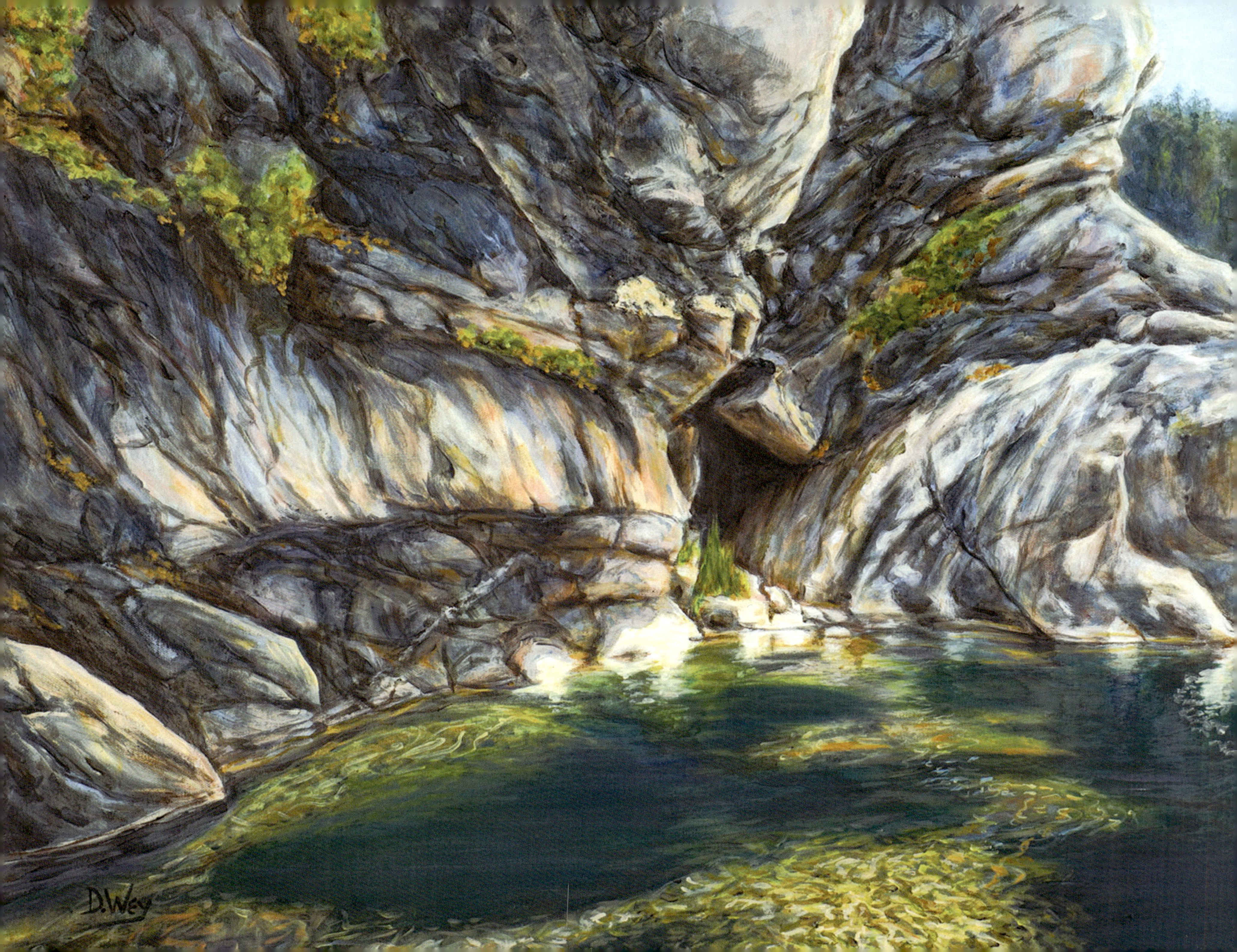
D.Wey

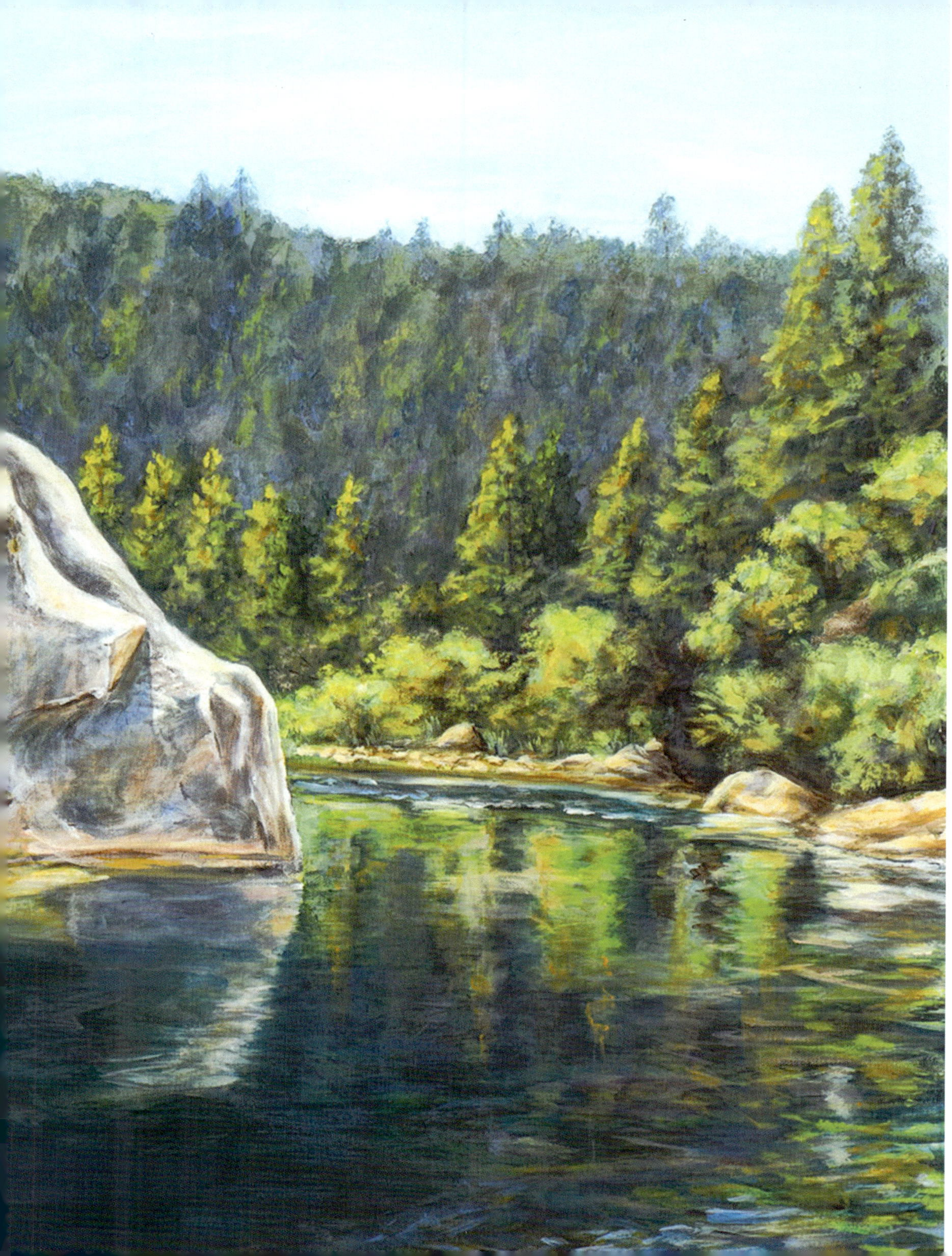

Contents

Shimmering Pool, #039
24″ x 48″
acrylic on canvas
private collection

FOREWORD by IVEN LOURIE

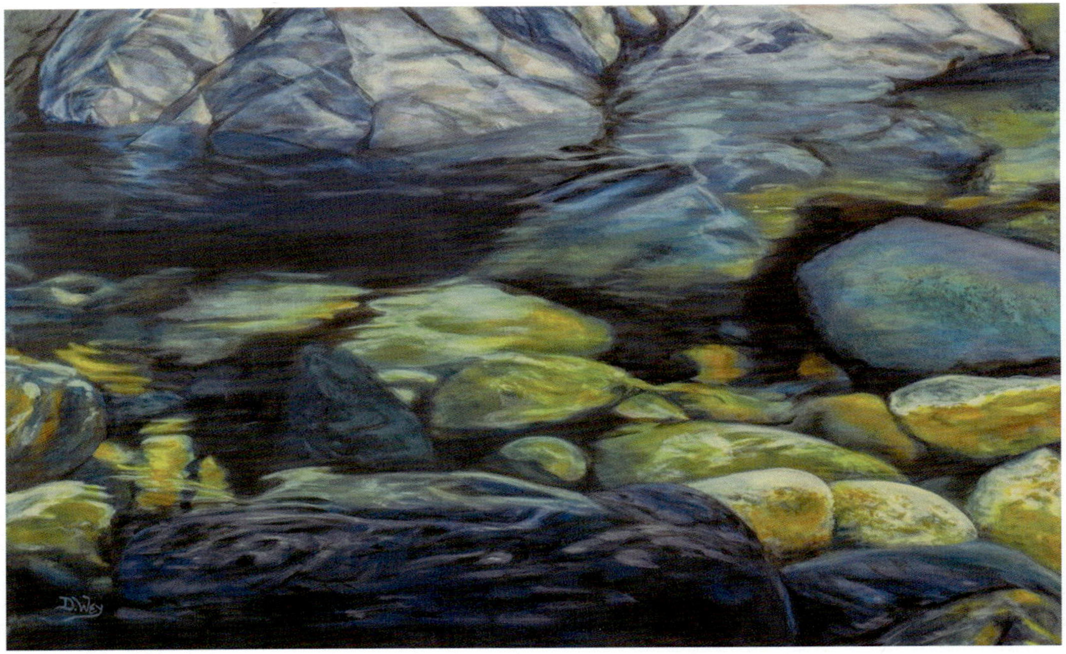

Yuba Love - Morning Whispers on the Yuba, #099
30″ x 48″ acrylic on canvas

"We live in a world of unreality and dreams. To give up our imaginary position as the center, to renounce it, not only intellectually but in the imaginative part of our soul, that means to awaken to what is real and eternal, to see the true light and hear the true silence. A transformation then takes place at the very roots of our sensibility, in our immediate reception of sense impressions and psychological impressions."
—Simone Weil, *Waiting for God*

Reading what Denise Wey has written in her "retrospective" summary of her painting practice immediately reminded me of the 20th-century philosopher and mystic, Simone Weil. "My work may look like art and painting rivers. But my soul's purpose is to grow and evolve through this," Denise writes. In this small but almost overpoweringly-beautiful book, she makes the admirable choice of tracking her development. She shares some of her lows and highs, her doldrums and her breakthroughs as a painter. The juxtaposition of Denise's paintings with the journal poems of Lil McGill, a fellow painter and adventurer, is also a gift to the reader.

I have had the privilege and the pleasure of seeing Denise develop this soaring landscape painting style drawn from the inspiration that she writes of here to paint the Yuba River both from memory and from photos.

You can trace with Denise her development from the emotional or dramatic versions of the landscape (after the ecstatic Bierstadt or the technical genius Monet, for example) to a more layered, nuanced—but also more vibrant and living portrayal of the natural world. I recall walking into Denise's studio one day and seeing one of the paintings in Chapter Two or Three, perhaps "Rocky Playground" or "River Music." I was excited, and I told Denise that this painting that was more exploratory, even analytic, reminded me of the lifelong experiments of Cezanne—no longer the idealized landscape or the exaggerated one, but the substantial, muscular, overflowing vision of the river and the land. I felt changed somehow to be seeing the river through her eyes and through her engagement with it at such a deep level.

Finally, the size of these new paintings is so effective. By working larger and larger canvases, Denise has broken ground on almost mural-scale paintings of the Yuba River, diptyches, multi-paneled works that will fill a wall. These do not resemble Bierstadts or fantasies like Maxwell Parrish's decorative wall paintings. These canvases are vibrant, subtle, colorful, and enlivening to the viewer. To me, Denise is breaking into the territory of Georgia O'Keefe and of Monet's very late, abstract work on the waterlilies: he created murals for curving walls so that they filled a room and surrounded the viewer, now at the Orangerie in Paris. His theory was that Parisian workers needed relief after their shifts, so they could walk through a Monet room that would soothe their eyes and souls, and support their mental health as working people. That may have been something of a reach—but the paintings are on display now for anyone and everyone to enjoy the immersive experience.

I recommend Denise Wey's painting to you on a similar, ambitious hypothesis: the work has a healing and invigorating quality. It reaches us through the eyes, but just as her practice of painting has been a lifelong soul-making journey for Denise, so then the quality of the work calls to us and calls to our larger selves, our better selves, perhaps to our drowsing souls that can use new vistas and windows to look through into greater worlds—starting with this very world of ours with its mountains and rivers. Congratulations, Denise! Please keep on painting....

Iven Lourie, September, 2020

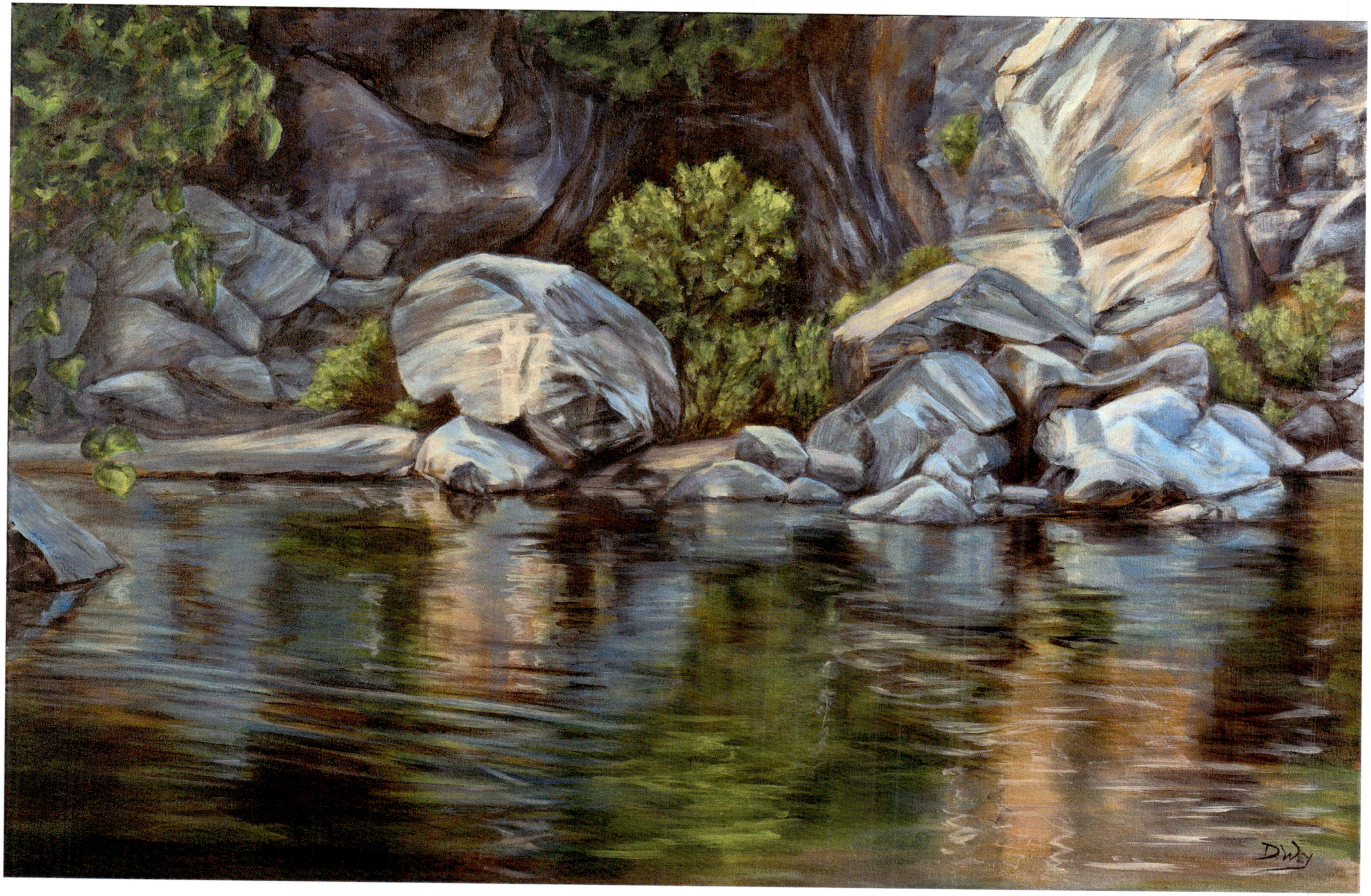

Yuba Moment, #090, 24″ x 36″, acrylic on canvas, private collection

INTRODUCTION

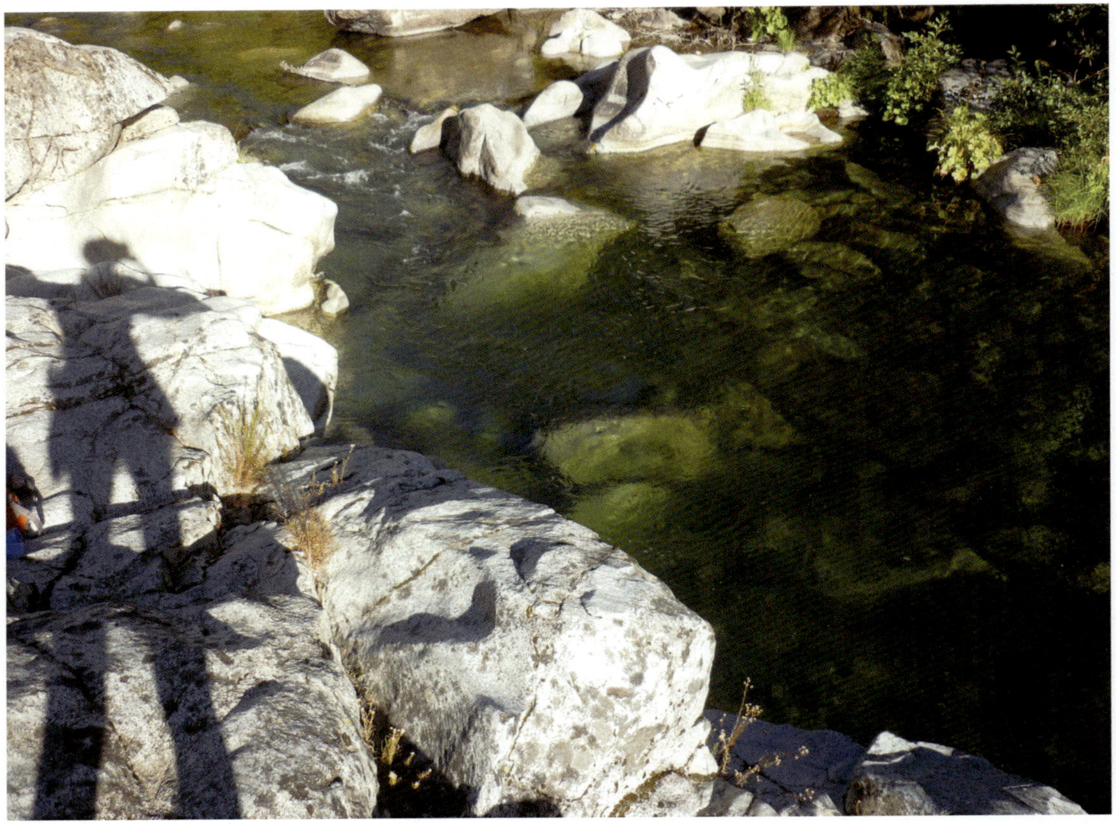

self portrait

Painting is my work—my real work. This book is about the journey I've been on these past two decades as a painter. I chose the format of a Retrospective to do so, as it appeals to my sense of order in the Universe.

A good friend once remarked, "Everyone has a book in them that is worth writing, even if it touches only one person in the world!" This statement motivated me but, not being a crafter of words, I could scarcely believe this was true for myself, even though the idea was compelling.

Now I understand his comment to mean that every life has a story to tell. Years passed; I ruminated. I never really thought I'd get past just the idea of a book.

At the beginning of 2020, after my most recent river painting was photographed, the printer's proof came back to me, numbered 100. I looked down at that number and felt pure joy!

Then the idea took shape; this would be a book about the 20-plus years of my journey of painting the Yuba River. It would be simple with lots of pictures, not too much to read and definitely not a book about my life so much as about my work as an artist.

My practical nature provided the momentum to manifest the idea which was that having a good many of those 100 paintings gathered in one place made sense, if only just for the sake of posterity.

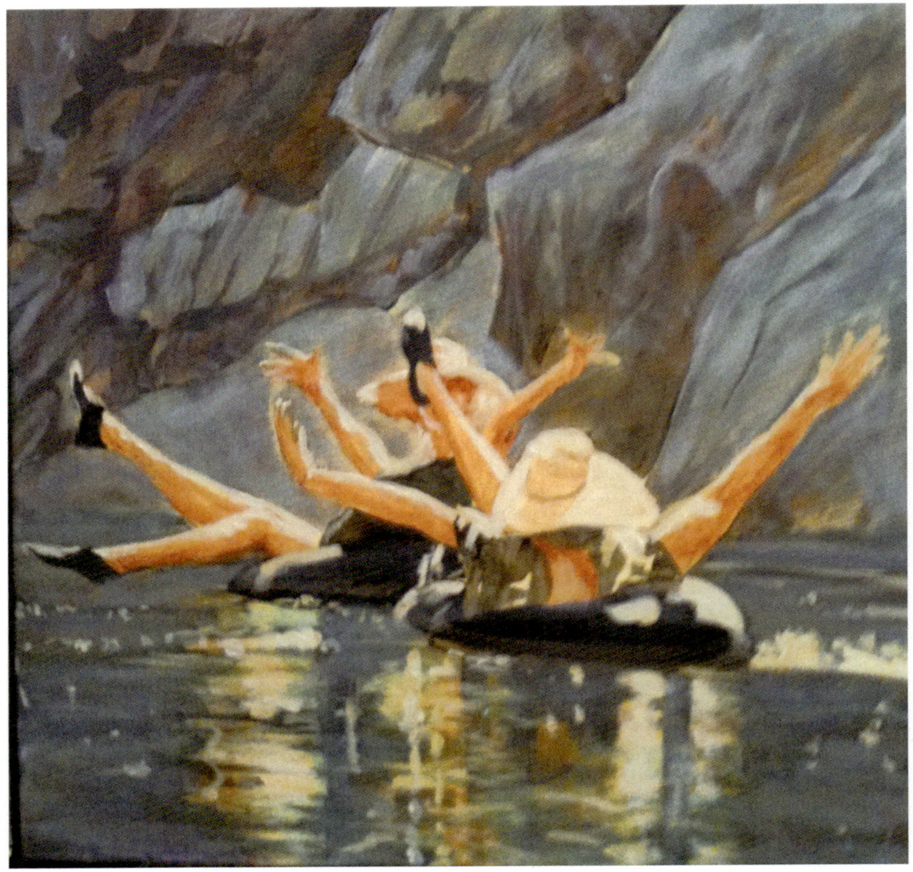

TUBING DELIGHT

on the Yuba River

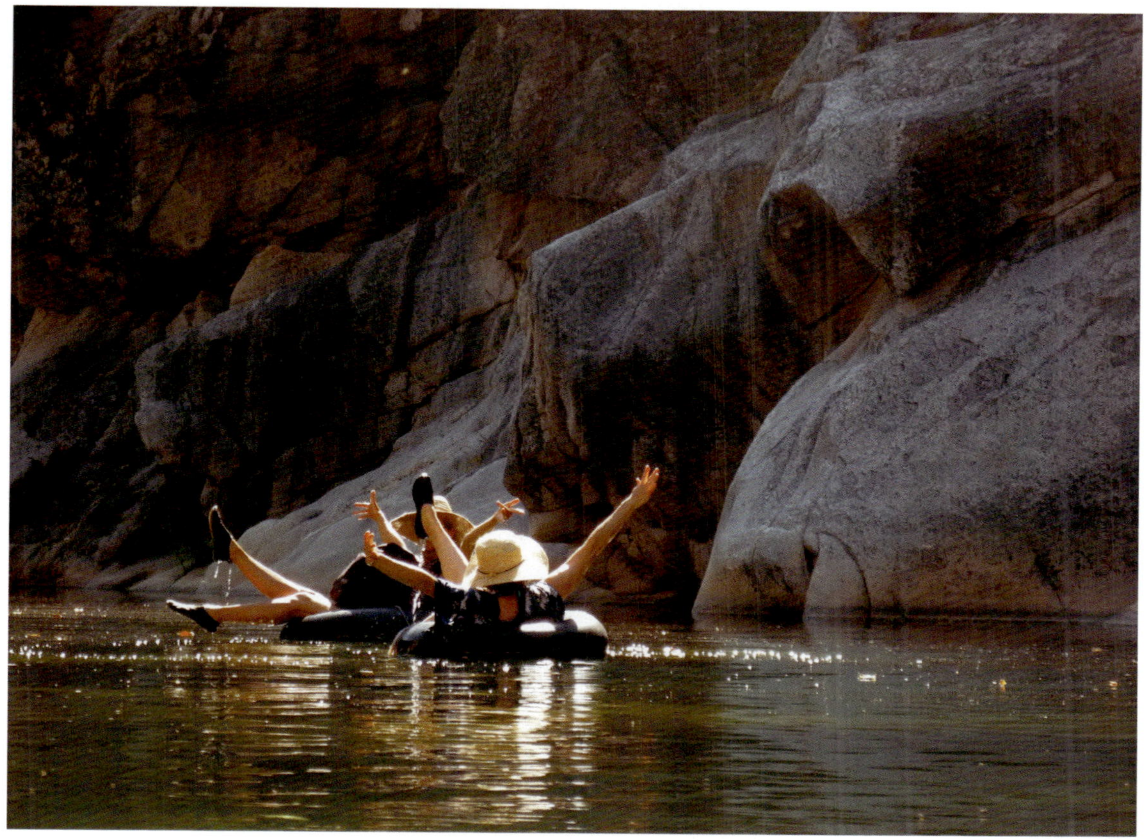

Chapter One: 1997 - 2006

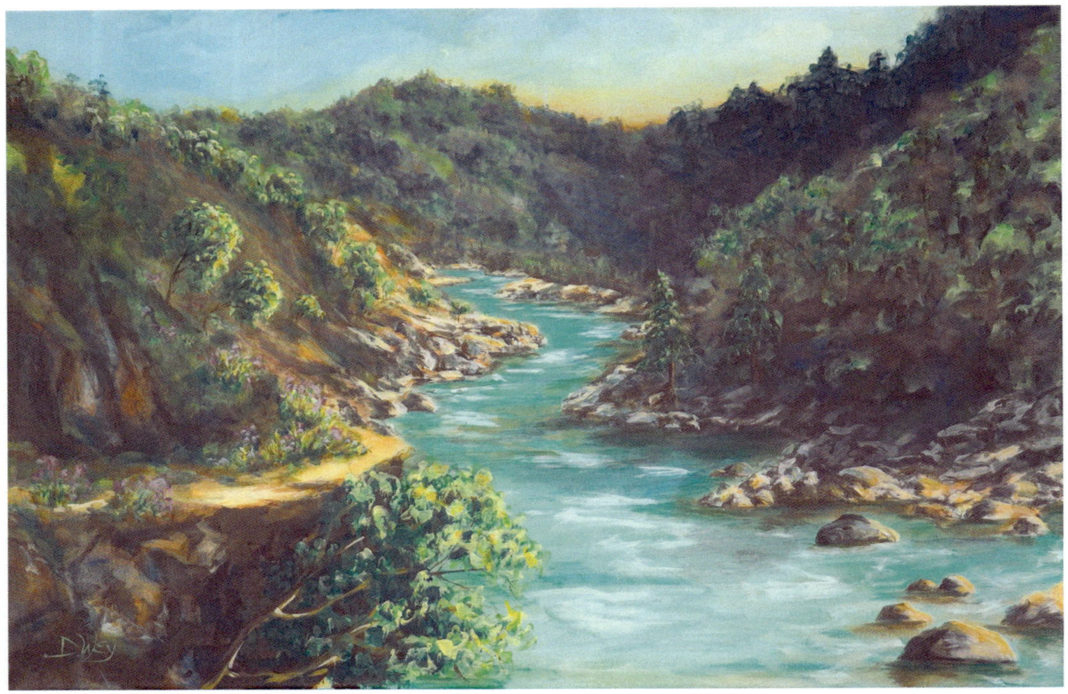

Wild Soul, Buttermilk Trail #003, 24" x 36"
acrylic on canvas, private collection

Morning River

we met early and drove
out to the 49 bridge,
the river quiet empty
before the weekend
started, soaked in the
water and sun rock
meditation, swallows
weaving a flight
pattern above us,
swooping high and
low then back to their
nests on the bridge,
and after our sweet
time together we wade
back to shore and
climb up the steep
stairs, I make it back
home to the studio
and get right to work

—Lil McGill

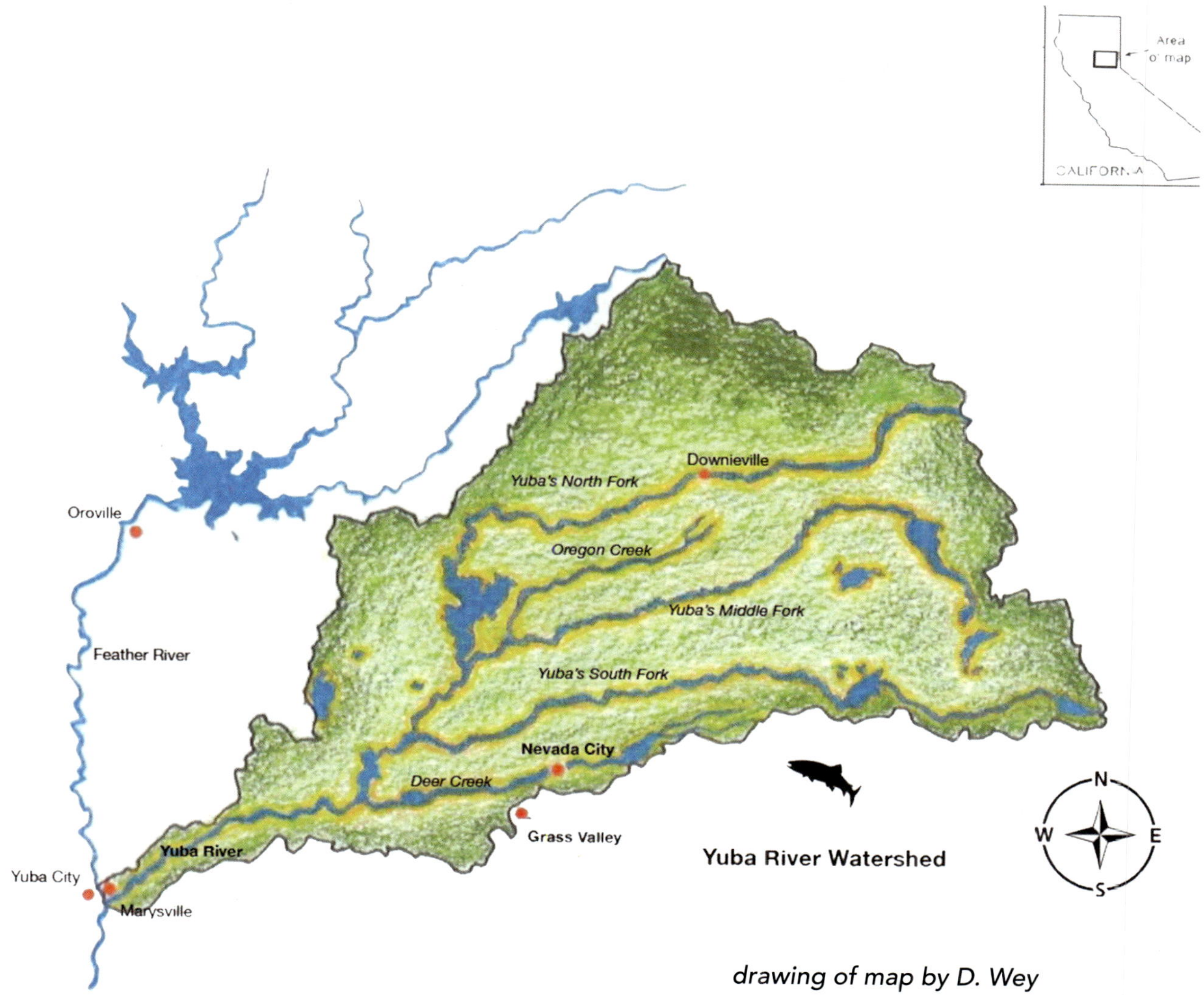

drawing of map by D. Wey

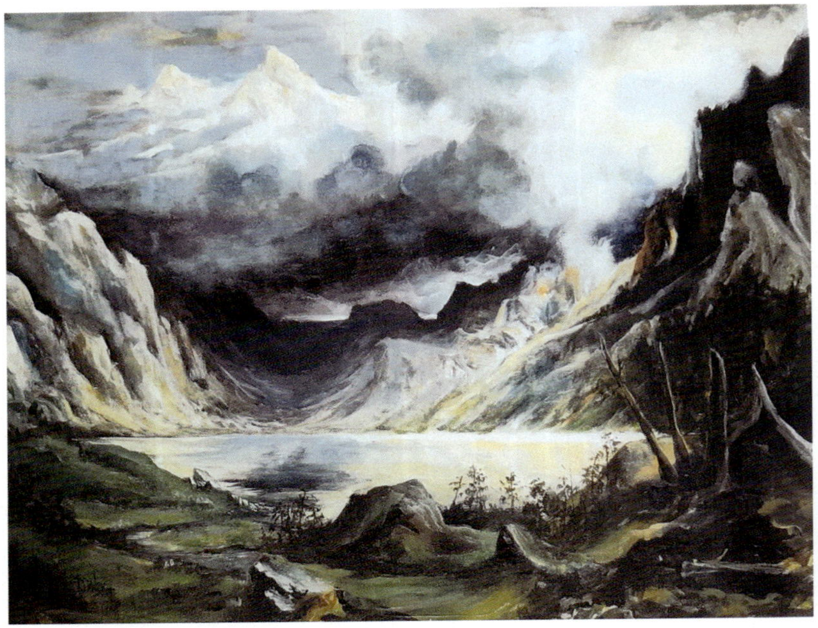

Denise Wey after Albert Bierstadt
8″ x 10″
acrylic on canvas

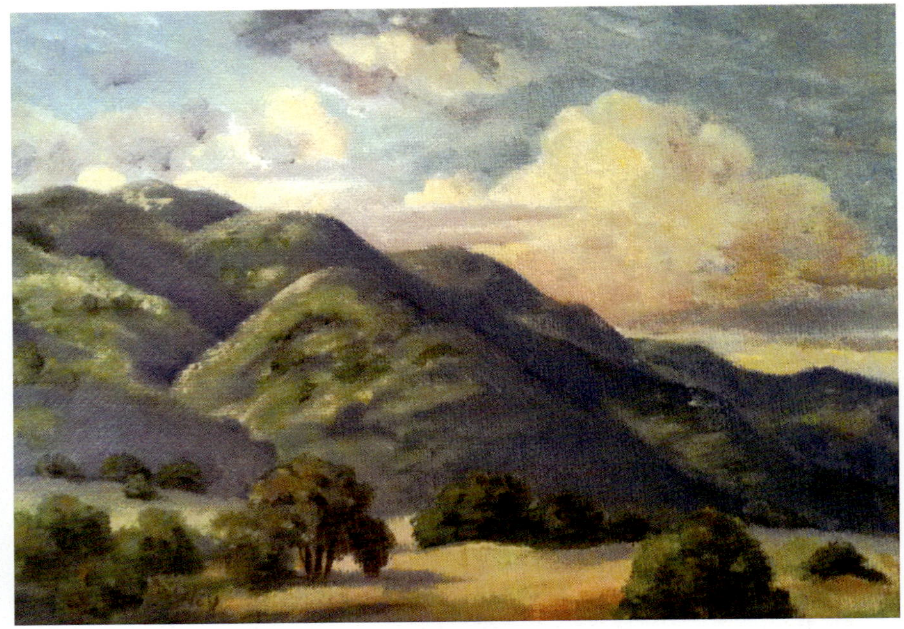

California Hills
8″ x 10″
acrylic on canvas

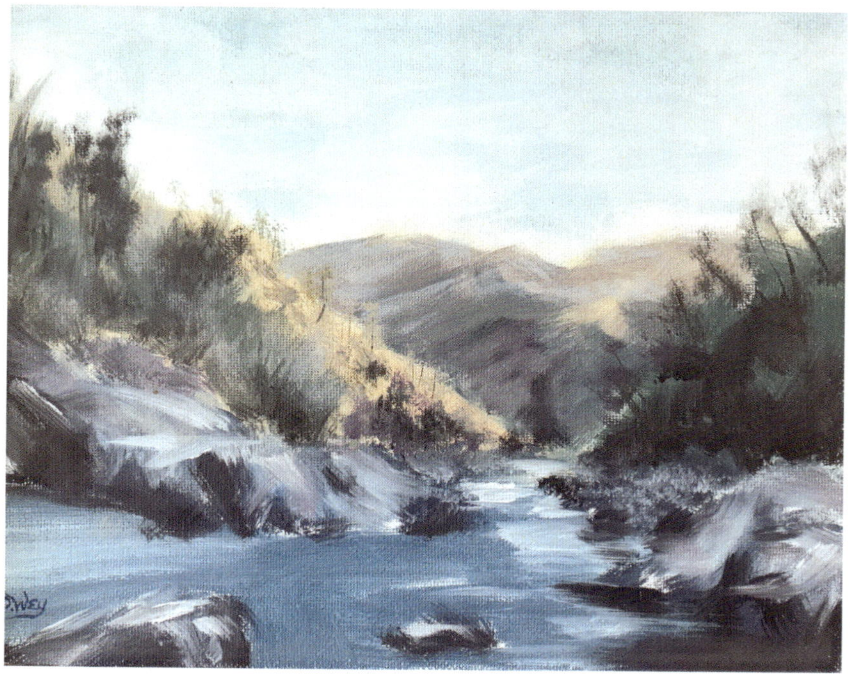

Yuba River Study, 8″ x 10″
acrylic on canvas, artist's collection

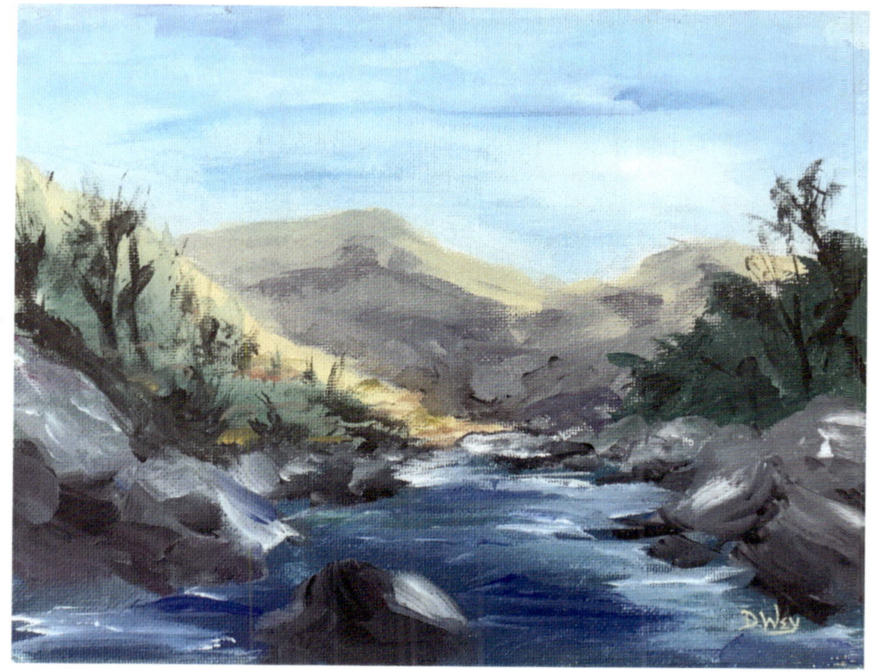

Yuba River Study II, 8″ x 10″
acrylic on canvas, artist's collection

In the springtime of 1997, my besties took me to the Yuba River for a hike…it was my first glimpse of this magnificent watershed and I fell instantly in love. Sometime later in my studio with photos of that day, two small river paintings poured onto the canvas!

From the lush province of British Columbia, I landed in the heart of an arts community in the Sierra Foothills of Northern California, circa 1990. This area is home to the majestic Yuba River, with its three forks flowing through and around it. This river is a local sanctuary...beautiful beyond description!

In the springtime of 1997, friends took me to the river for a hike...it was my first glimpse of this beautiful watershed and the heart connection was instantaneous. Sometime later in my studio with photos of that day, two small river paintings poured onto the canvas!

The grip and pull of a certain destiny flashed in that moment and I felt that I had a mission to paint the Yuba.

Being a creative as long as I could remember, I had explored many mediums: jewelry making, screen printing, working with clay, watercolors and of course drawing! But once painting in acrylics revealed itself to me, the desire for anything else fell away.

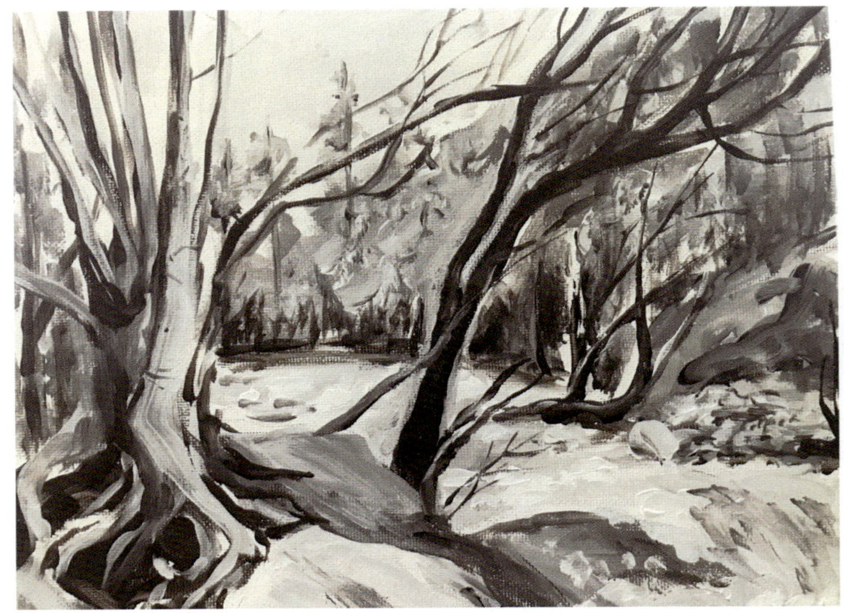

value study for *Winter Yuba*

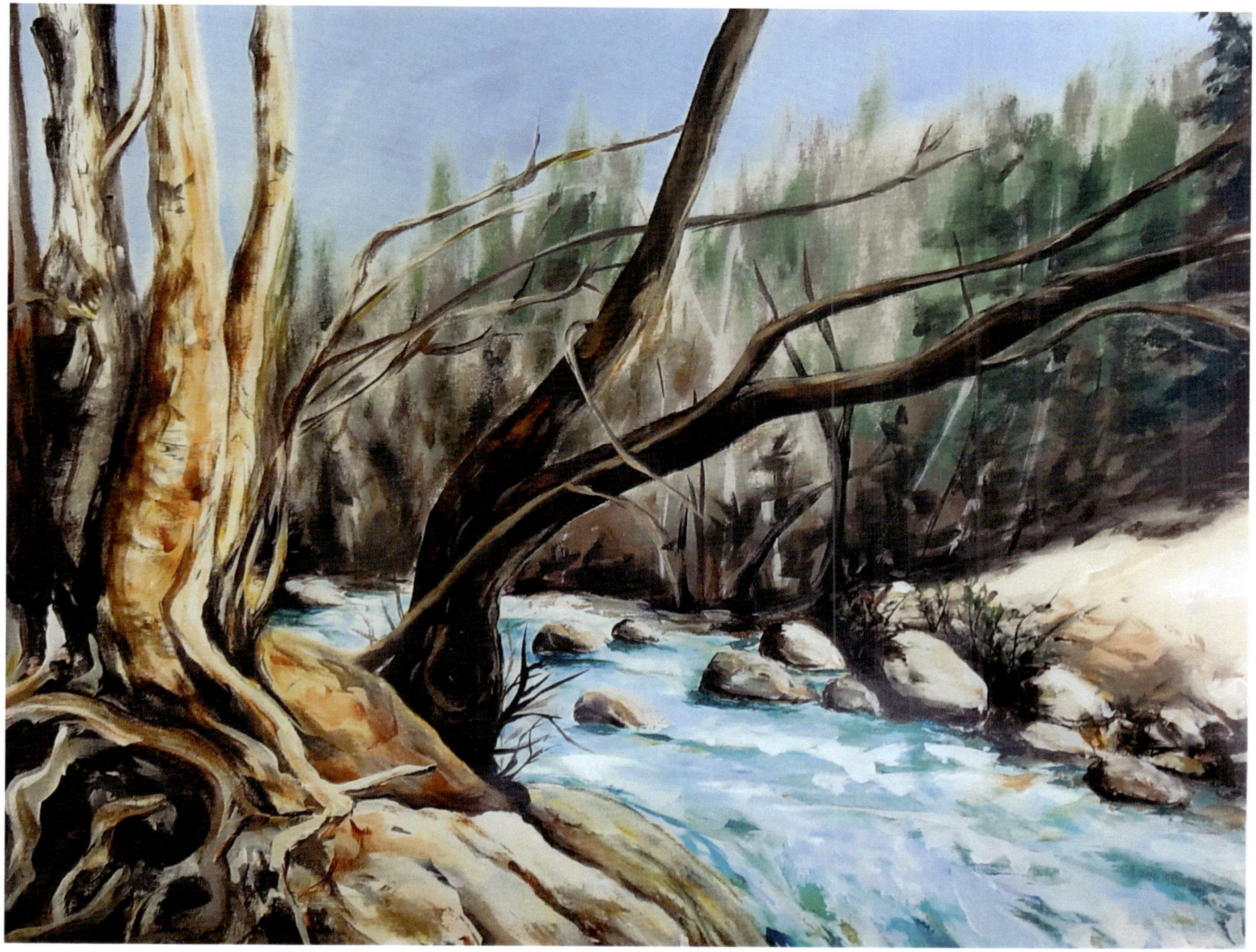

Winter Yuba, 9″ x 12″, acrylic on canvas

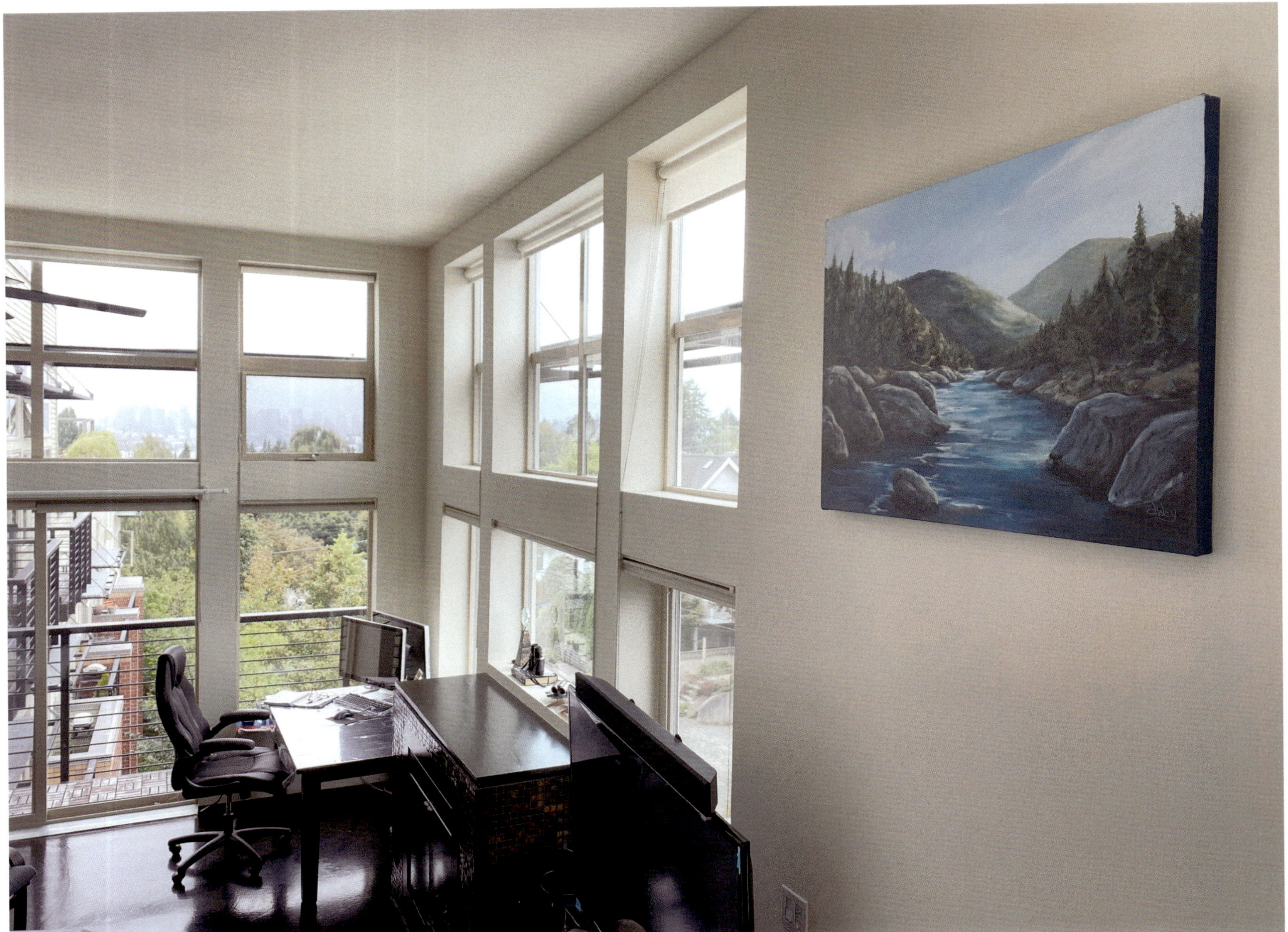

in situ

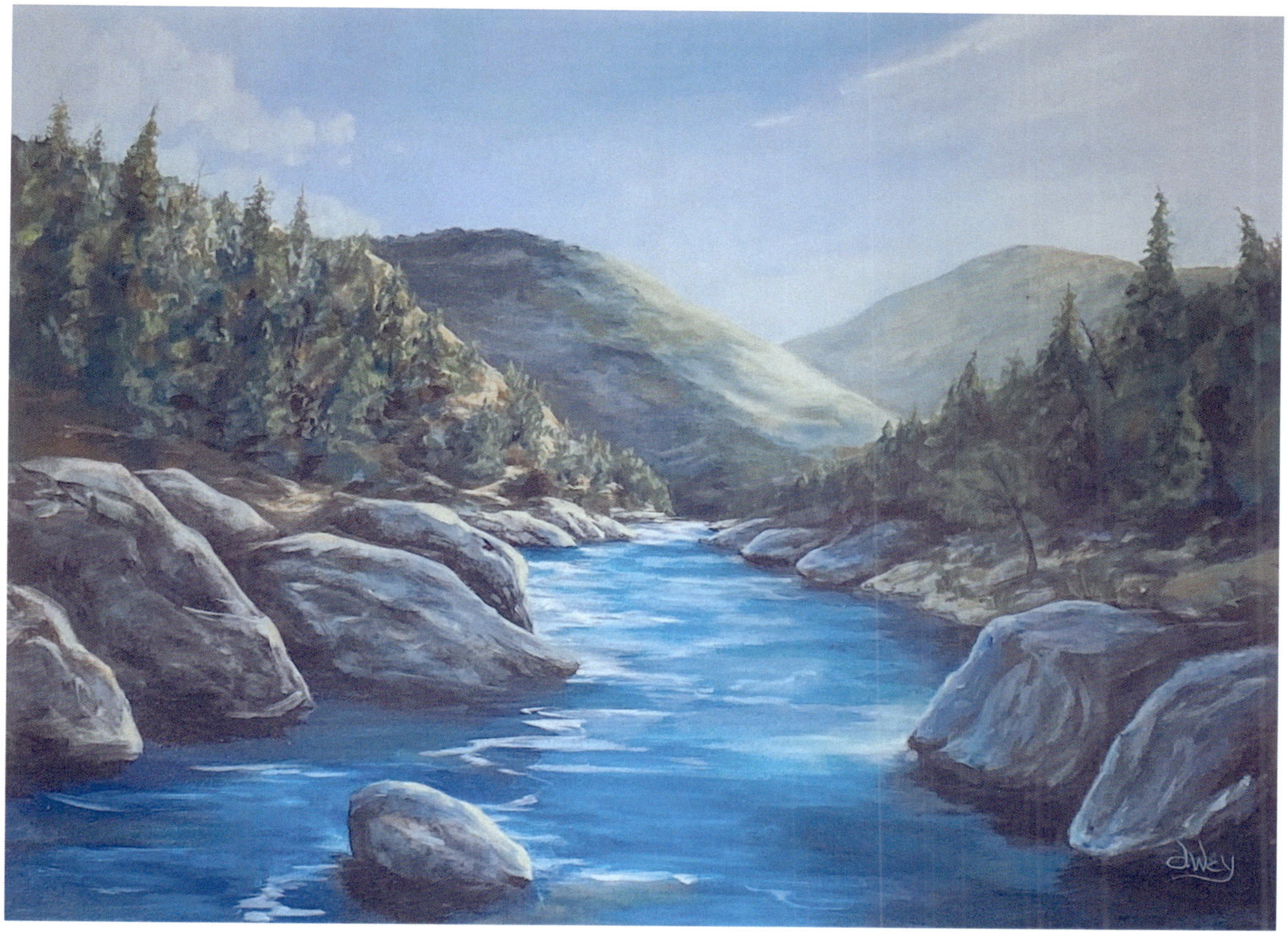

Yuba River, 24″ x 36″, acrylic on canvas, private collection

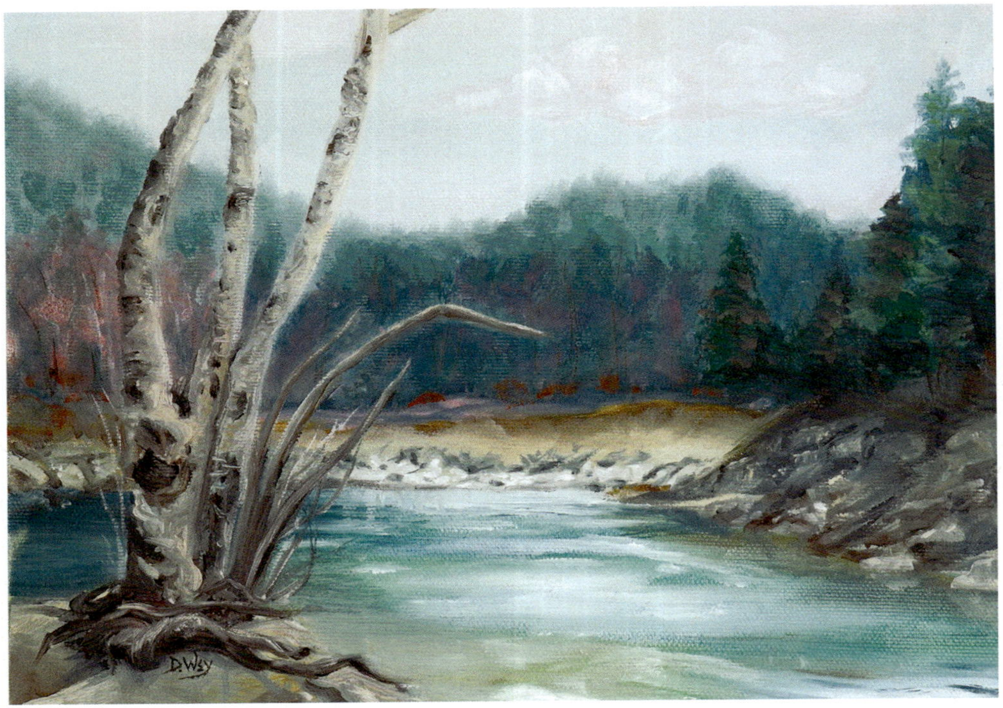

South Yuba, Early Spring, #008**,** 9" x 12", acrylic on canvas

The first decade of painting was all about learning to handle the medium: the paints, colors, lights and shadows…trees, sky and river water. I painted fairly small and my work was tight…I was a detail person. Thanks to kindred art and river-lovers, who bought my early work and commissioned paintings of the river from me, I was encouraged to keep on.

I really wished to paint like my favorite painter Monet, whose works I would study at the museums. I was always good at copying from sight so I felt I could attain this goal.

Concentrating on Monet's style, I would begin with my sky and then lay in the trees, blending the sky in with the tree tops, like he did. Feeling encouraged that I'd caught on I'd continue down through the painting, only to lose Monet and have it turn into a Denise Wey. Every single time!

Coming to this understanding that I could only paint like myself no matter how hard I tried, was my first breakthrough…I continued to press on with my mission of painting the Yuba River… but now, only like Denise Wey.

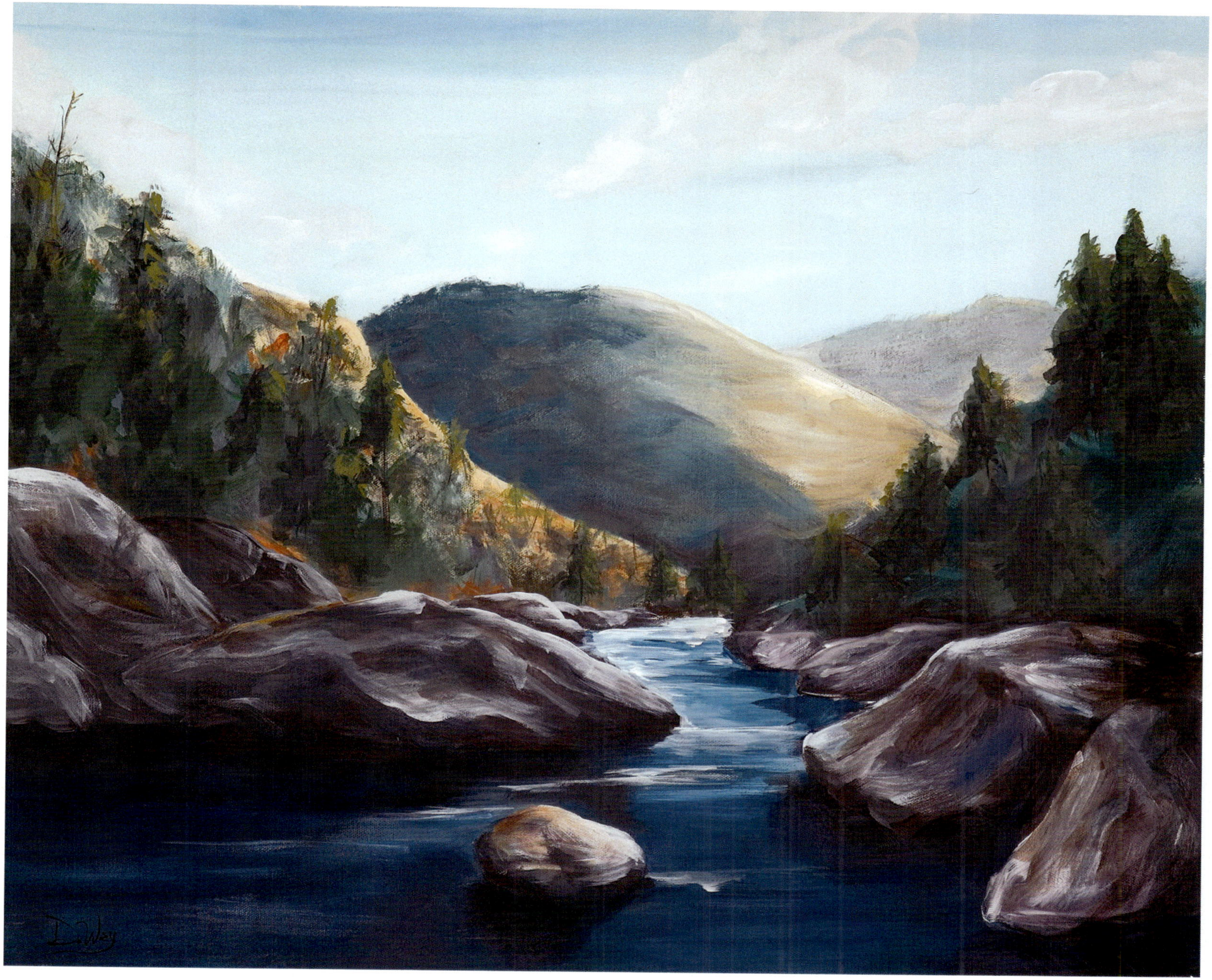

Ancient Whispers, #004, 20" x 24", acrylic or canvas

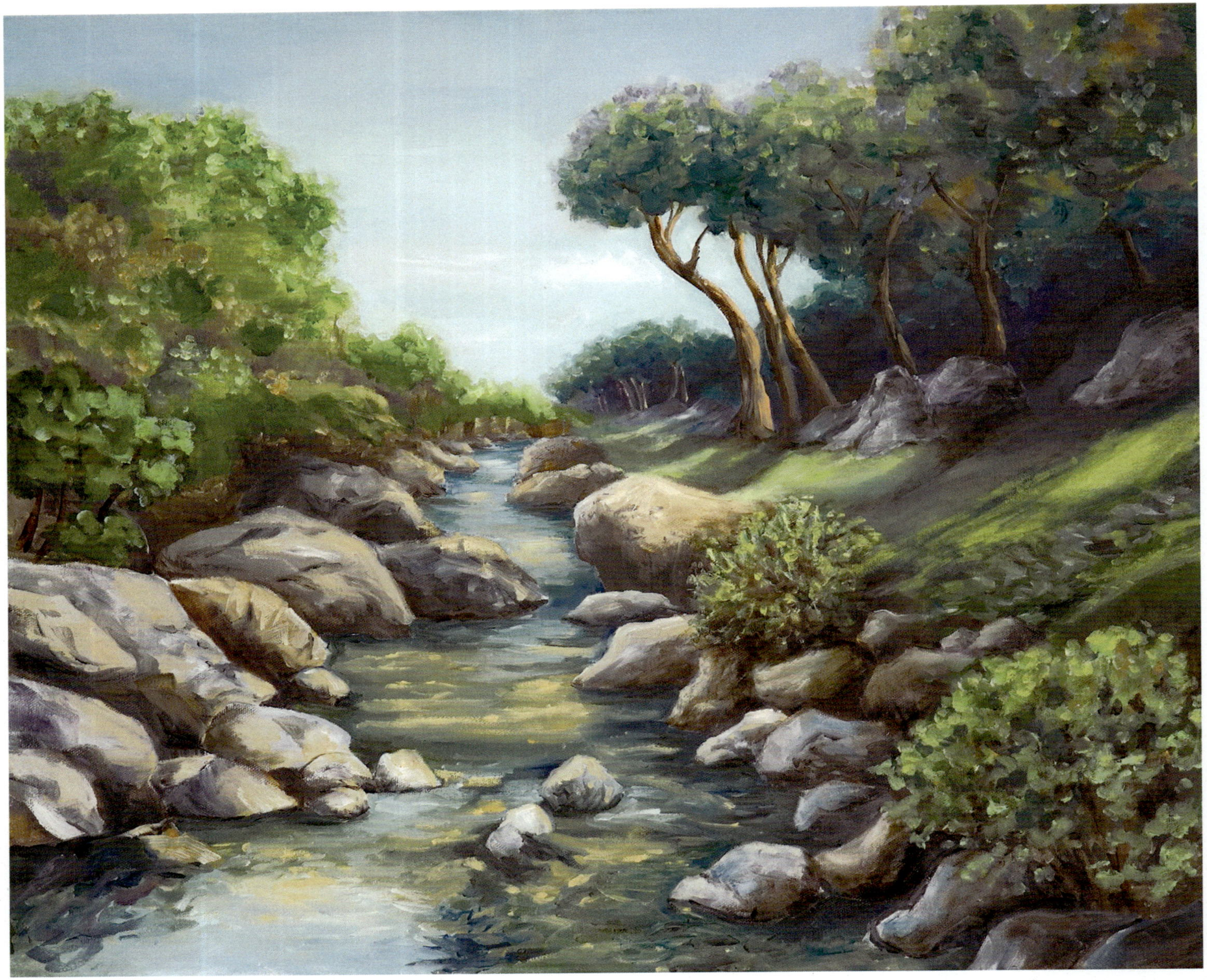

"River Dreams" was one of my Painting-like-Monet attempts! Note how the trees-into-sky is rendered in similar style to how Monet did his. This also came from my imagination.

River Dreams, #005, 20" x 24", oil on canvas

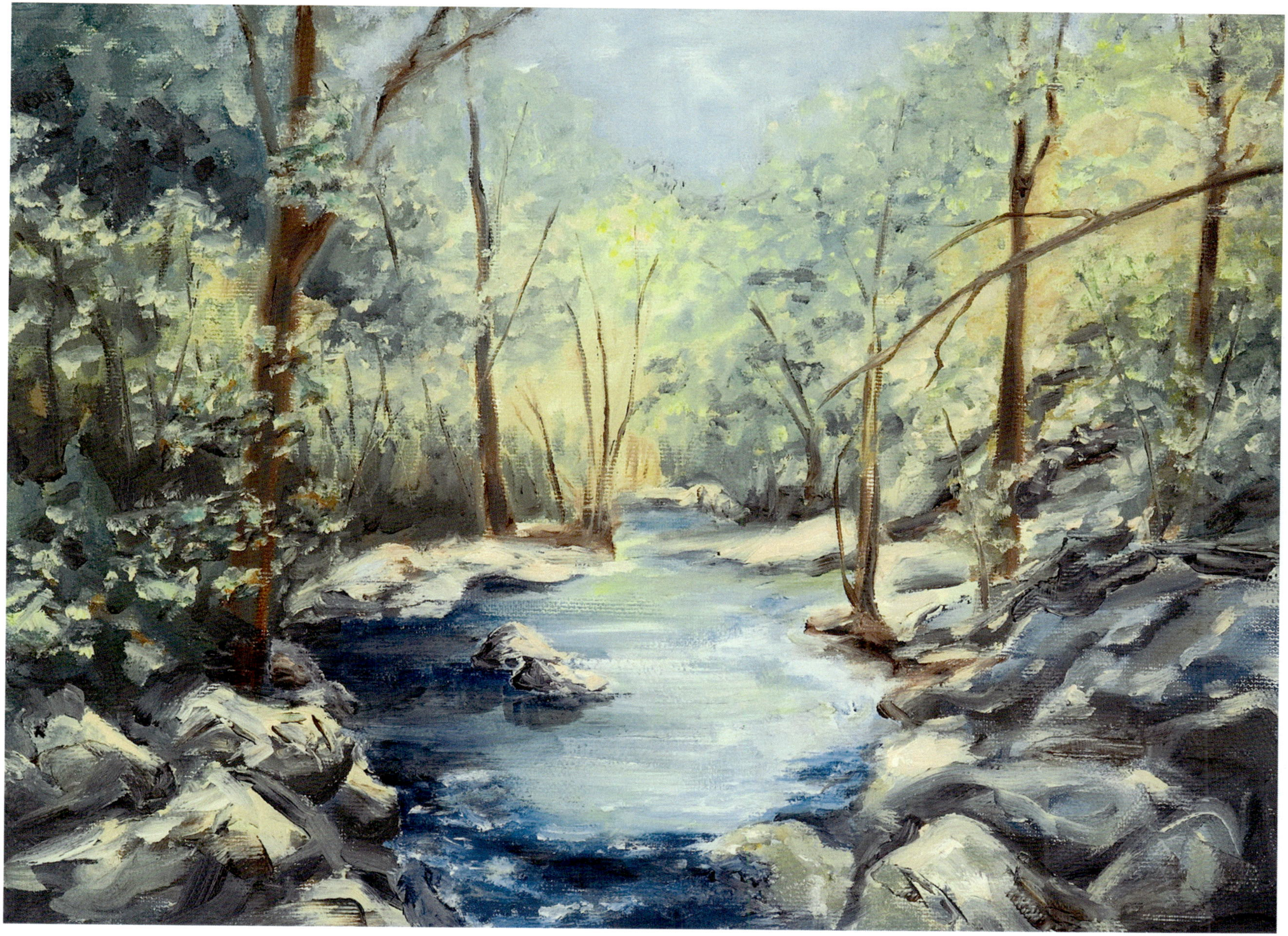

Tranquil Pool, #001, 9″ x12″, acrylic on canvas, private collection

This river painting came from my imagination one day.

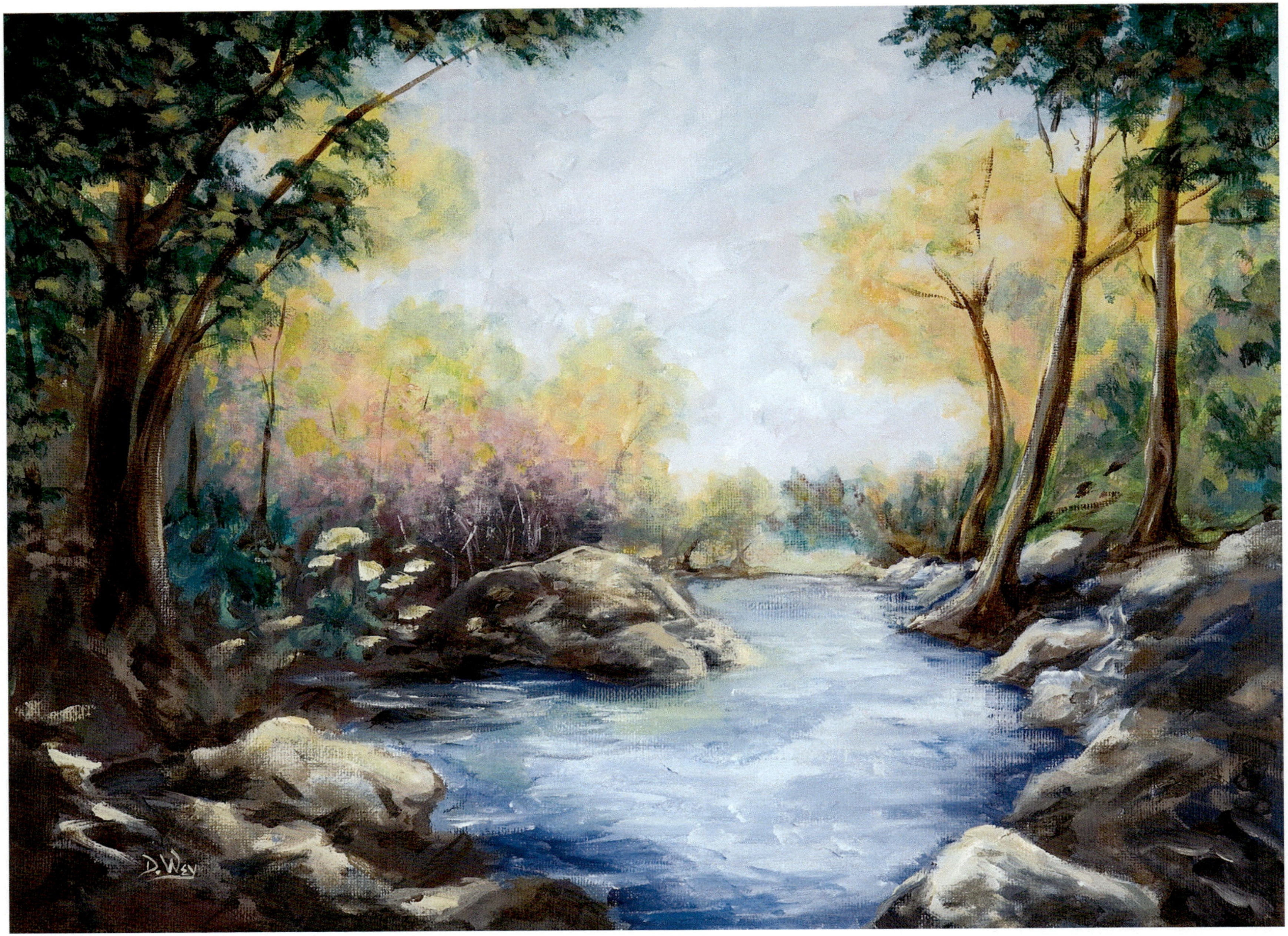

Deep Within The Light, #006, 12″ x 16″acrylic on canvas.

In the early days, I was still going for impressionism.

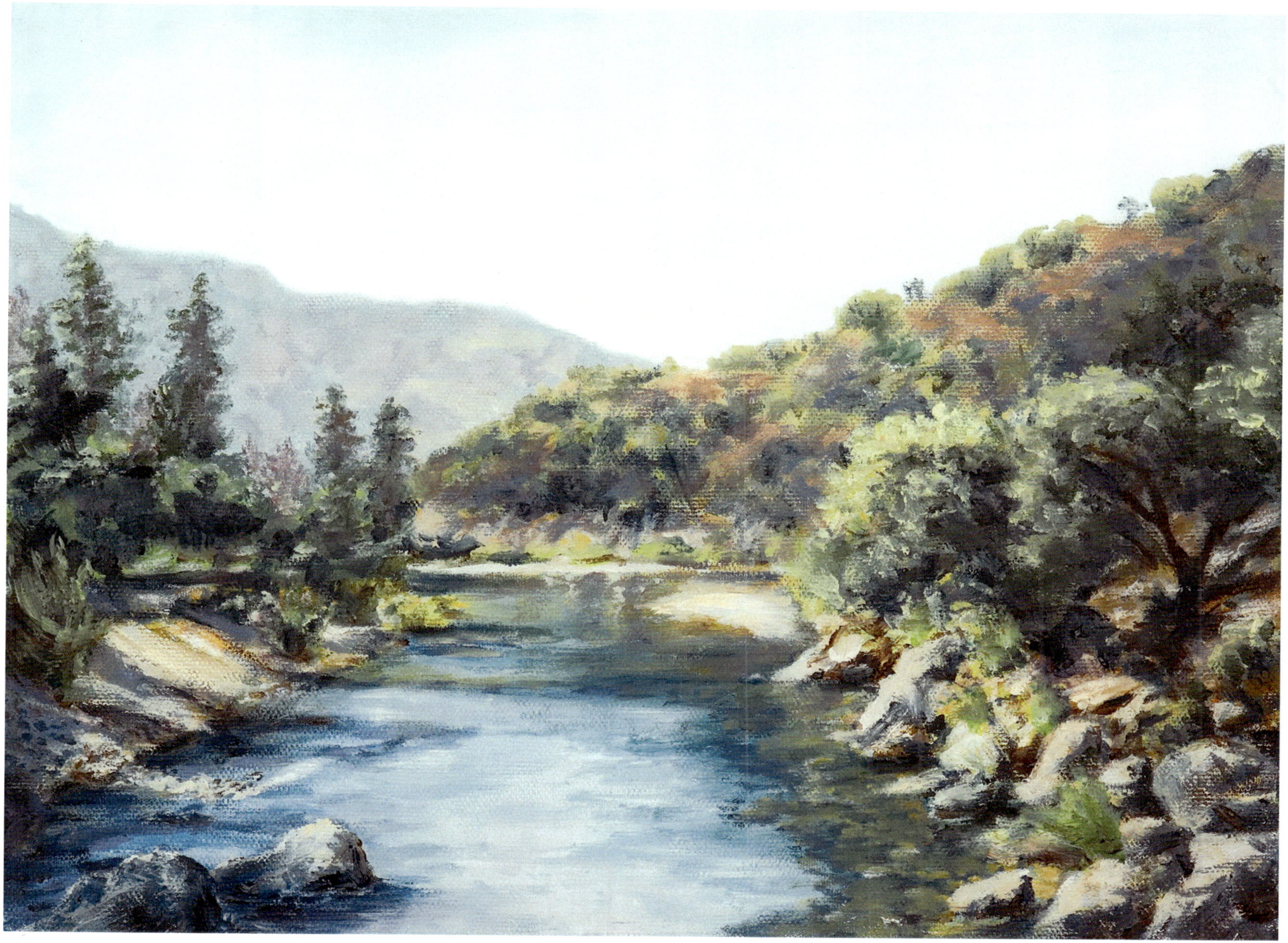

Peace of the Yuba, #002, 9″ x12″ acrylic on canvas, private collection

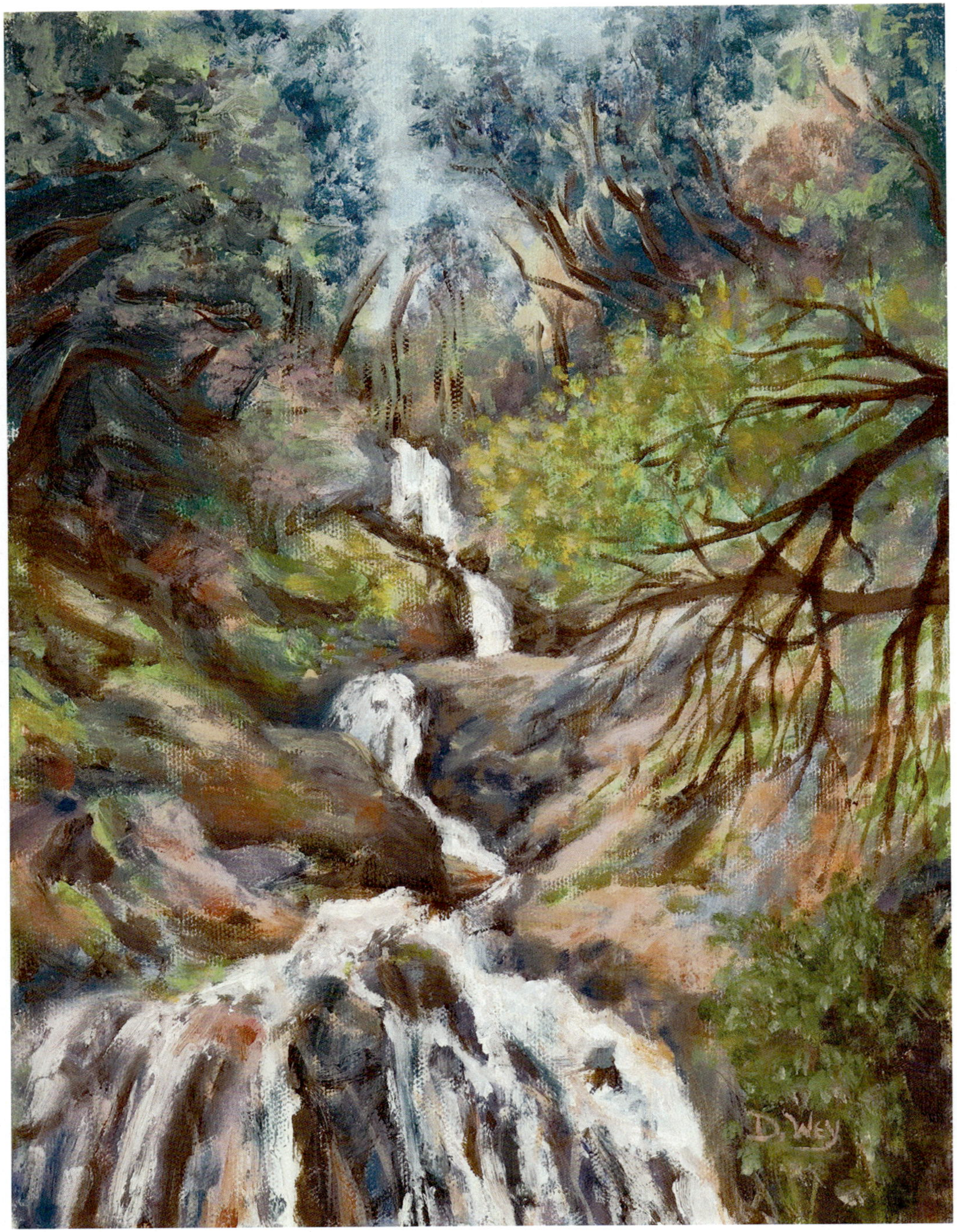

Sacred Water, Sacred Earth, #009
12″ x 9″
acrylic on Canvas

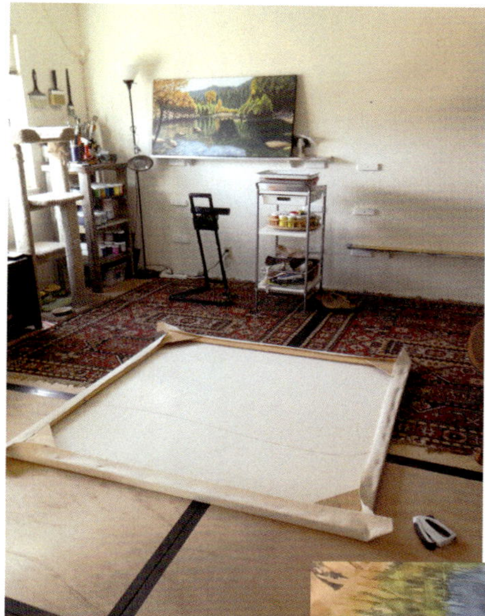

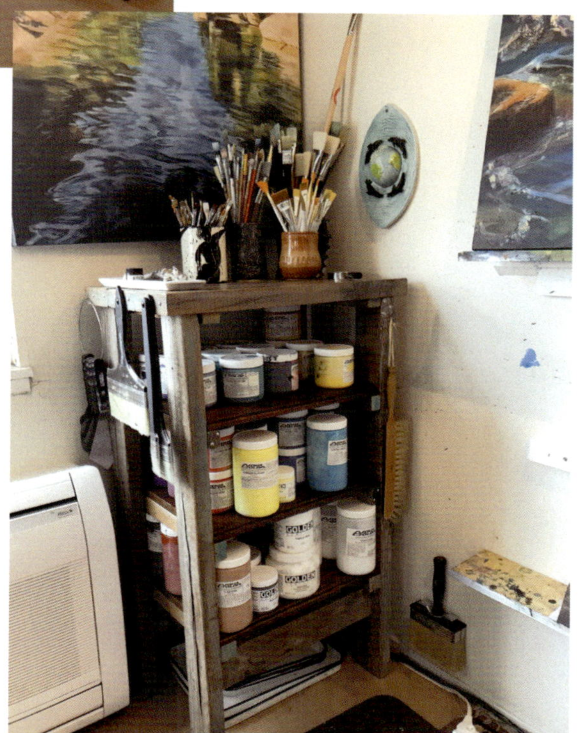

current paint studio

studio assistant for artist, E.J. Gold 1990s

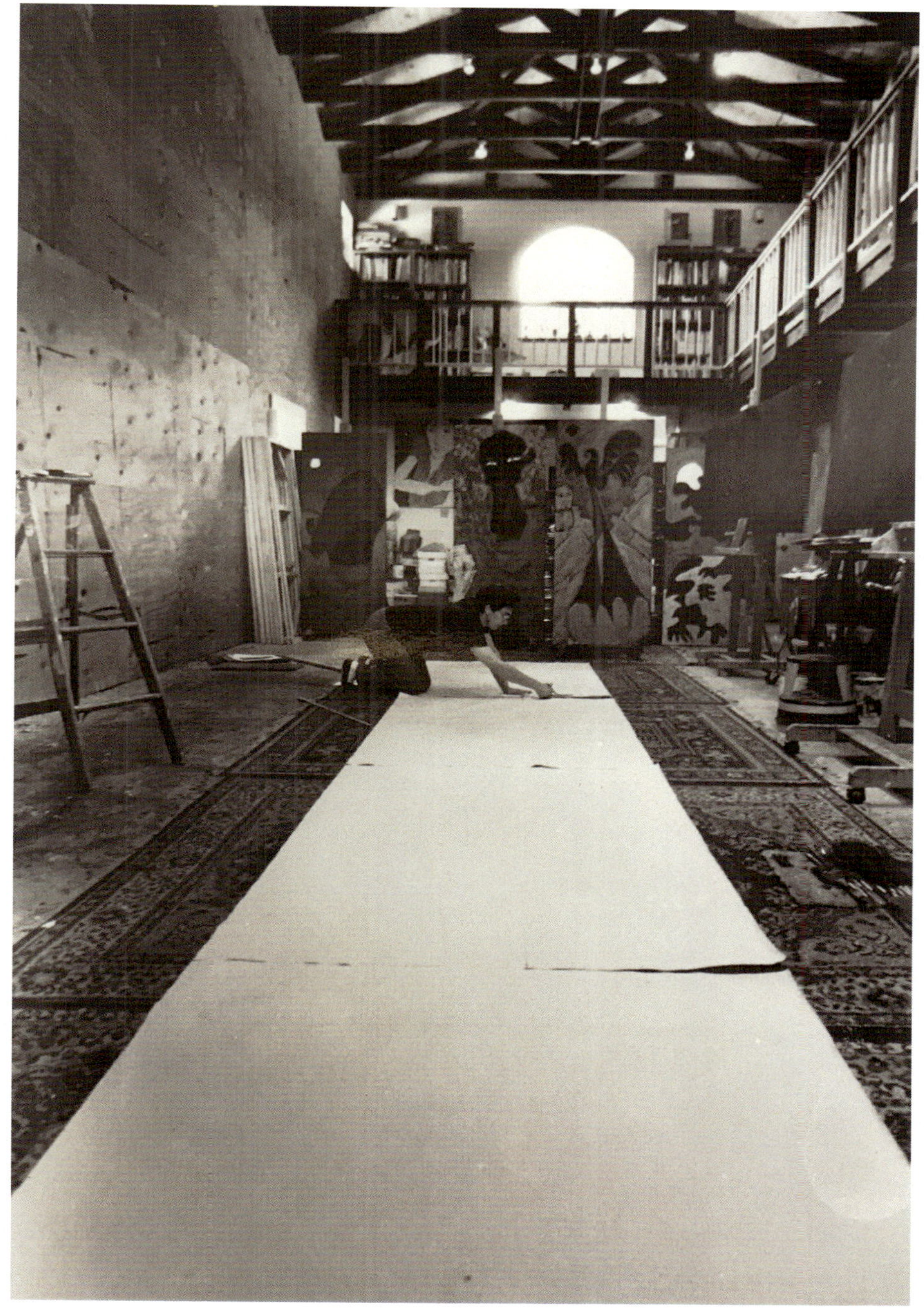

Chapter Two: 2007 - 2012

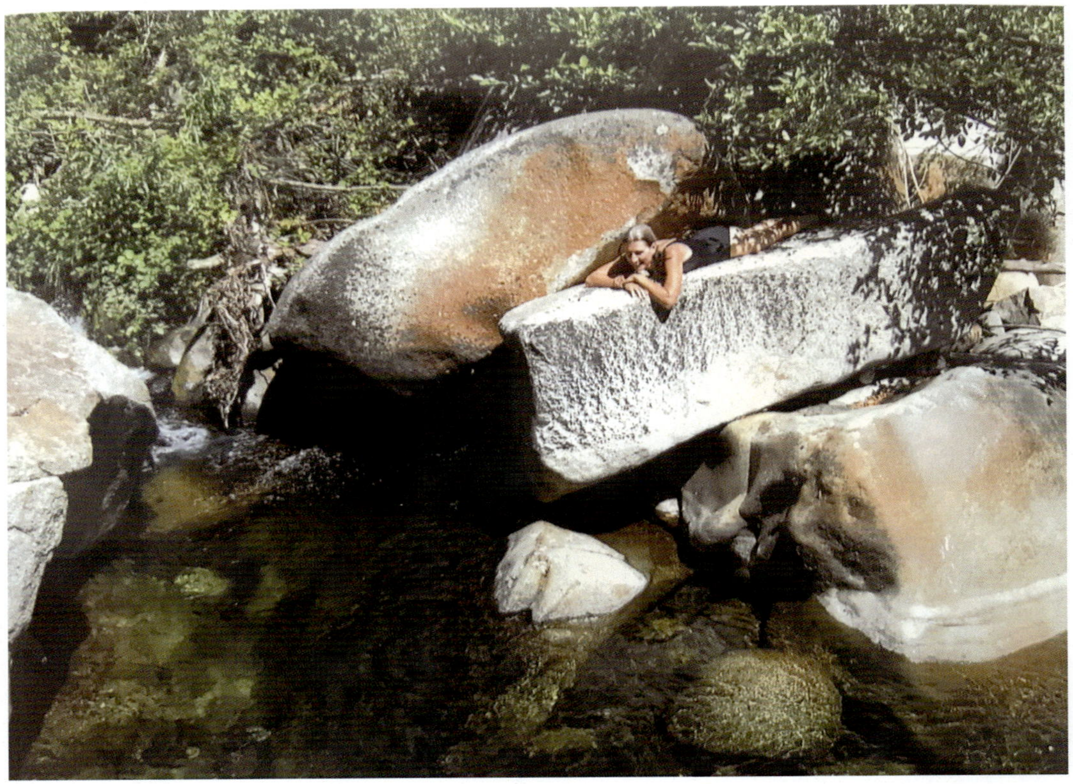

My friend on her rock on the Middle Fork.

Bridgeport Dreamtime

friday opened up
so of course we three
drove out to the river
which is running
so high after this
epic winter that we
still can't get to my rock,
but closer this time,
and i am glad for
so much water,
the roar of the current
listening to della's dream
of a woman with cornflowers
braided into her hair,
and we all happen
to be wearing periwinkle,
to match the tiny butterflies
that alight on the strap
of my backpack
and linger long enough
to whisper our thanks
to the great spirit
we feel so keenly here,
shaking out energies
to release what
we dare not keep
any longer
bare feet in cool water
warm rock
washed clear

—Lil McGill

Ascend to Sky, Granite Point, #011
36″ x 24″
acrylic on canvas, private collection

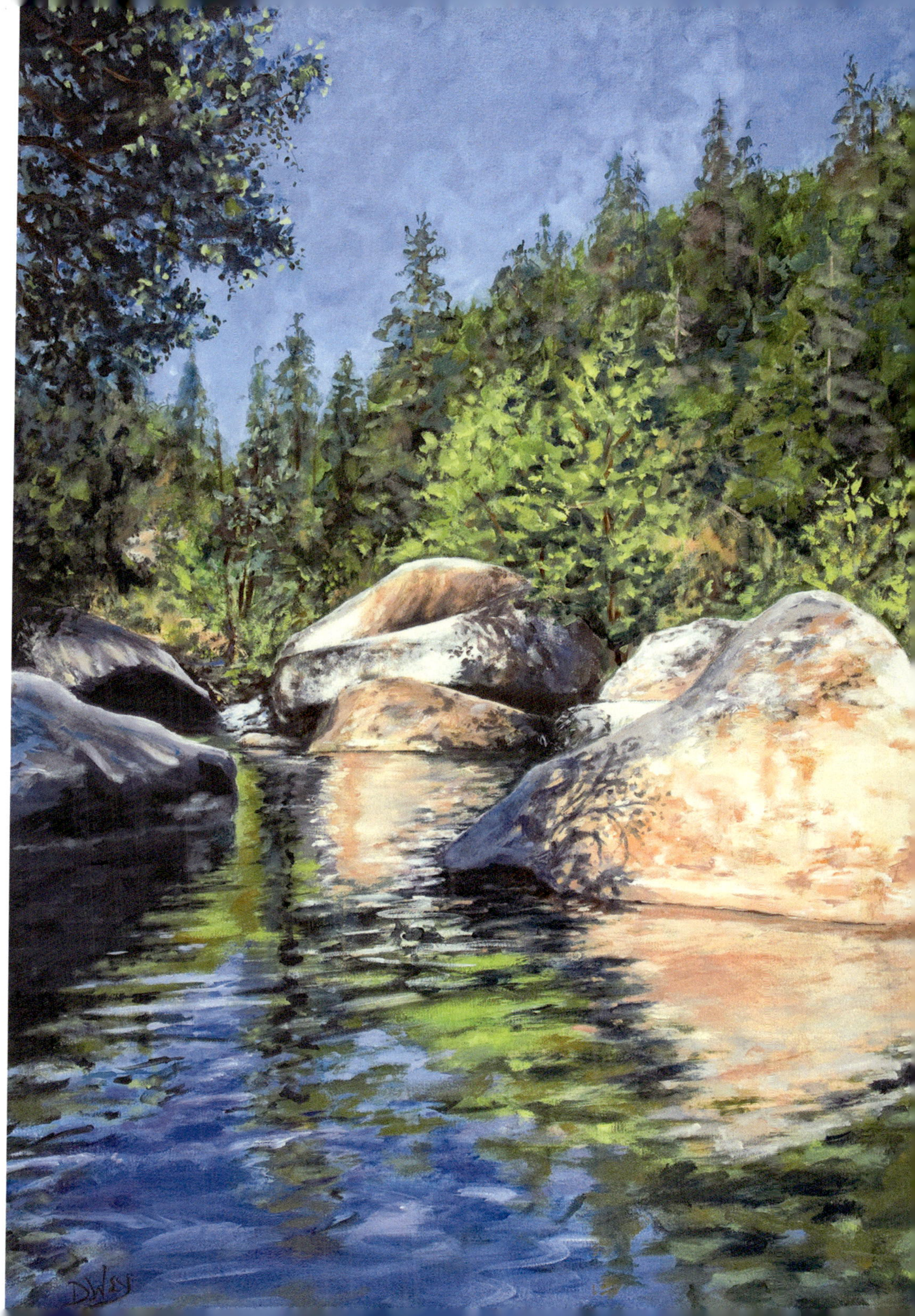

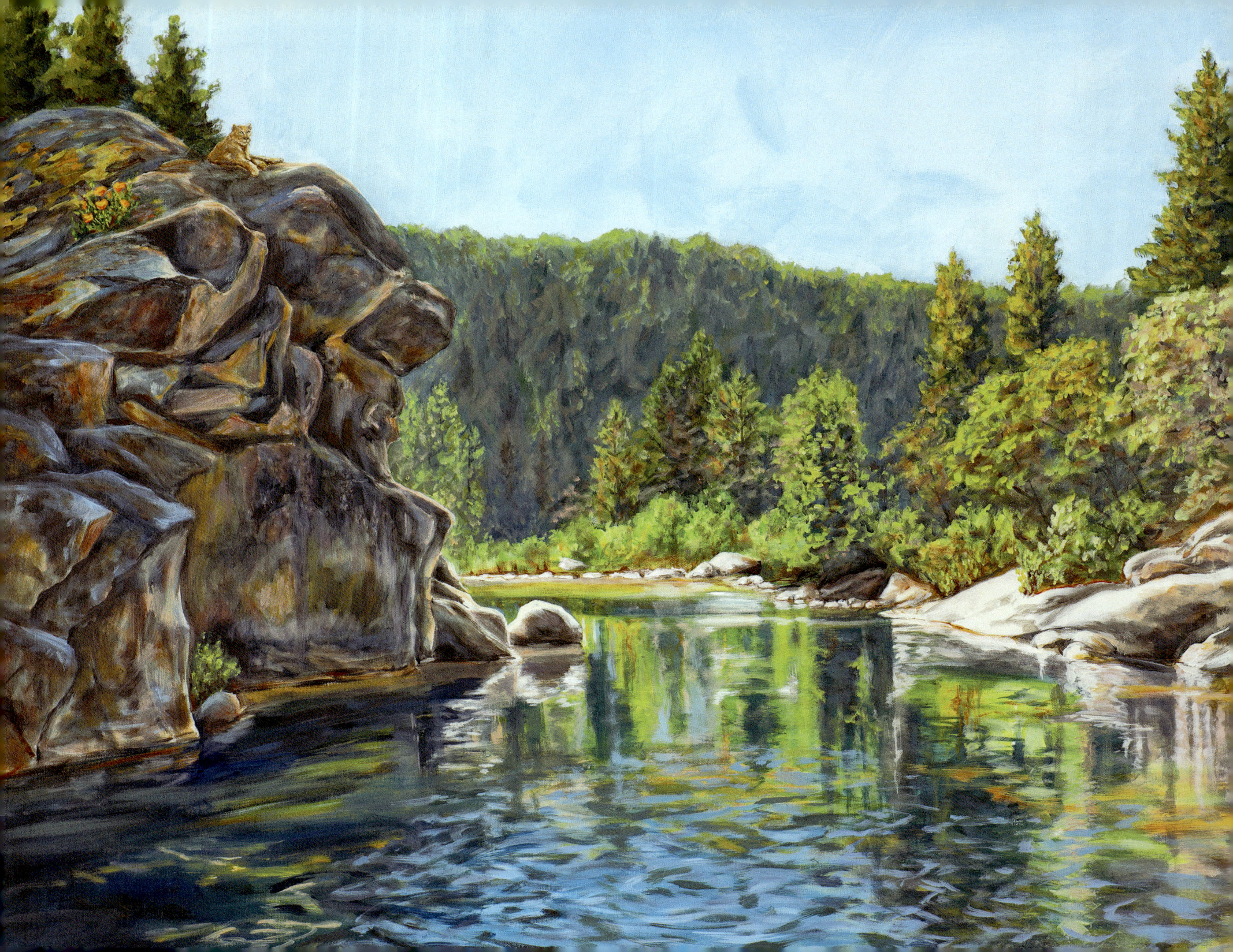

I rented a tiny studio in town with great lighting and a little kitchen, up above a used bookstore. I loved it there! Up until this, I painted quite small; usually the 9x12 size and once in a while I'd paint a 20x24.

But within the magic of these walls the muse visited, whispering to have courage! In this teensy studio I decided to paint really big and stretched some 36x48 canvases. This led to another breakthrough for me. I had to paint very differently to paint large…it was an enormous task and I had only so much patience.

Details were now too tedious to render…bold strokes with big brushes and many coffee breaks to refresh my vision became my new normal.

And I had my second painter's breakthrough. I discovered that I did my best work in a time-frame of about two hours or until I felt slightly confused about my next step. This I took to indicate that, for the moment, my brain was tired of making all the infinitesimal decisions that go into a painting and I'd best stop now, for the painting's sake.

So much happened for my artist-self in this studio above Booktown and Coffeetown!

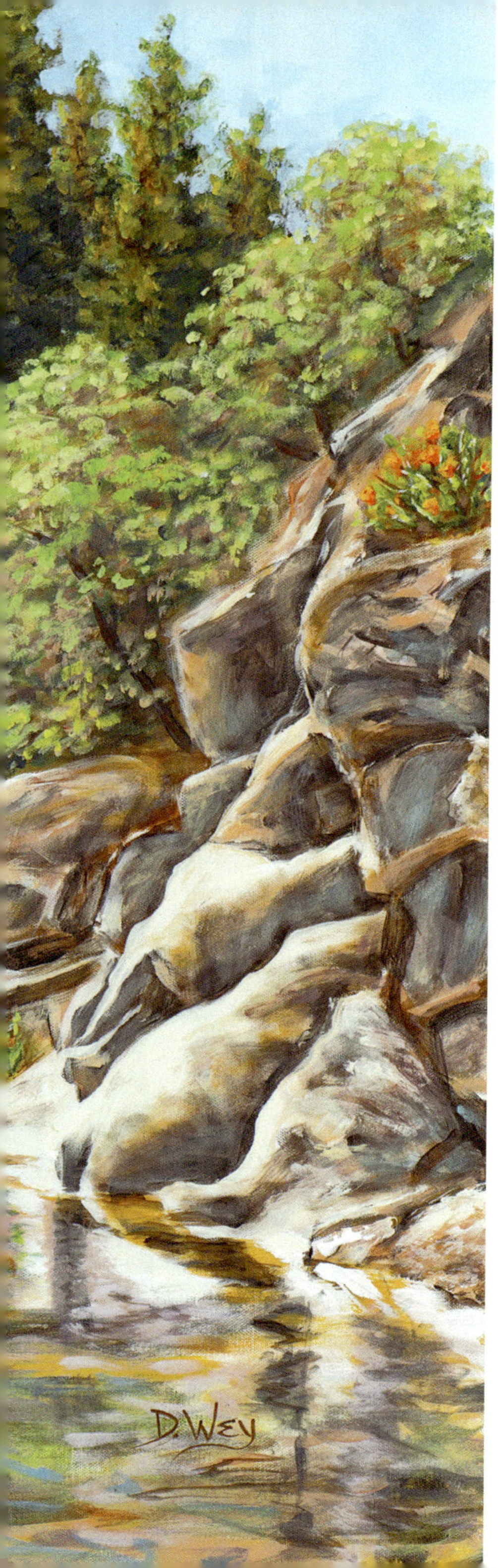

Wild and Scenic, #017
30″ x 48″
acrylic on canvas
private collection

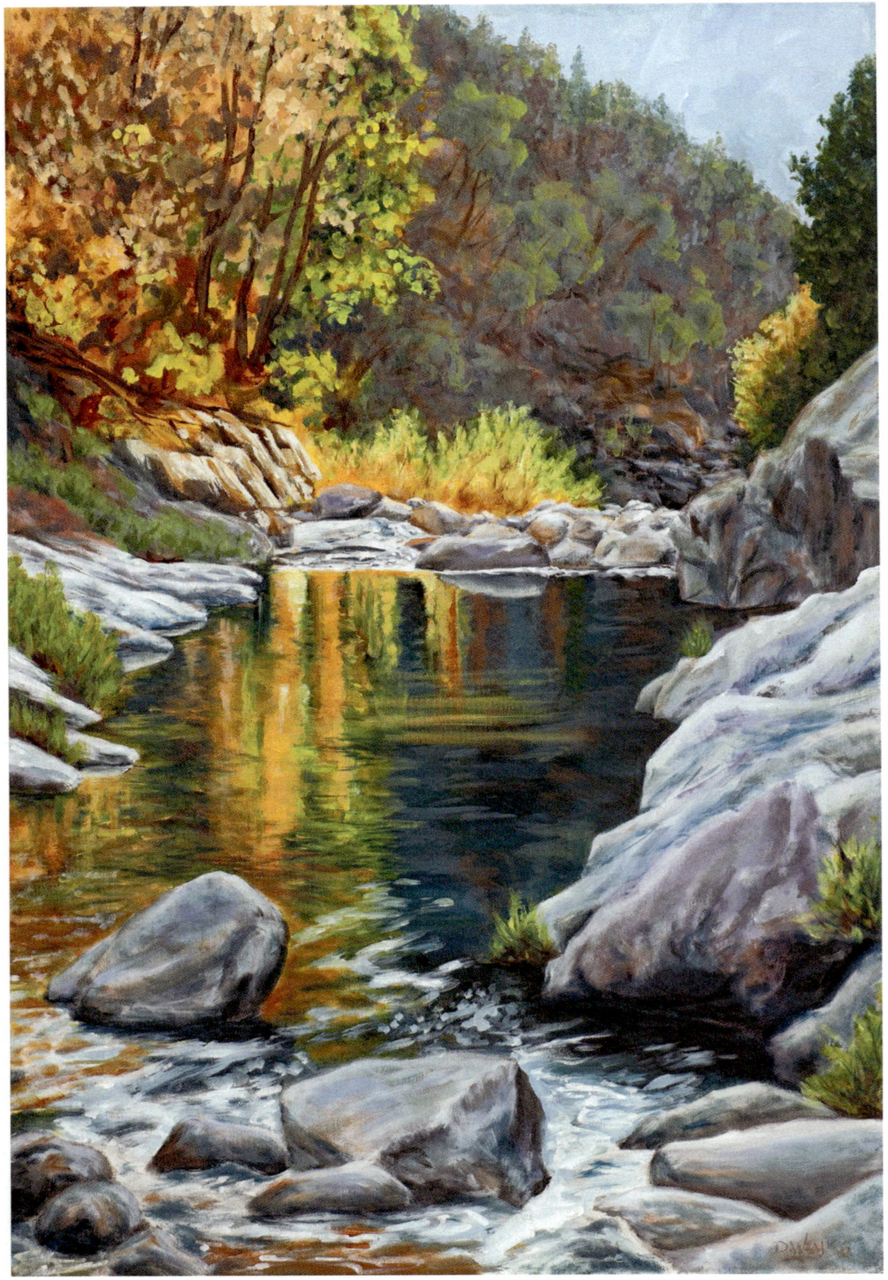

In 2008, a friend took me camping on her property on the shore of the middle fork of the Yuba. Previously, I'd only been to the South Fork. The middle fork was exceptionally breathtaking with huge walls of rocky cliffs staggered with sweeping bouldered shores and tumbled granite sculpture everywhere.

No one else was around for we were in the Tahoe National Forest with little public access to the river. There were deep swimming pools in between a series of shallow rapids that were perfect for tubing downstream. I officially became a river rat…tucked my camera in my hat whilst tubing and got some good shots… painted and swam and laid on rocks in the sun.

A Labor Day tradition of camping on the river began and the rest of the year I'd paint from the photos and memories.

The River's Song, #014
36" x 24",
acrylic on canvas
private collection

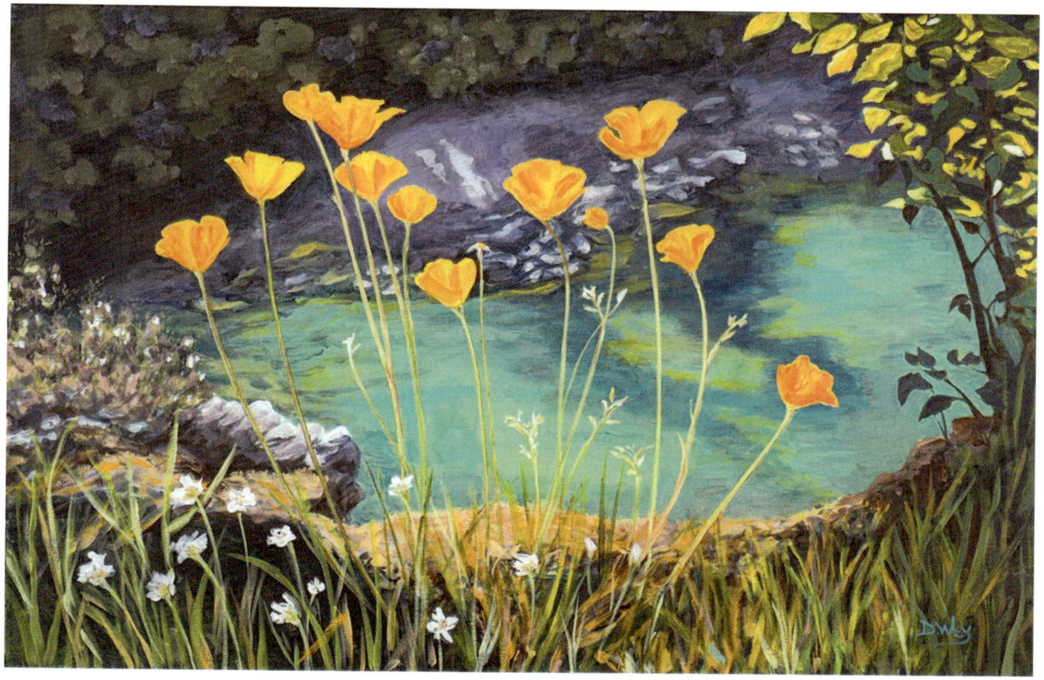

Poppies on the Yuba, #027, 24" x 36"
acrylic on canvas, private collection

My year is punctuated by the Open Studios Art Tour that occurs every October, — and for two weekends, I assimilate, summarize and celebrate my work year as a painter with this event. I see old friends and make new ones. We discuss art and life and some people happily find paintings they must take home.

The paintings from this time period were somewhat large and impressionistic as I was attempting to capture the feelings the river stirred in me at the middle fork…I think because I was living on the river… sleeping there, bonding with my surroundings, the experience was deeper, richer.

I felt so healthy after camping and filled with much to express! I remember how happy I was with the brushstrokes in "*Ascend To Sky*", with getting that concave rock shadow in "*Down Moonshine Road*", the early autumn light in "*The River's Song*" and the rock cliff in "*Shimmering Pool*".

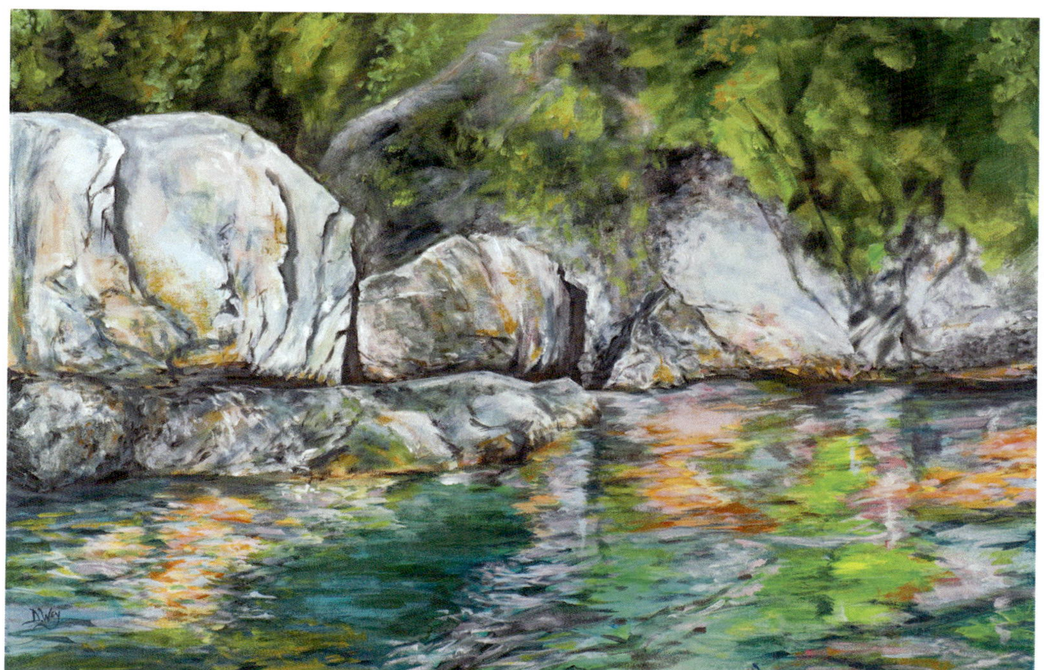

Harmonies, #015, 24" x 36", acrylic on canvas

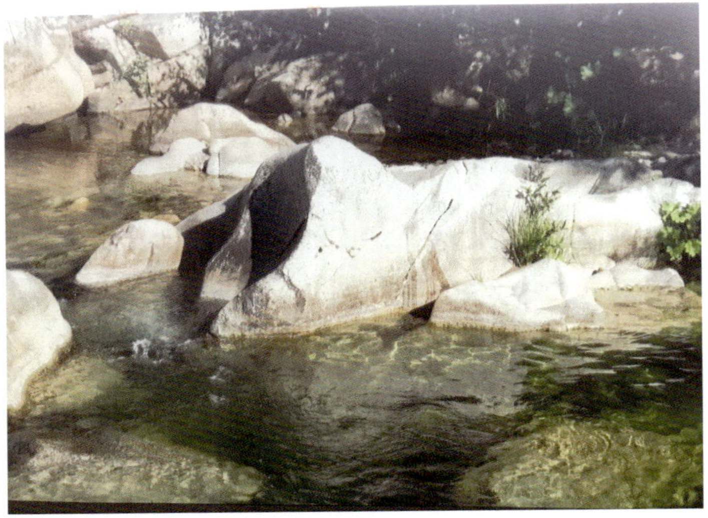

The concave shape in this rock proved to be a great lesson in modeling form in the painting, "Down Moonshine". It was also the first time that I painted shallow submerged rocks. I was very happy with how this painting turned out because I really love the middle fork of the river!

reference photo
for Moonshine

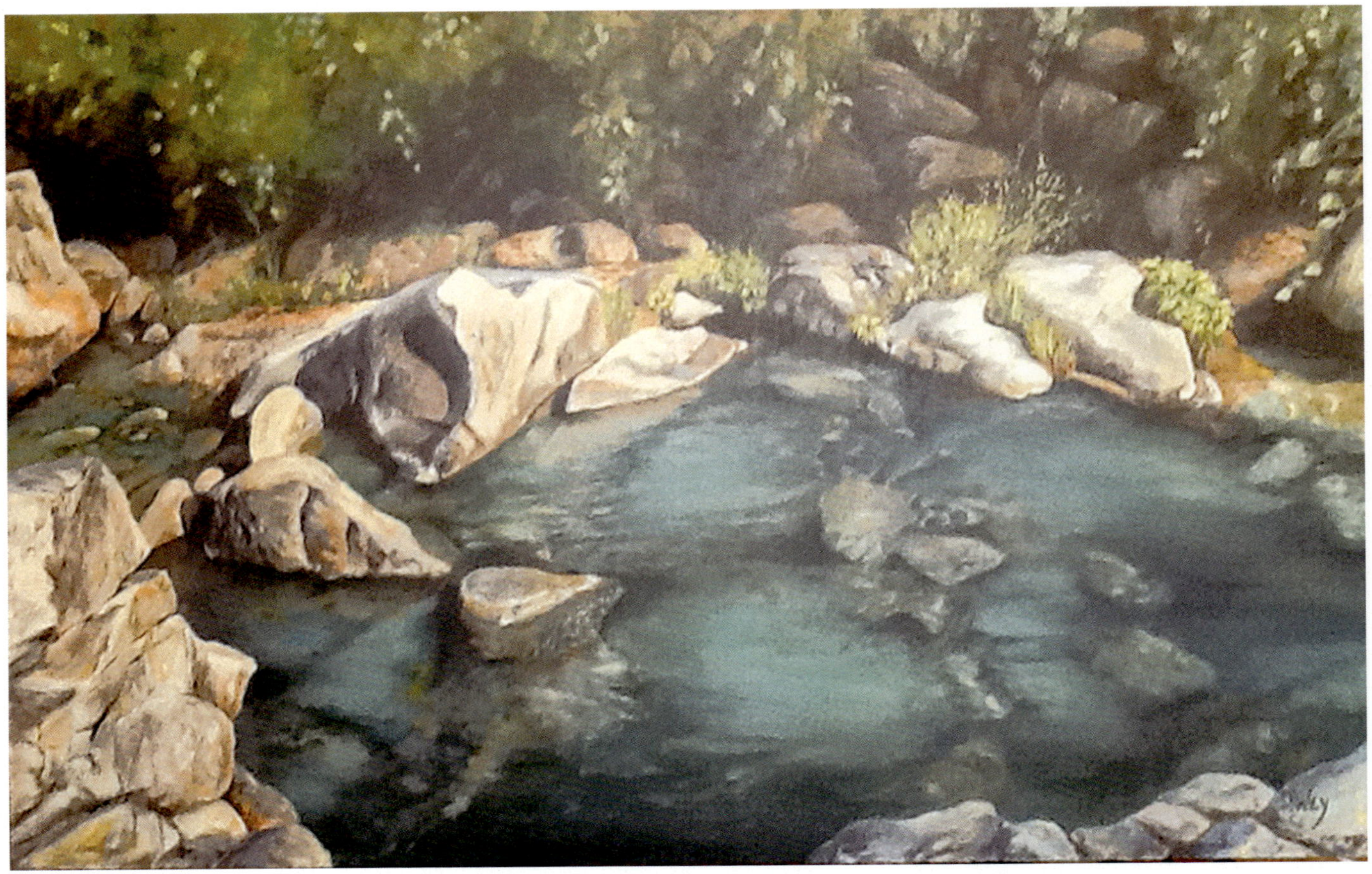

Down Moonshine, #013
30" x 48"
acrylic on canvas
artist's collection

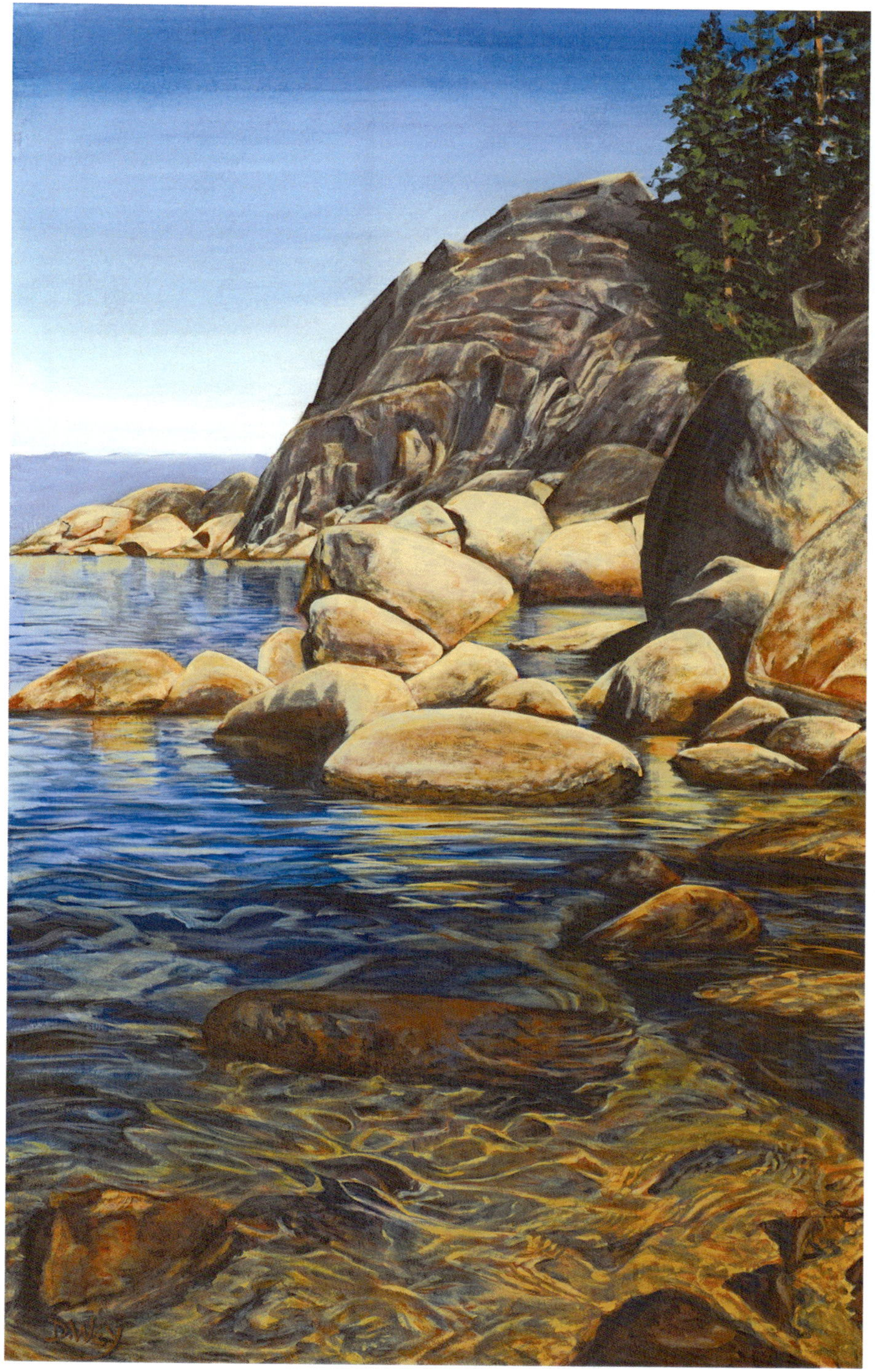

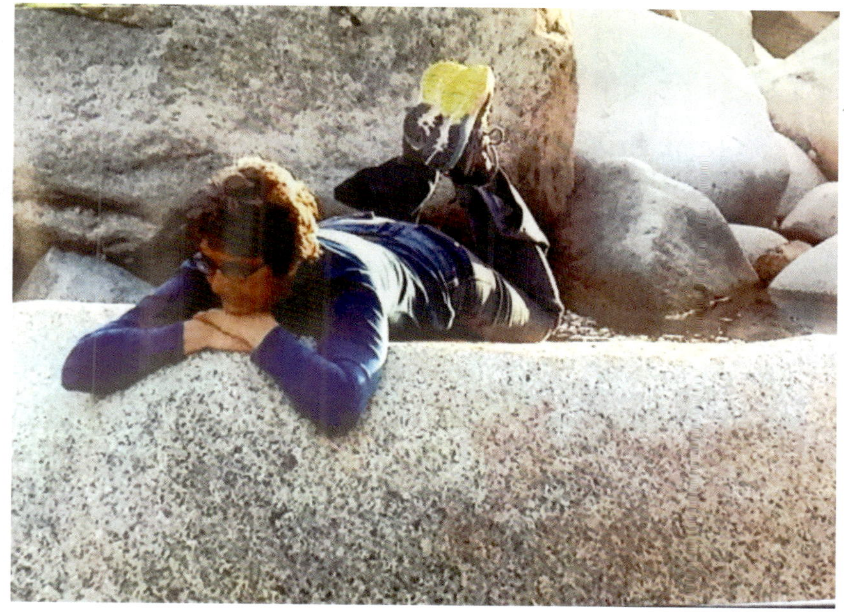

Denise on a rock
photo credit: Lil McGill

Tahoe, #077
"48 x 30"
acrylic on canvas
private collection

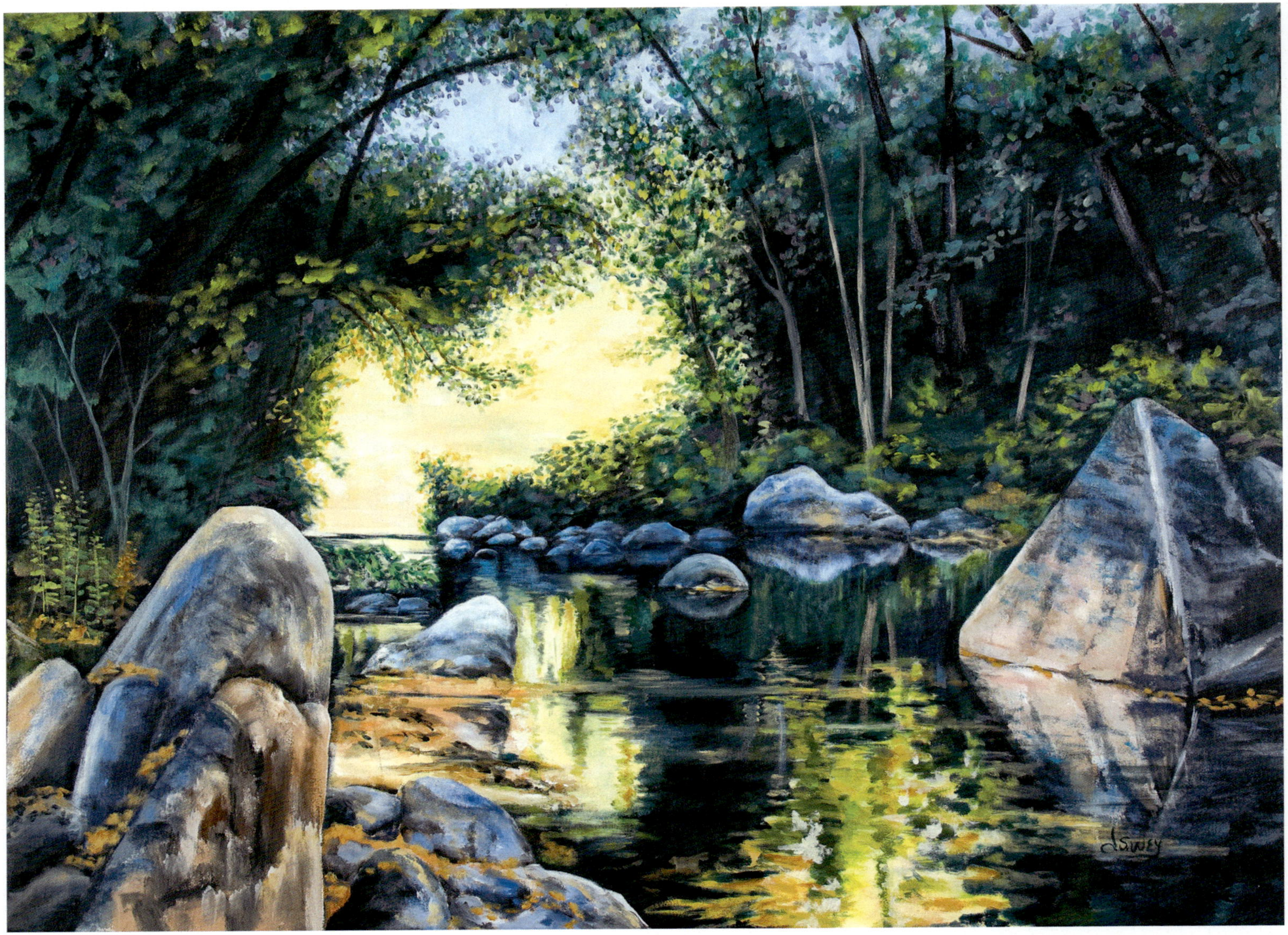

Pyramid Rock on Deer Creek, #012 , 36" x 48", acrylic on canvas, private collection

in situ

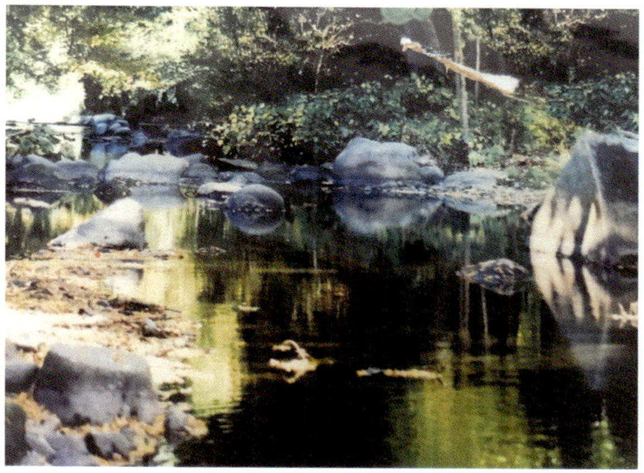

photo credit, Barbara Dean

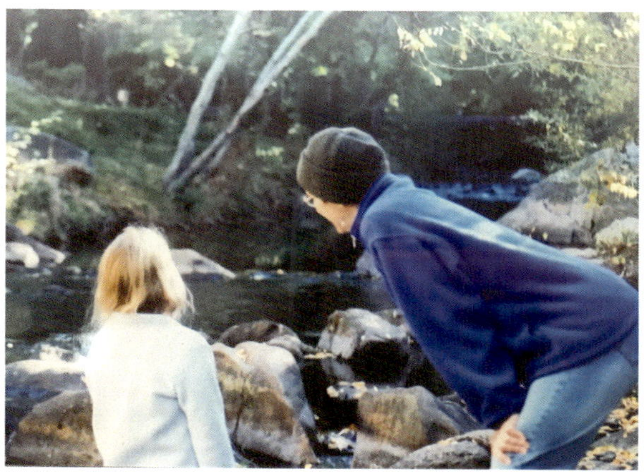

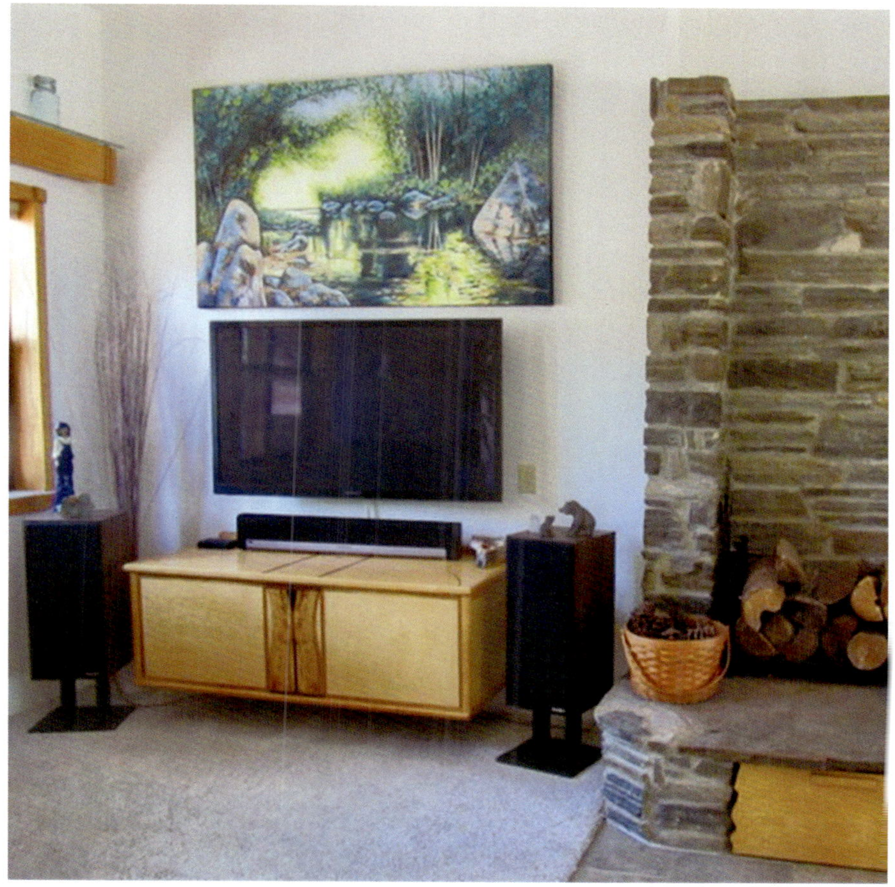

I was at Deer Creek one sparkling spring day with some children doing a watercolor class and one of the grandparents took the photo I would use for inspiration.

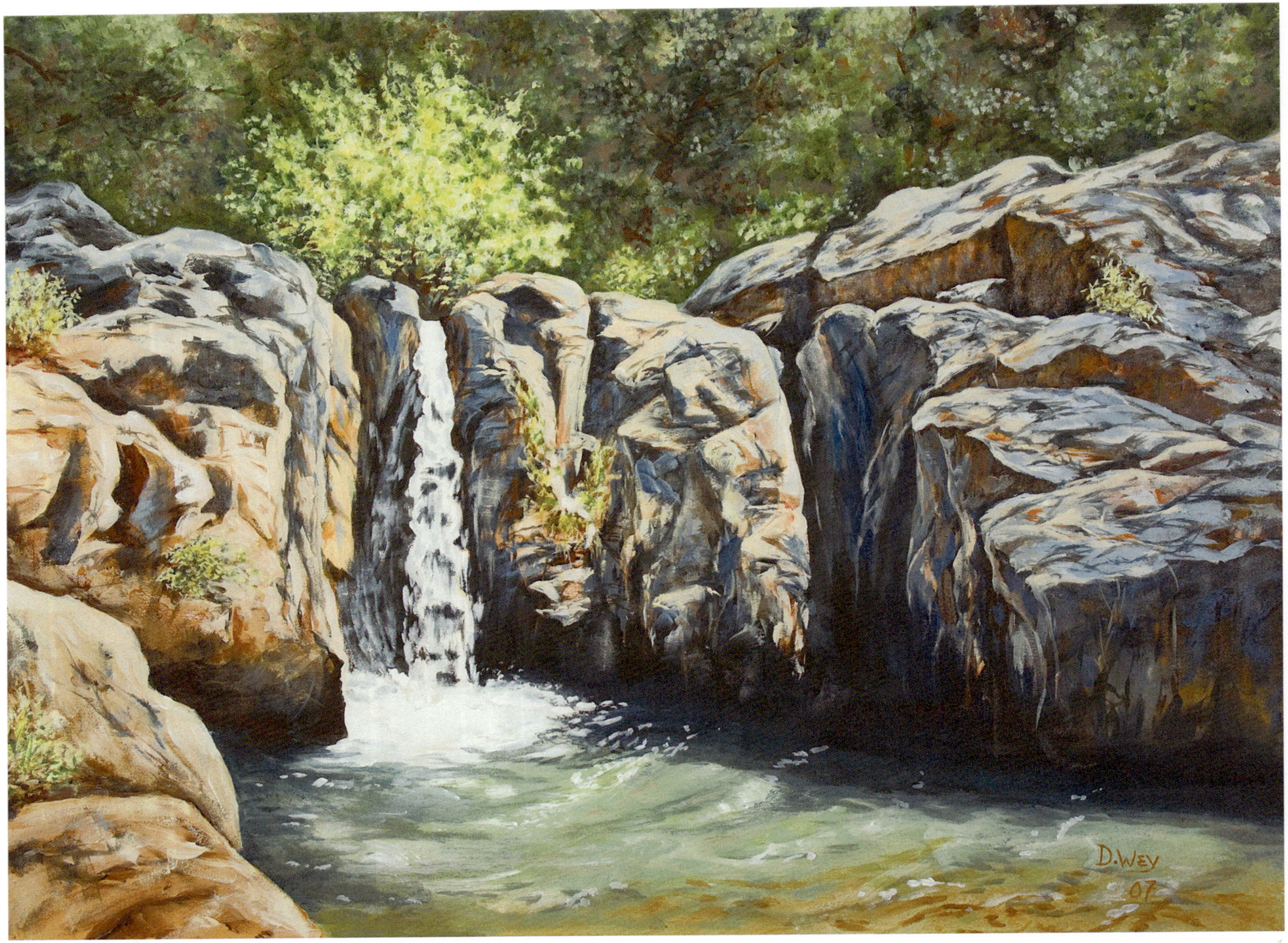

Downstream from Edward's Crossing, #010, 36″ x 48″, acrylic on canvas

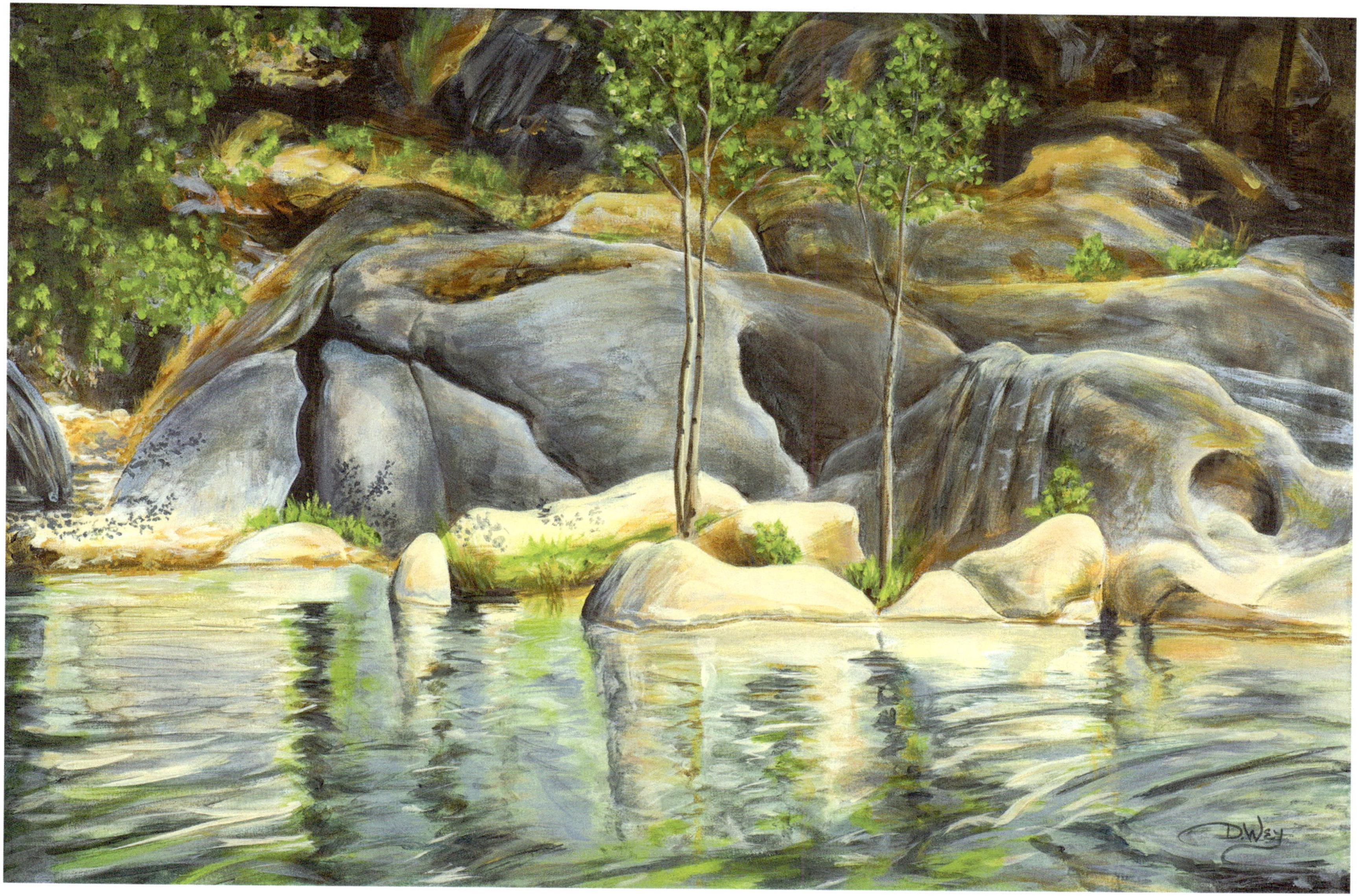

Repose of the River, #029, 24″ x 36″, acrylic on canvas

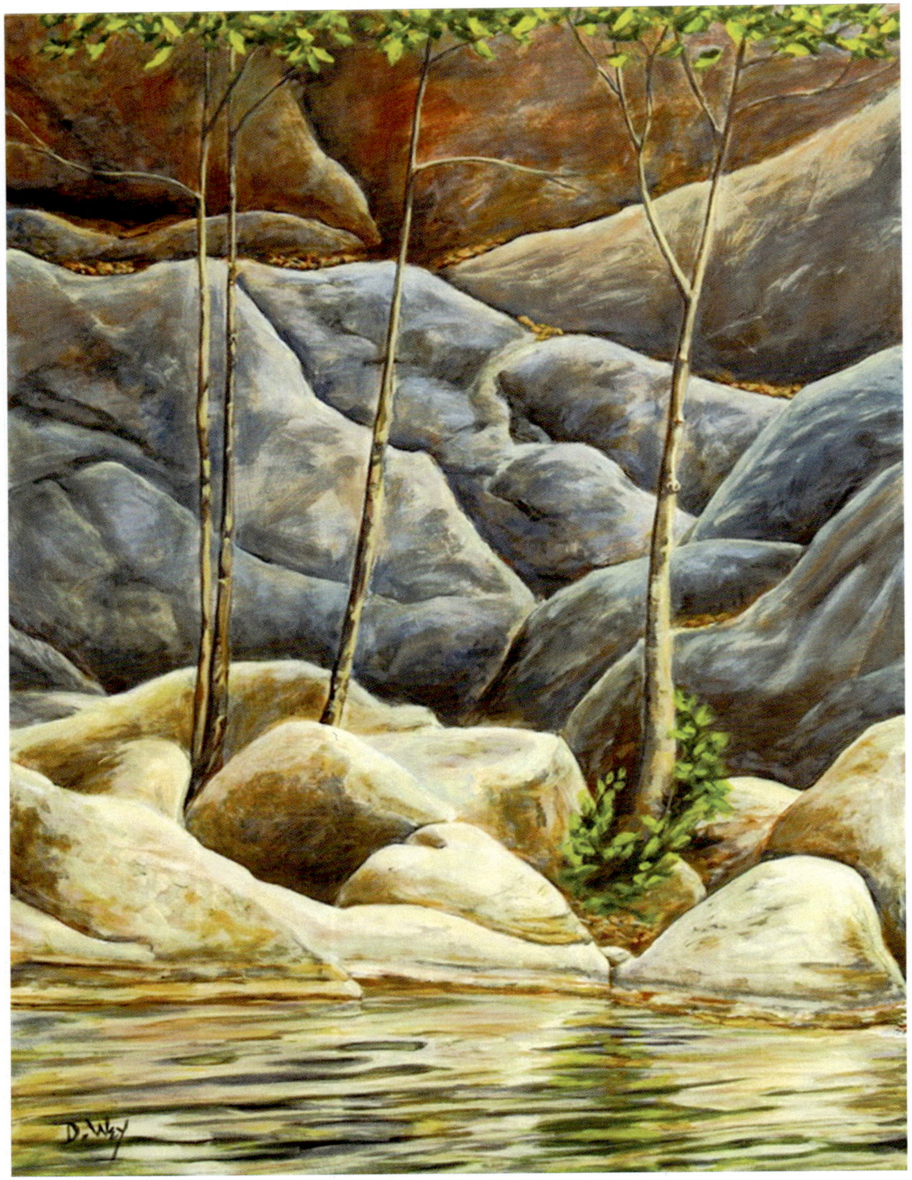

Down to the River, #018, 40″ x 30″
acrylic on canvas, private collection

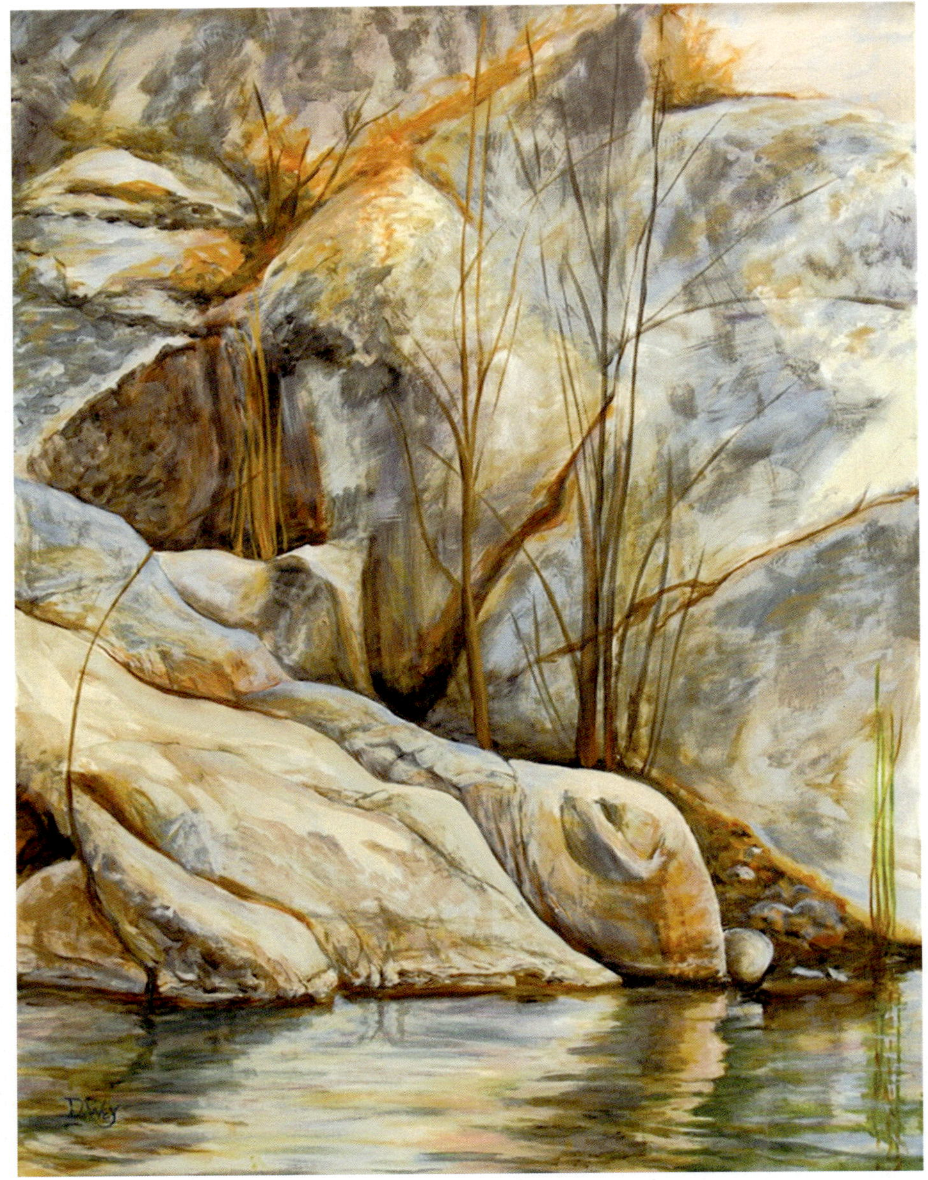

Rock Temple, #020, 40″ x 30″
acrylic on canvas, private collection

These two paintings are what I call "sister" paintings, in that they're from the same litter! They were begun and finished together. The one painting, "River Temple" has a very special significance for me: I wanted this set for the annual Studio Tour, which was coming right up but I couldn't seem to "finish'"them. I had mostly laid in the under-paintings. Next, I planned to lay in all the beautiful green foliage. But I couldn't seem to bring myself to lay a brush on "Rock Temple". I'd study it and leave and come back again to view with fresh eyes.

I came to the conclusion that it might be done for now, even without the foliage, though it was an unusual direction for me. On the first day of the Tour, someone remarked "Oh, I like the woman in the painting!" I said, "What woman?" And he proceeded to show me the hooded woman who appeared to be blowing a shell.

Once I saw her, I couldn't not see her. She was very much present in the landscape of my painting and was also in my reference photo. Had I painted the foliage, I may have obscured her image! By the second day of the Tour, the painting went home with a happy patron and I haven't seen it since.

I'm more aware now of process; that paintings have a life of sorts, if the painter can be the instrument and allow the painting to flow and "come into being".

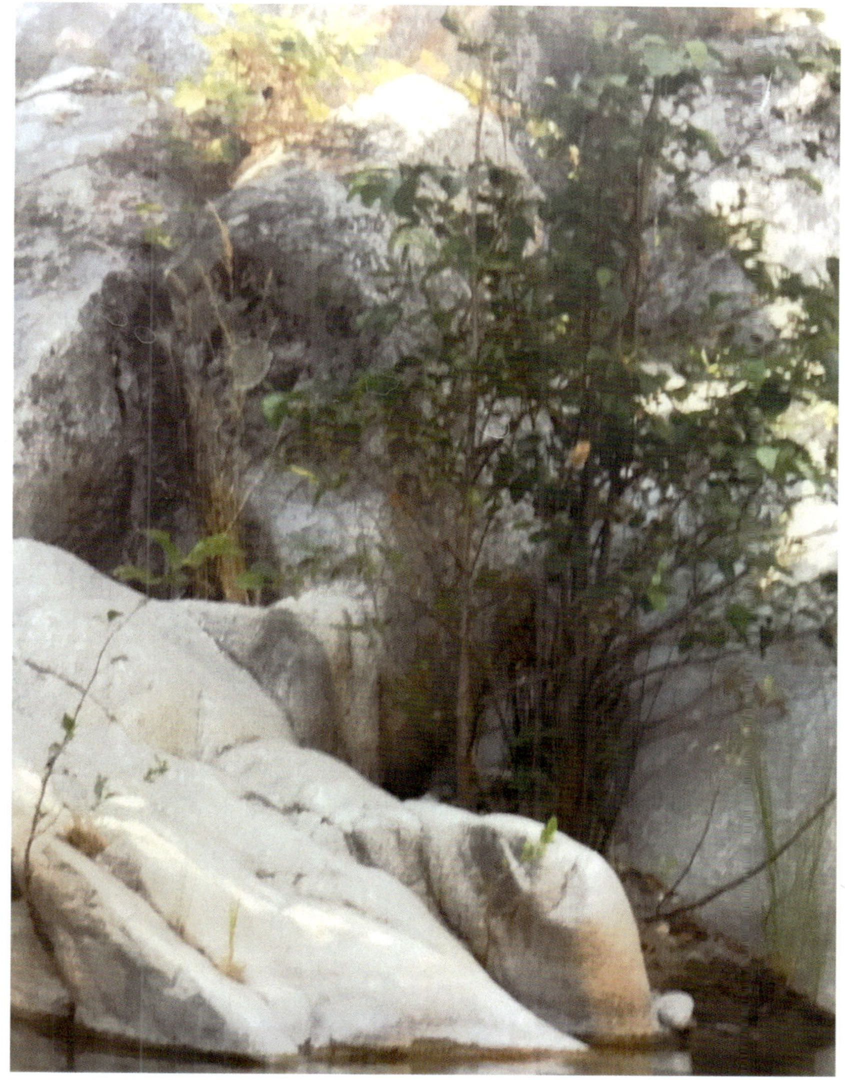

photo reference for *Rock Temple*

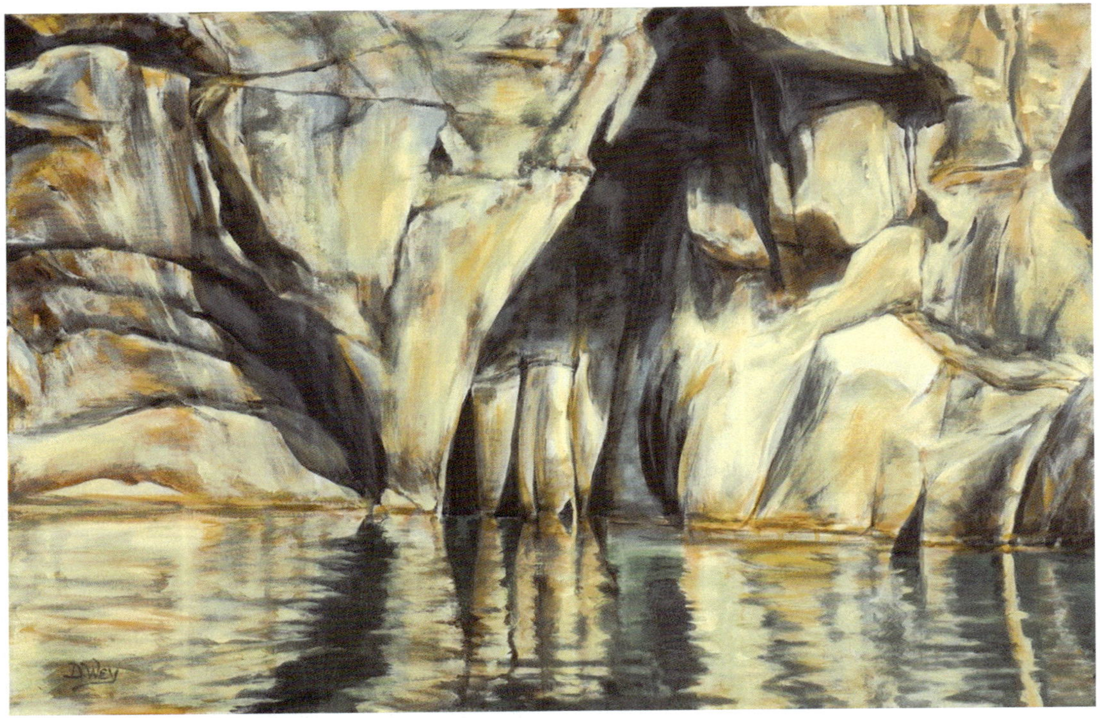

Rocks and River, #021, 24" x 36"
acrylic on canvas, private collection

This river has astounding rock formations that are uniquely "Yuba". This happens to be another favorite spot where we tube downstream to float and swim in large deep emerald pools. The painting of "River Caverns" happened whilst I was participating in the Studio Tour. I usually set up to paint because it keeps me busy during the slow times and people love to see the process. When I paint there where there's constant distractions, I usually only manage to begin a painting. Finishing a painting takes much more concentrated focus than can happen at a public event. It was quiet and I got out my paints and used a big brush to block in my underpainting. It was very fast and before too long, I put my brush down because some people came in and I went to the other side of the room to speak with them. I glanced over at my easel for a moment and couldn't believe my eyes...the painting was mostly finished! It was so loose and almost abstract, which appealed to me. Once I got it home, I painted in the green water and it was complete. I found it so interesting that again, here was the lesson... that less can be more. And often, that many breaks and lots of looking will allow the painting to "come into being." For, had I sat there and continued painting, I may have moved forward in a direction that might have dampened it's wild spirit. Now I spend more time studying a painting than I do painting it.

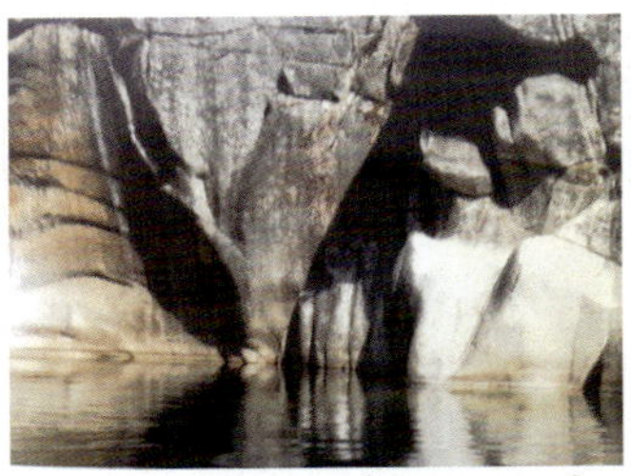

photo references for *River Caverns*

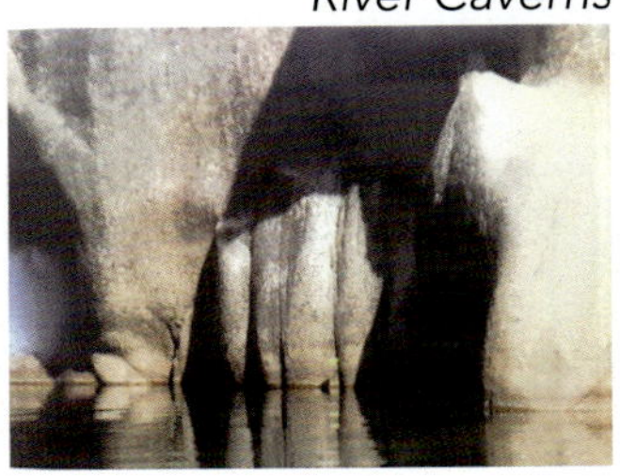

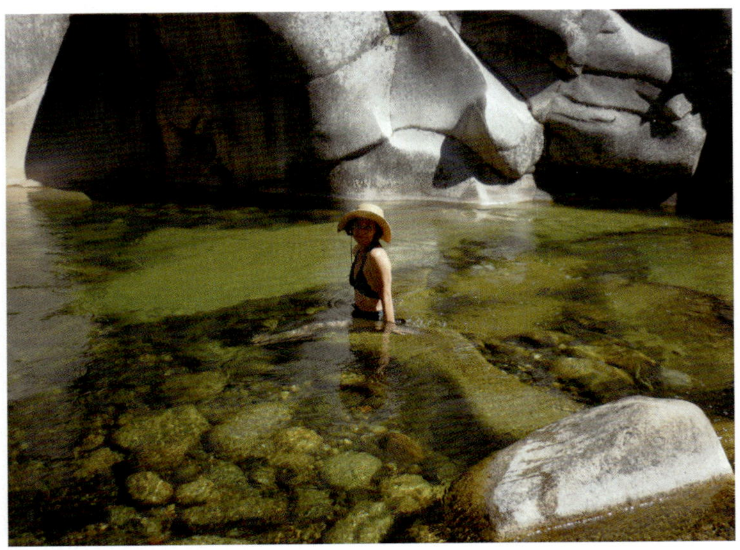

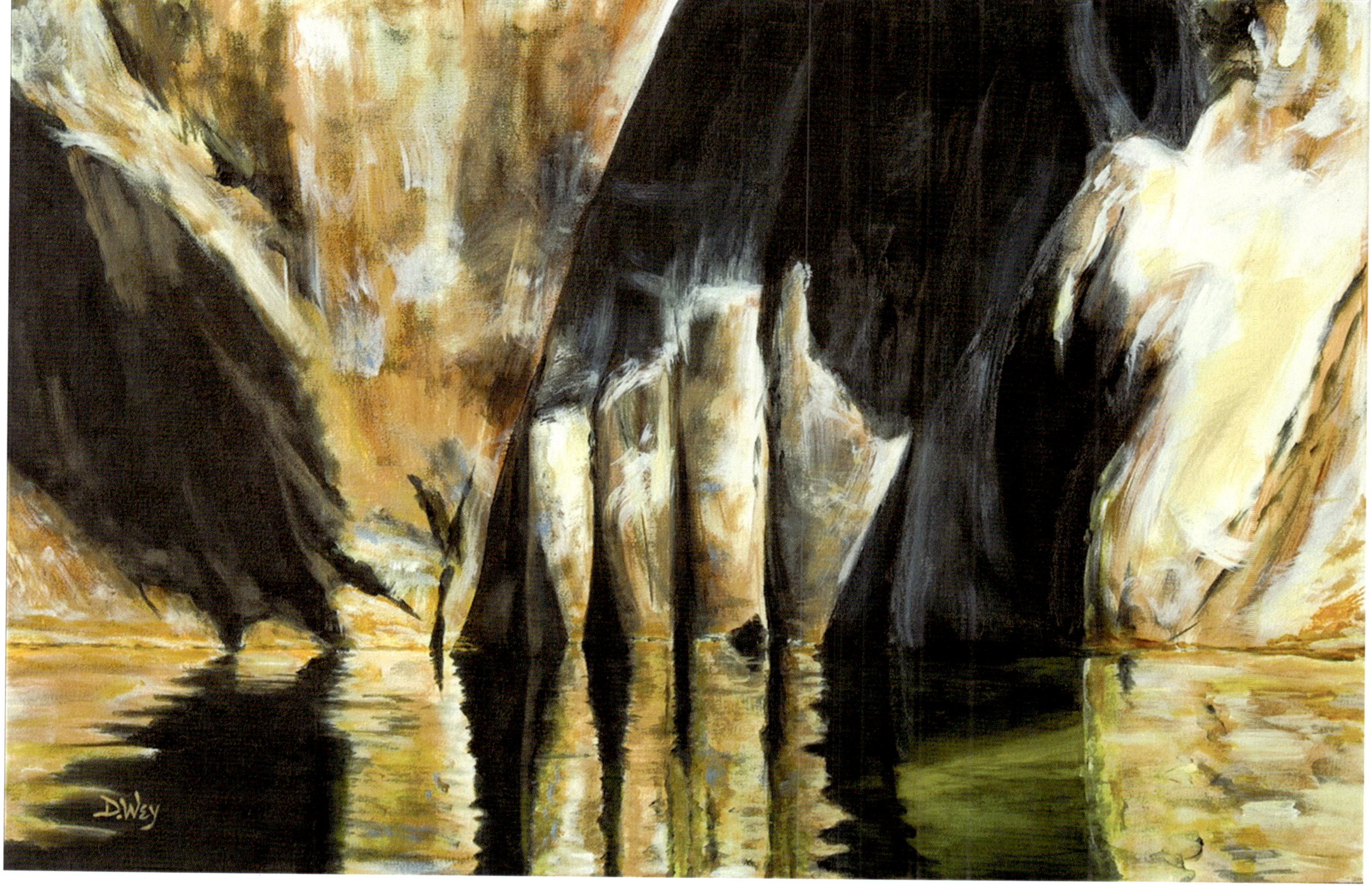

River Caverns, #019, 24" x 36", acrylic on canvas, artist's collection

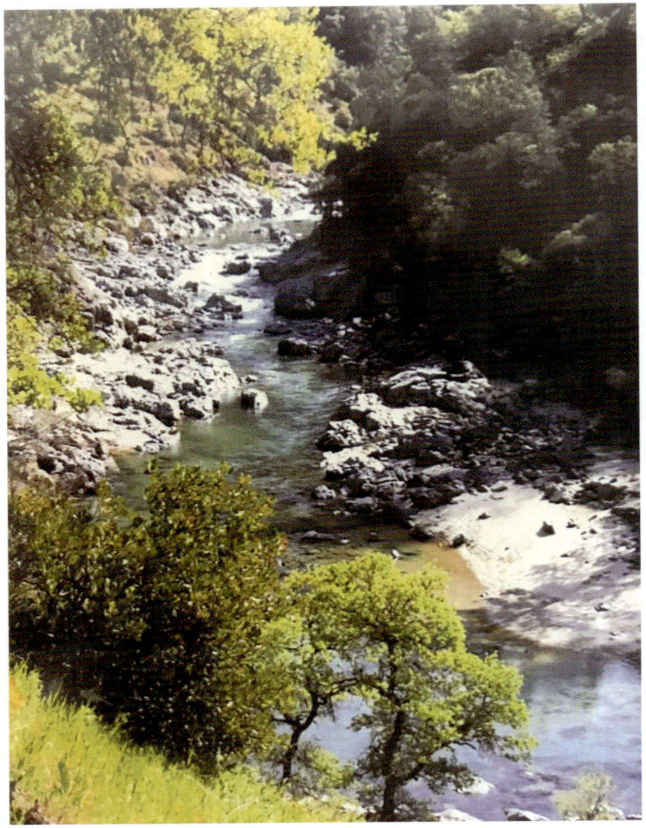

reference photo

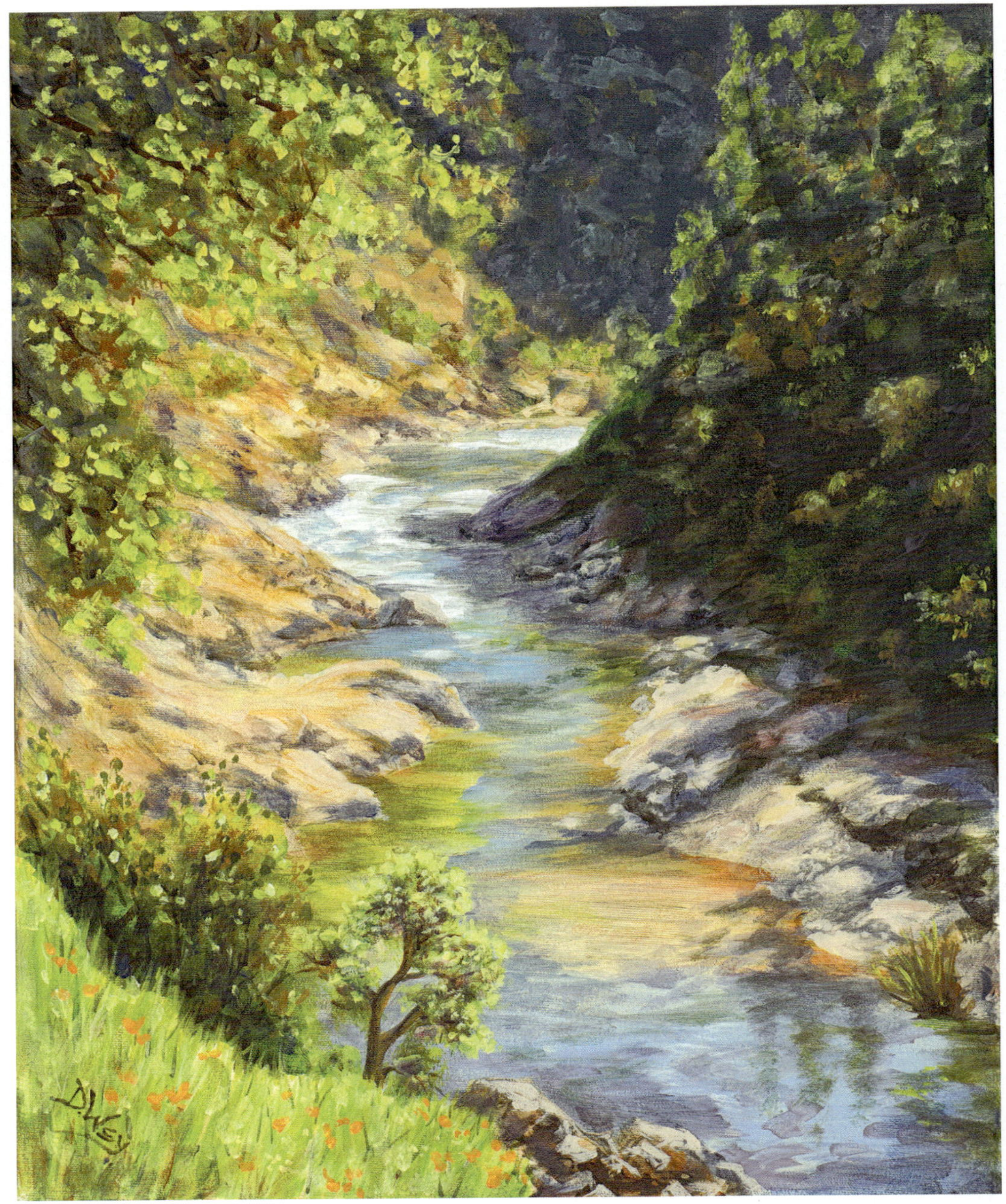

Buttermilk Trail, #024
20″ x 16″
acrylic on canvas
private collection

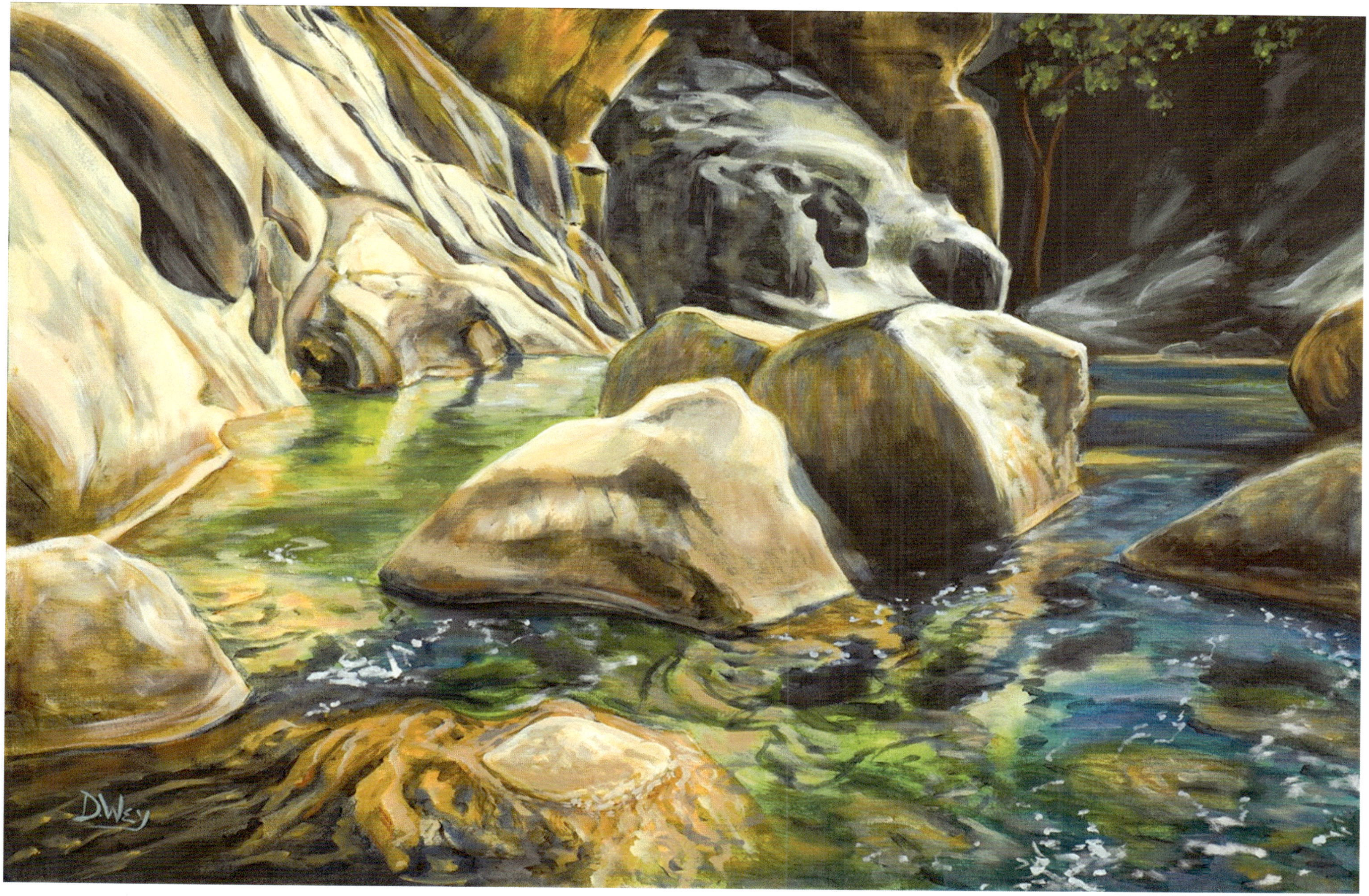

The Singing River, #022, 24″ x 36″, acrylic on canvas, private collection

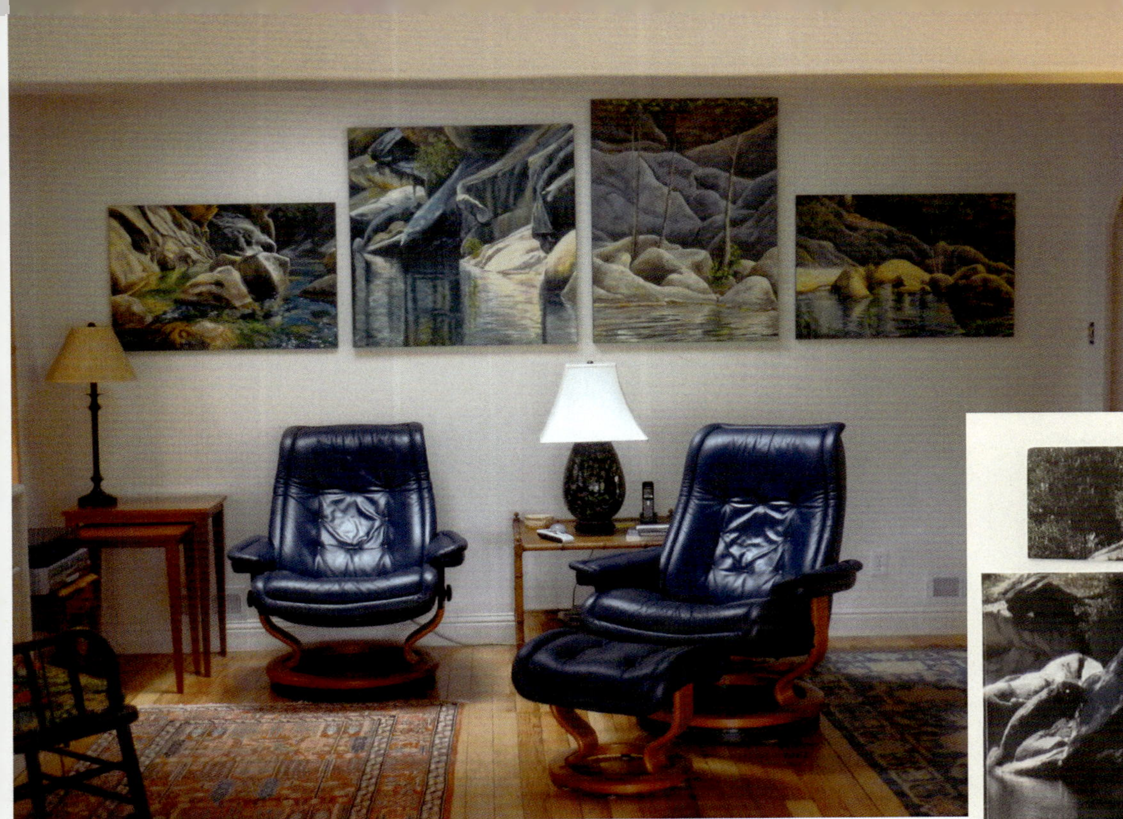

in situ

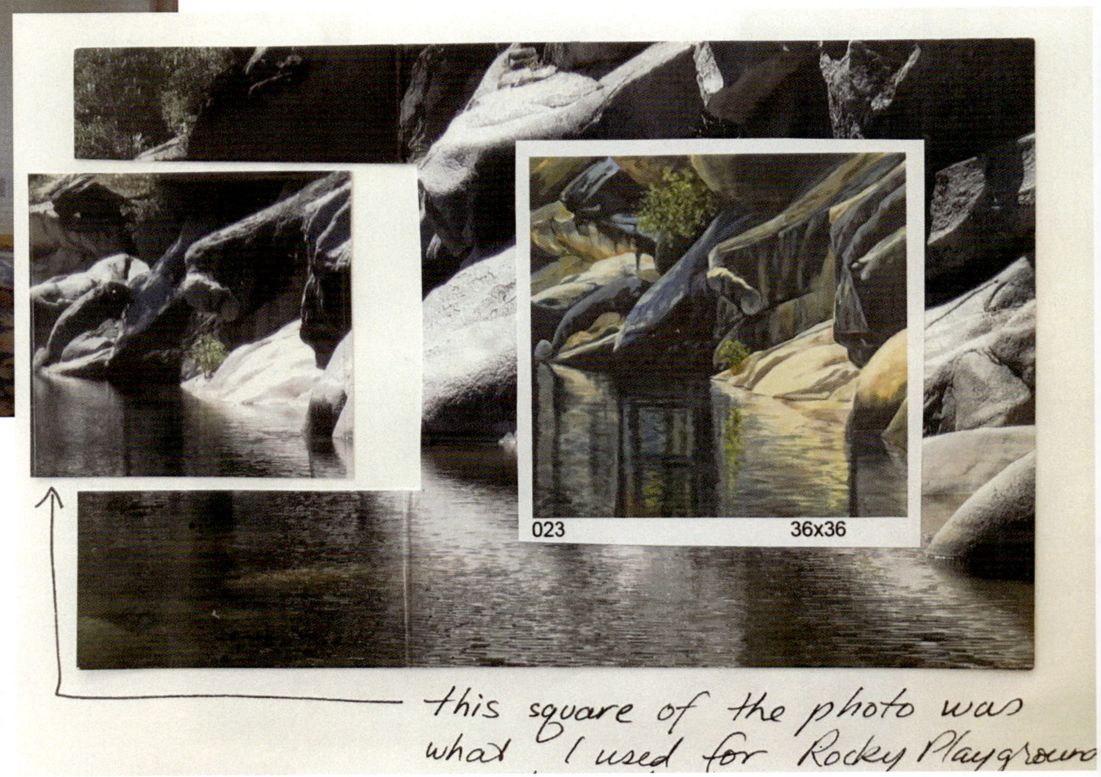

page from scrapbook
showing photo reference

The painting, Rocky Playground, to me, is an example of a painting's will to survive! Had it not been for the fortuitous drop-by of a creative friend whom I hardly see, this painting would have been gessoed over! I did not draw his attention to the painting but he noticed it leaning against a wall and his insightful remarks stayed my hand. I learned right then and there to get second opinions when I reach a wall because a painter can be so close to their work that they cannot see it anymore. Or they may have a major breakthrough, but not understand it at the time. This painting is one of my favorites now.

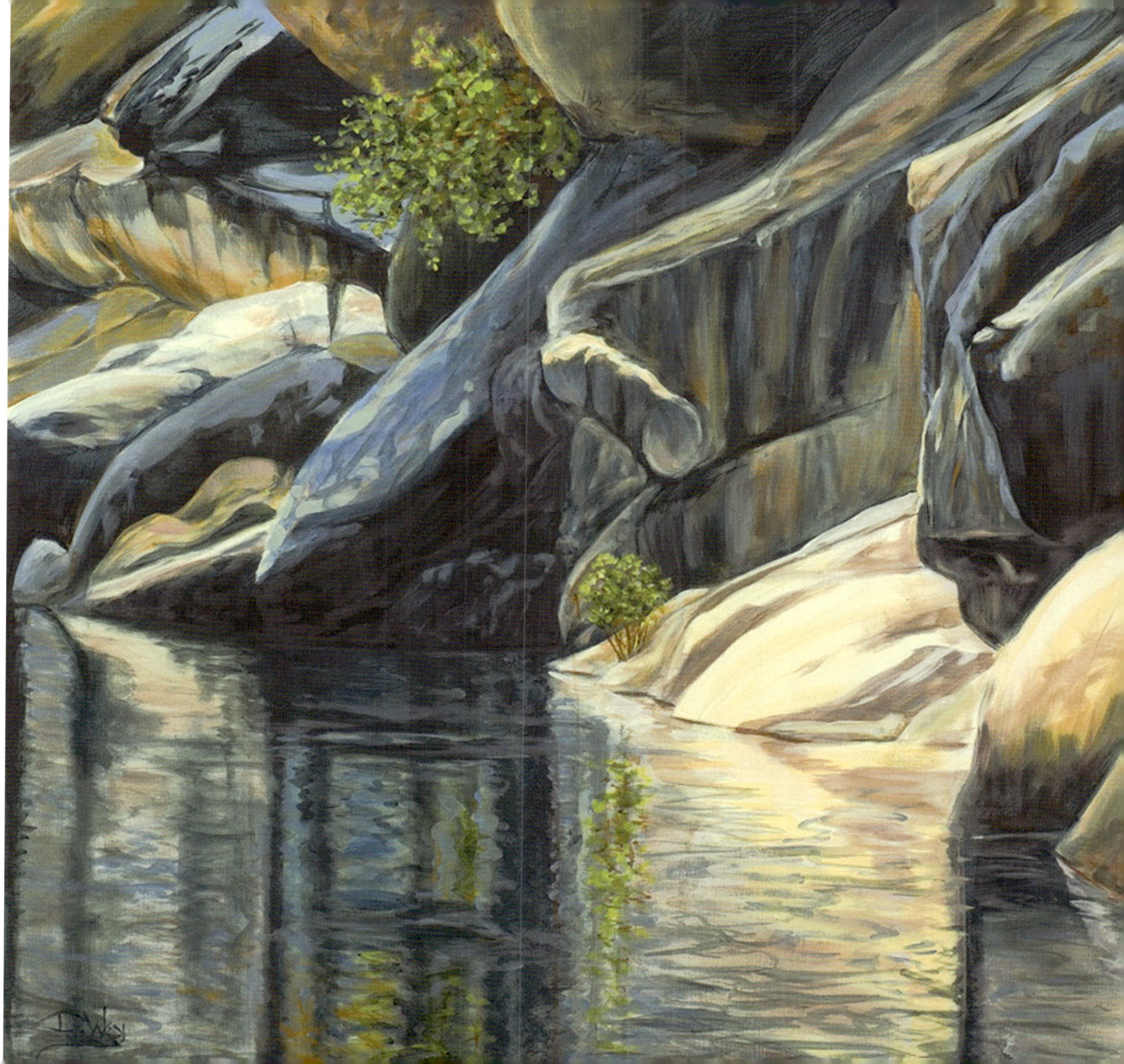

Rocky Playground
#023, 36″ x 36″
acrylic on canvas
private collection

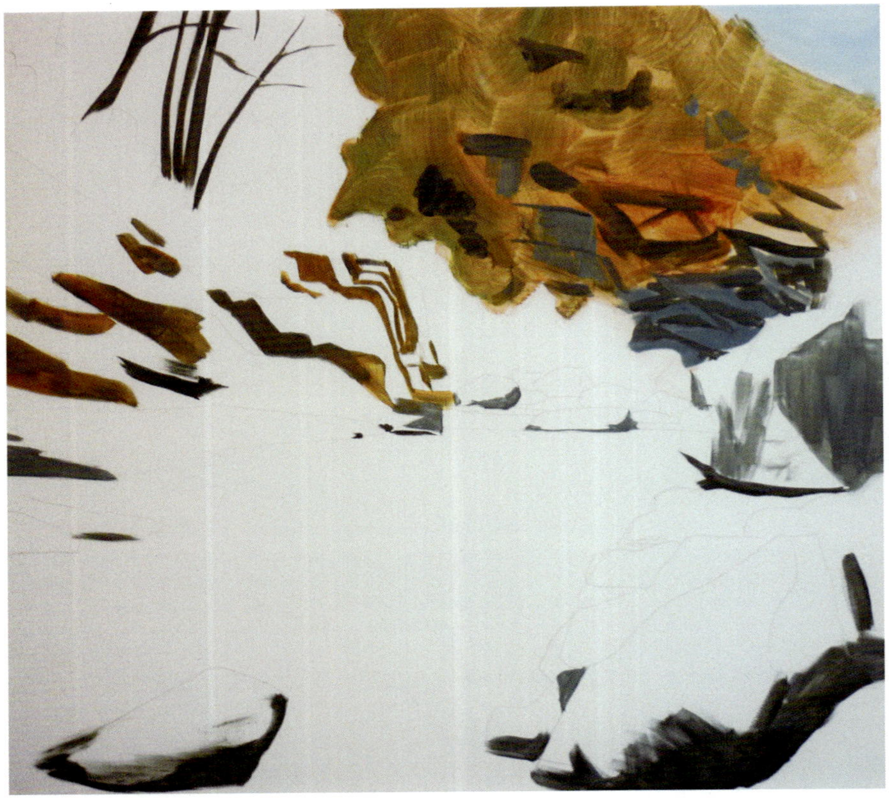

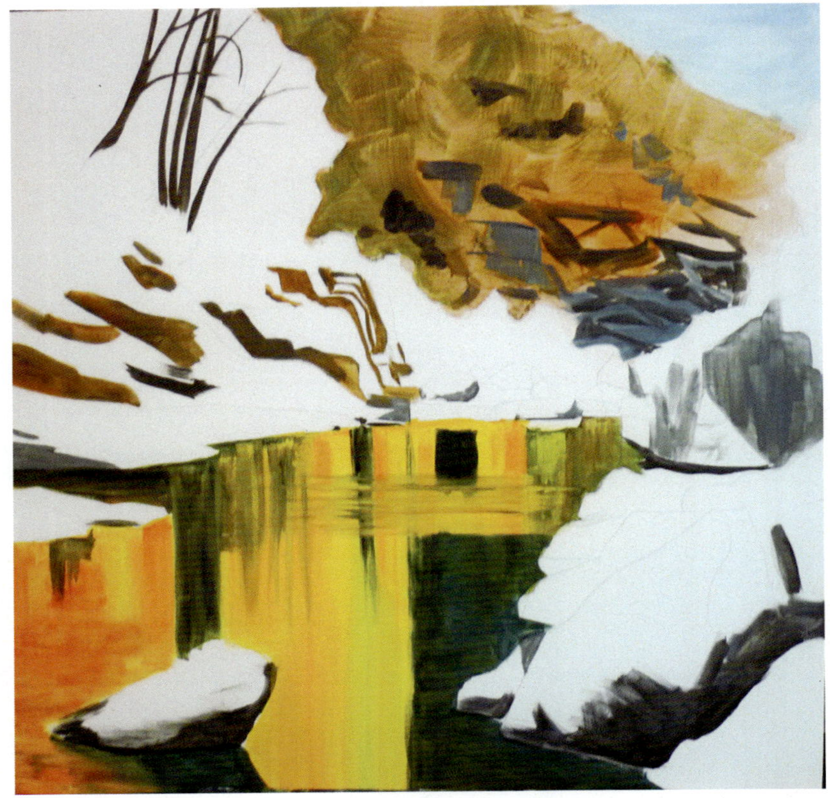

The River's Song, an autumnal view of the Middle Fork with a couple of 'in-progress' photos.

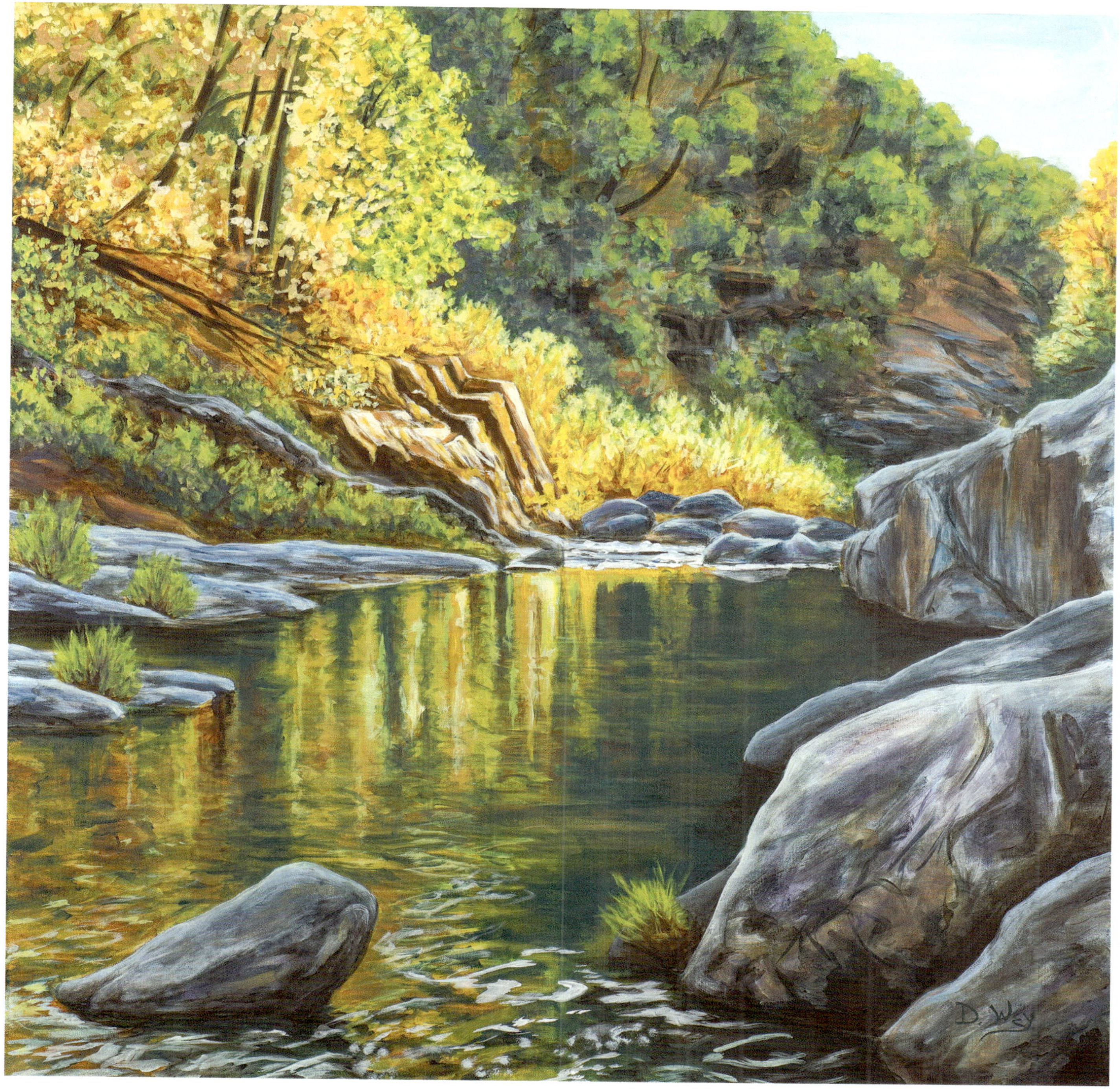

The River's Song II, #031
36″ x 36″
acrylic on canvas
private collection

Chapter Three: 2013 - 2015

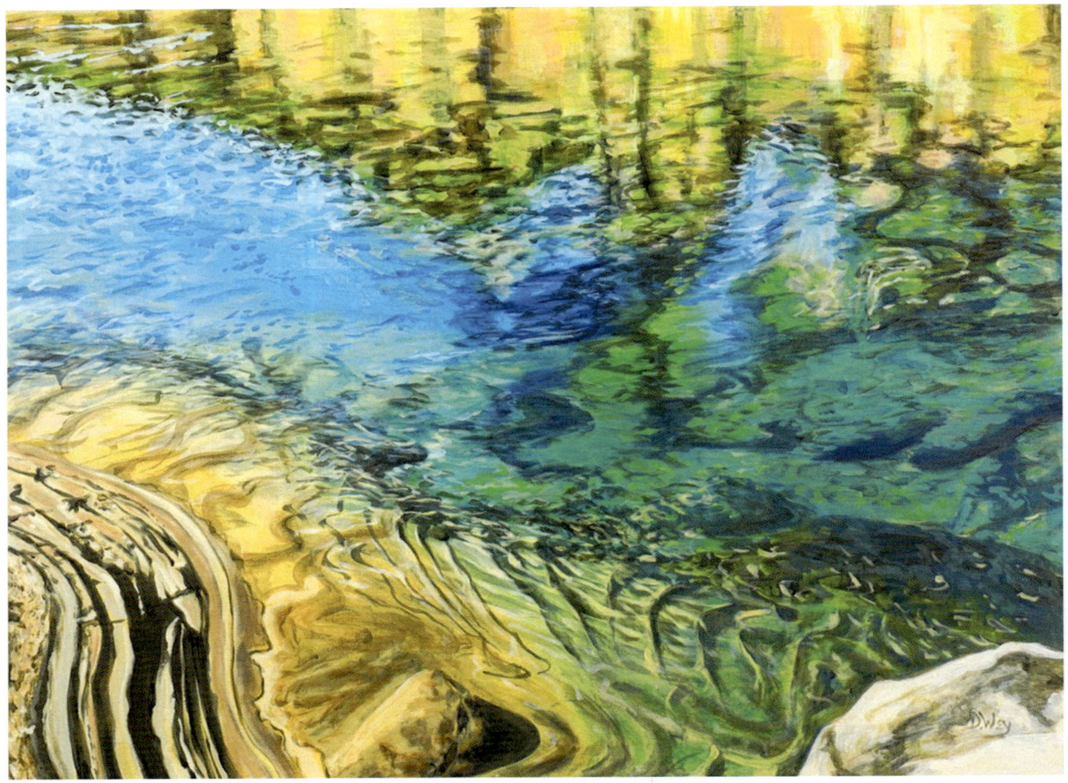

Emerald Pools, #040***,*** "36 x 48", acrylic on canvas, private collection

Emerald Pools

i was hoping you'd want to change
our original plan and take a spontaneous
trip to the river instead, you were right
there with me so we jumped in the car
and drove the windy road to bridgeport,
digging the dollar bills out of our pockets
for the parking fee, walking under the bridge,
past the wintering figs and blackberries,
along the path to the empty beaches,
the riverbed carved so wide and high
from the storms last fall, ravaged,
rebalancing, i expected more rushing
water after all that but you say the
snowpack is still holding on, hasn't
begun its melting, but still the swimming
holes are deeper than summer, quiet,
finding a sunny rock to lounge on,
doing nothing, letting the universe
handle all the stuff to be done at home,
gazing for an hour into the many greens
and watching the changing currents
and patterns on the water's surface,
wondering if we caused the chaos that
formed as we spoke of the darknesses
in our culture, and how it's affecting
the children, so we began chanting love,
singing love is all your need, you hopped
down to inscribe love in the silky sand

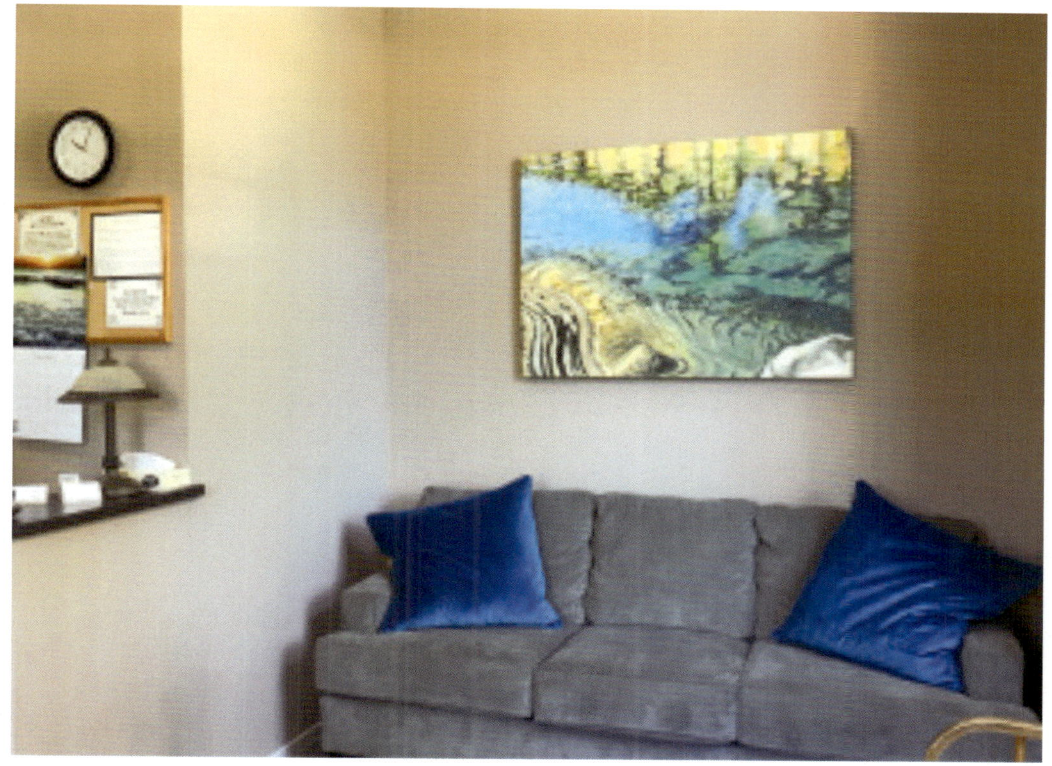

in situ

of the shallows, glinting pyrite, radiating,
finding the mother bird in the ferned
rock formation, the divine feminine
in all its aspects, all part of us, dark,
light, letting go our grievances, our
worries, for a time, water, earth, sky,
february sun rock, emerald pools

—Lil McGill

In 2013-2015, I was finding my stride as a painter…the impressionistic brush strokes would peek through every so often. But something else was happening…my "style" was emerging. A friend and mentor used to say "Don't worry about finding your signature style…it's already there, embedded in you… just paint a lot! And when you find it, you won't be able to get rid of it!"

Since I've been teaching art, I've come to see this to be true! It's why we never have to worry about someone copying us. Though a very good copy of a piece might be produced, the copying of the style is practically impossible.

You may see influences of past artists/mentors in the work, but really, each person's art is a window into how they see and like a snowflake it is unique. It's a good thing.

During this time, I was enjoying teaching art in many mediums to children and adults alike which, I believe, helped me become a better artist.

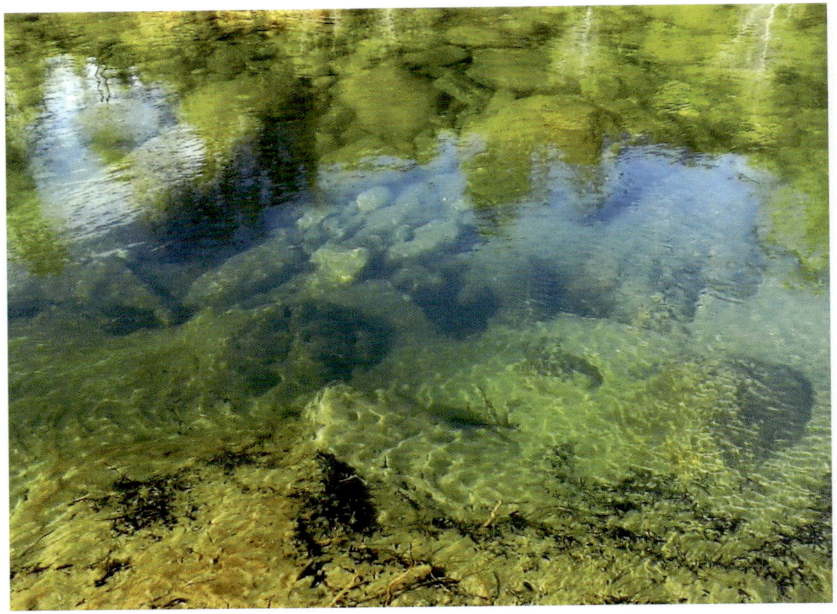

reference photo by Lil McGill

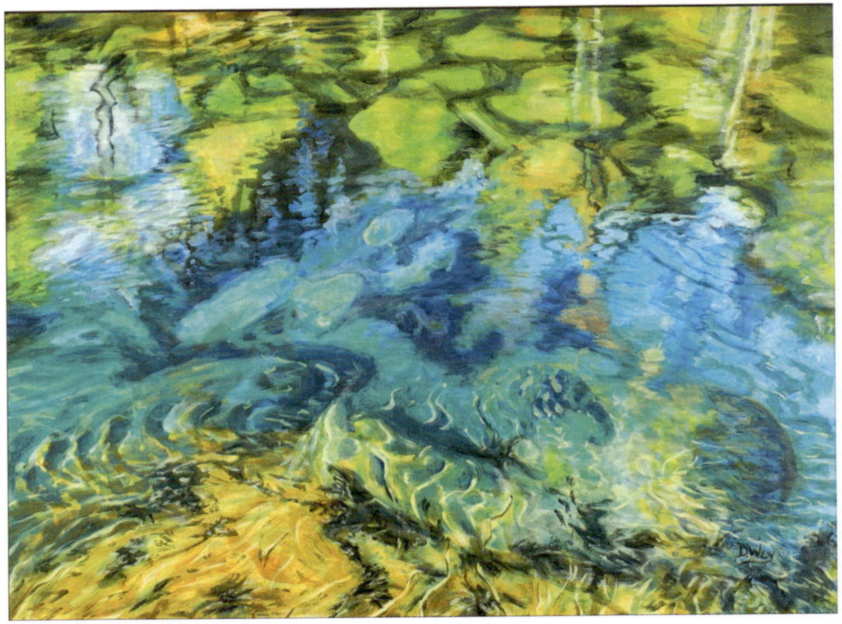

Emerald Pools II, #041, 36"x 48"
acrylic on canvas, private collection

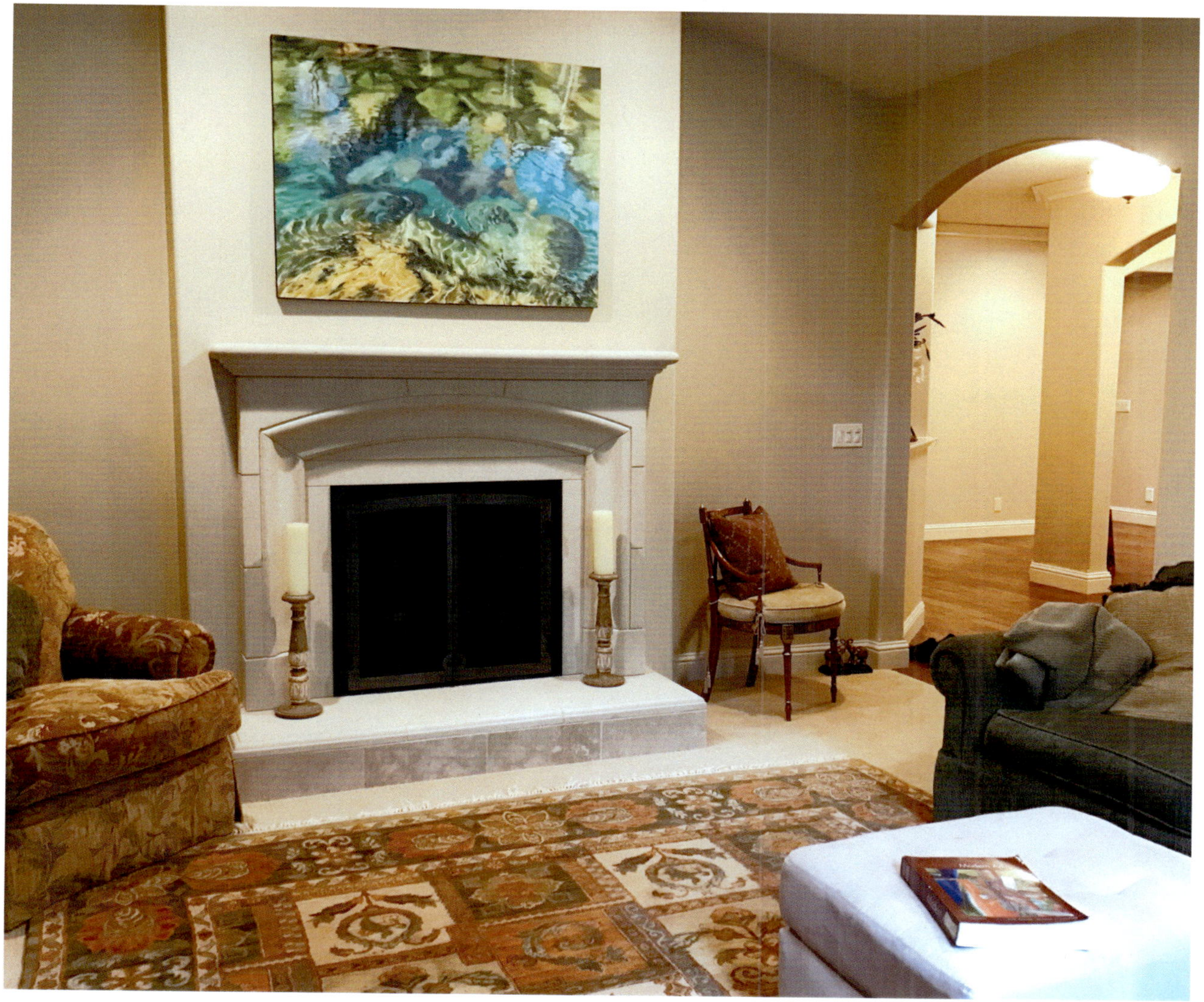

in situ

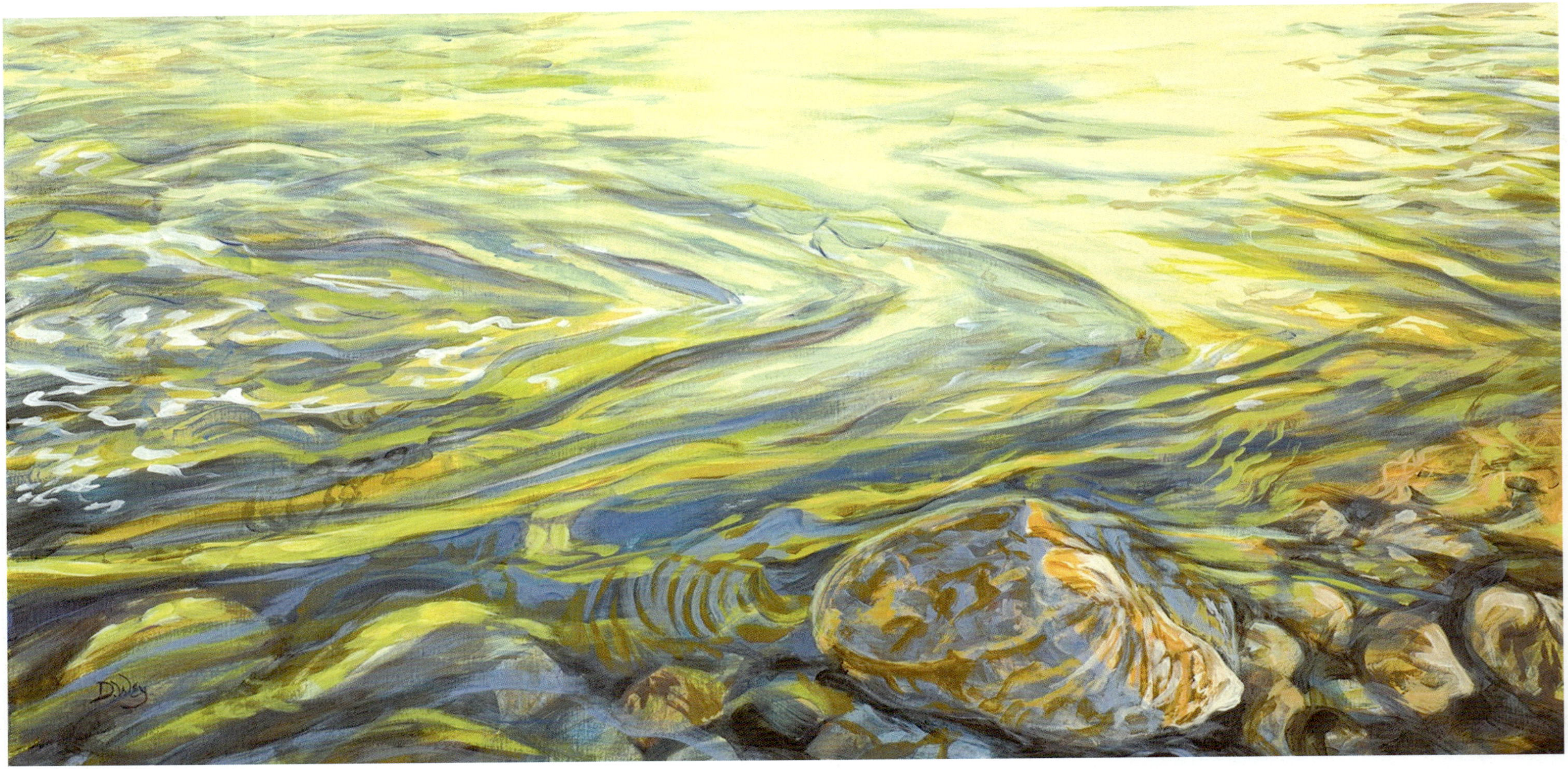

River Running, #028, 18" x 36", acrylic on canvas, private collection

These years were exciting for me as a painter. I didn't set out consciously to choose this direction. It felt a bit like I was riding the crest of a wave...the force and momentum was tangible. And I felt another presence strongly with me during these times; energizing me... helping me. Was this the Muse that some artists talk about?

Maybe...whatever it was, I was paying attention to the painting and what it was communicating. I now learned that some of the best paintings came forth when they were hardly touched by me...when personality got out of the way and the artist functioned in the present moment of No-Mind, connected to Source. I have a taste for this natural essential state of being—I lived to paint and was loving it!

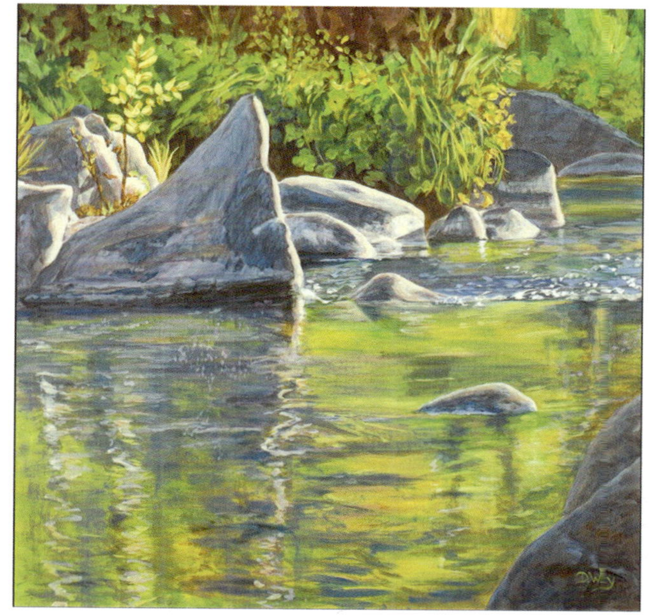

River Time, #033, 36" x 36",
acrylic on canvas, private collection

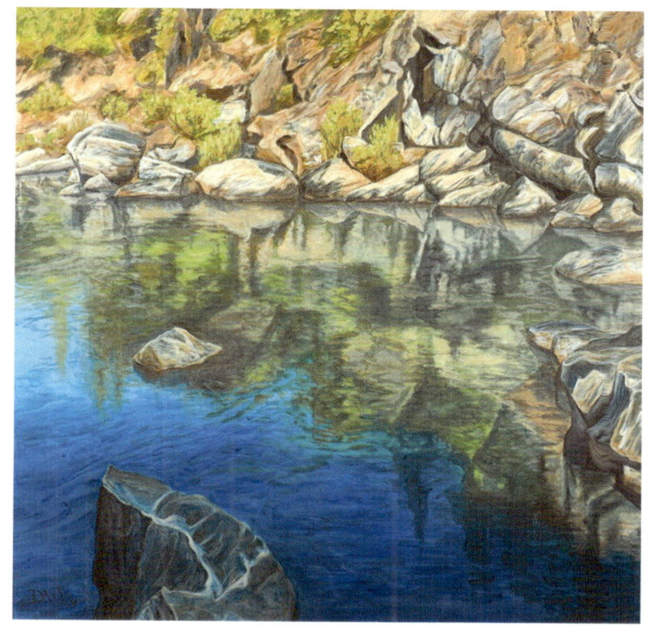

River Mirror, #037, 36" x 36",
acrylic on canvas, private collection

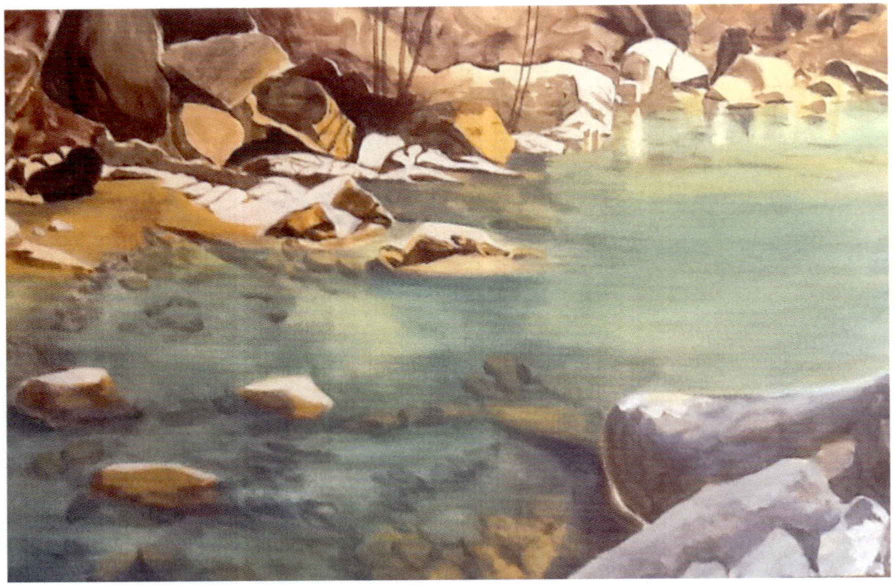

River Beach in progress, first layers

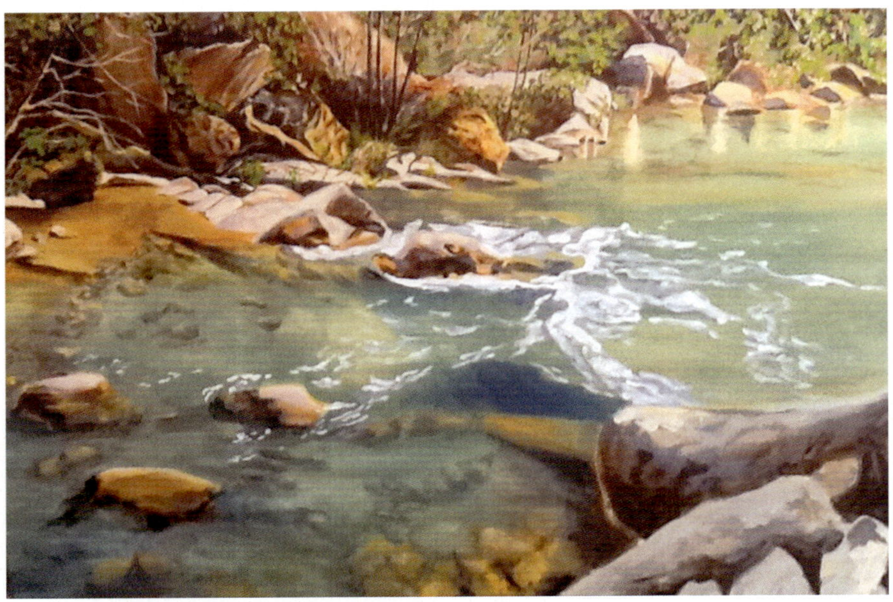

River Beach in progress, four layers later

A personal favorite, River Beach was a photo I'd taken and the color foundation for this painting rested on the natural dynamics of the complimentary earthy versions of red and green.

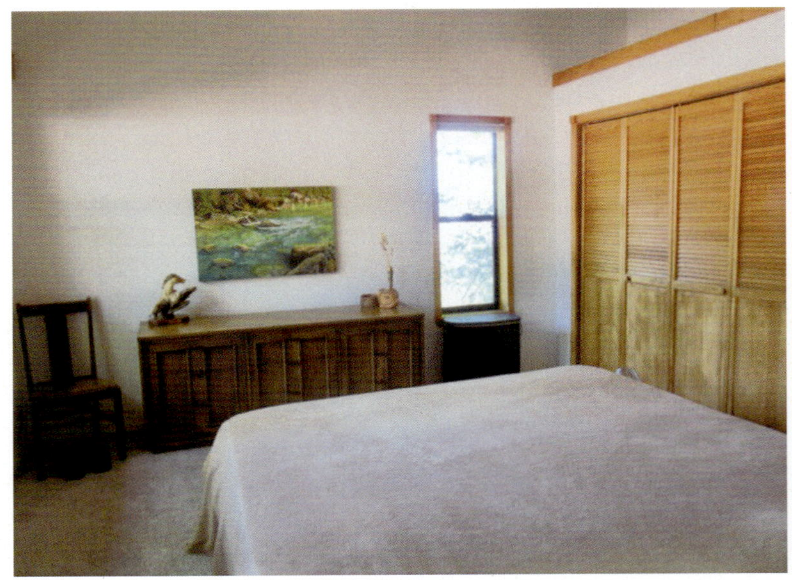

in situ

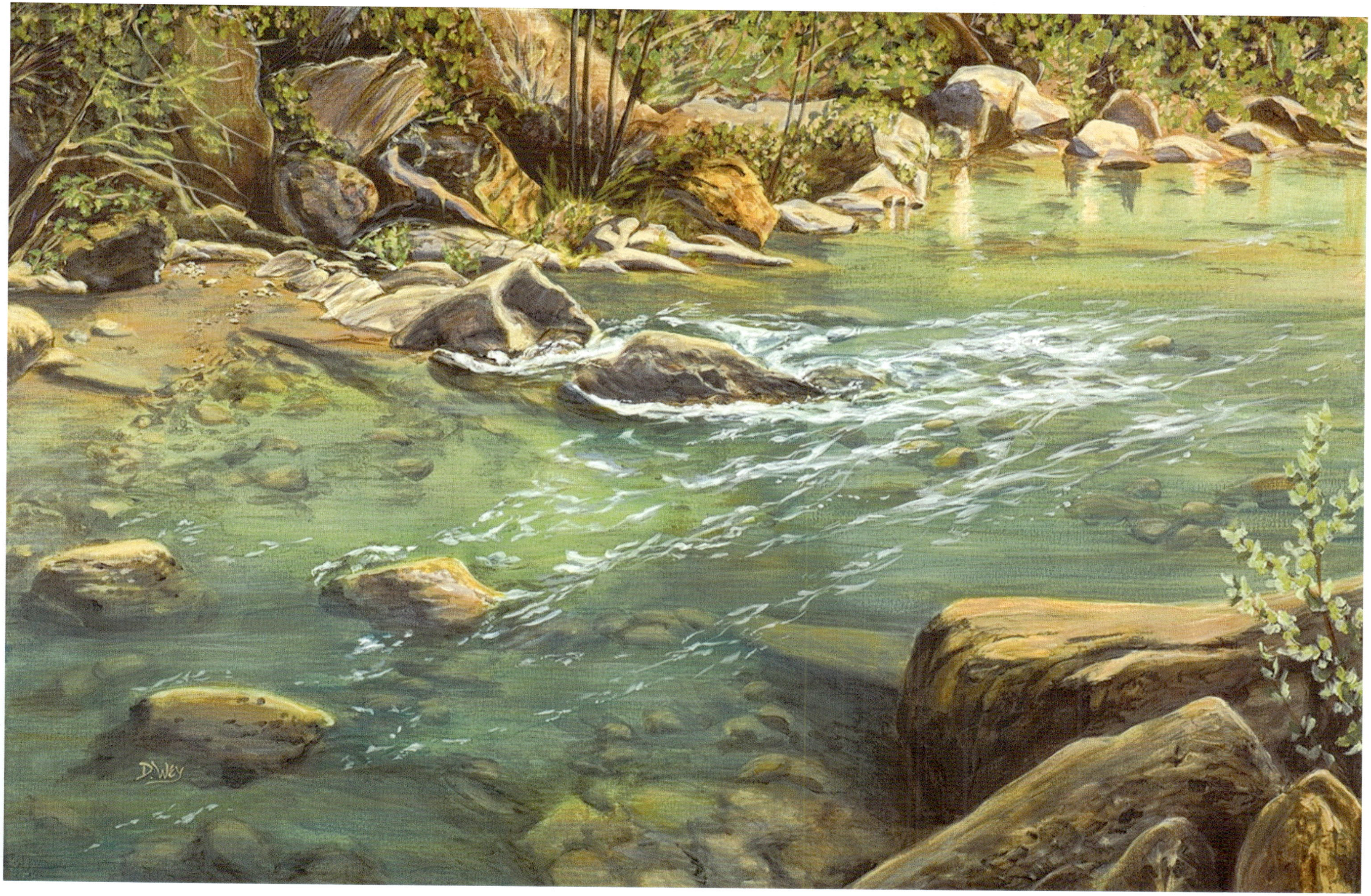

River Beach, #036, 24" x 36", acrylic on canvas, private collection

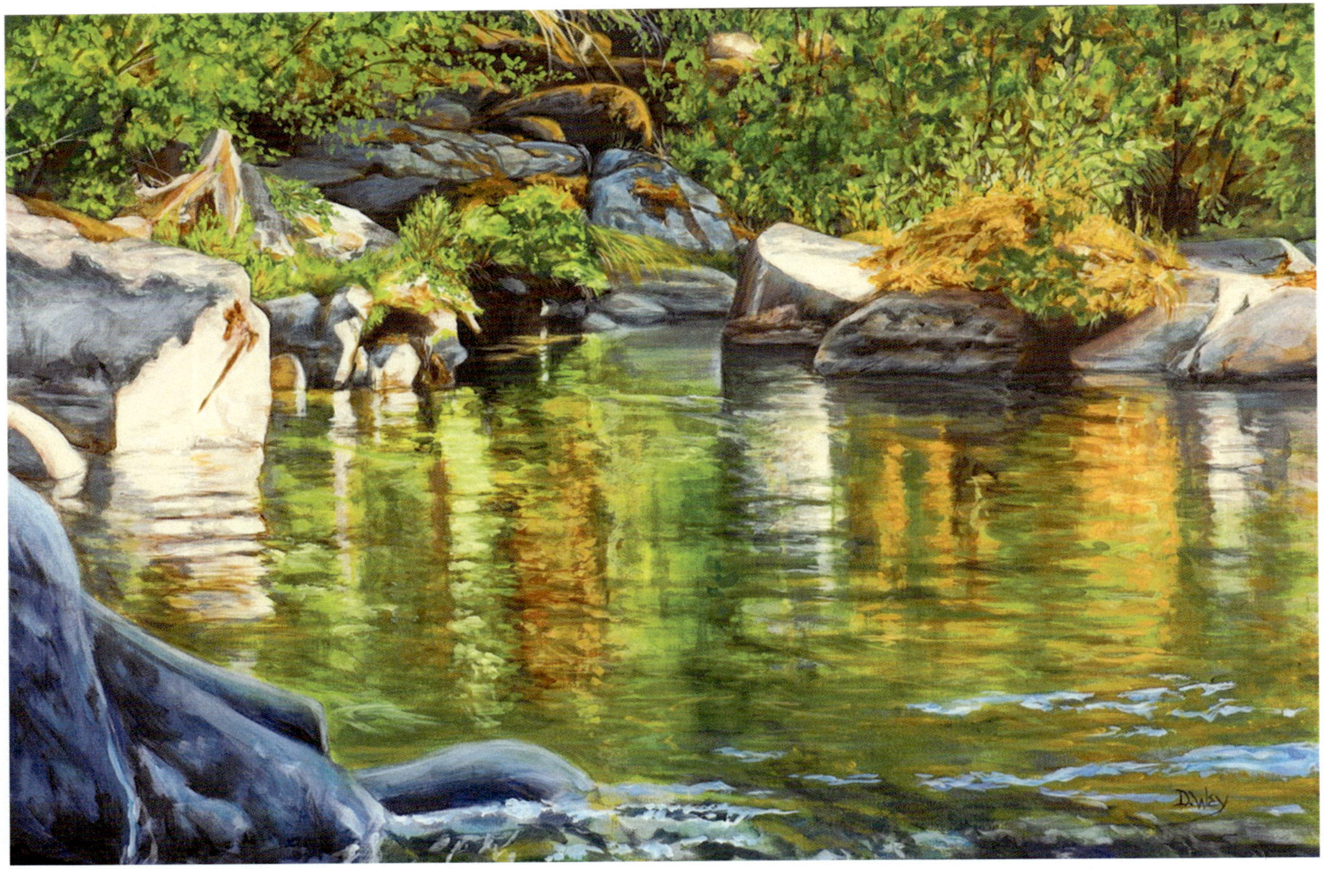

Yuba Golds, #038,
24" x 36"
acrylic on canvas,
private collection

photo reference

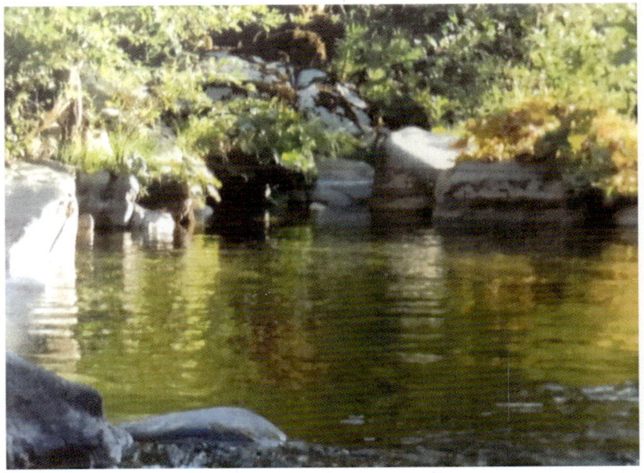

in situ

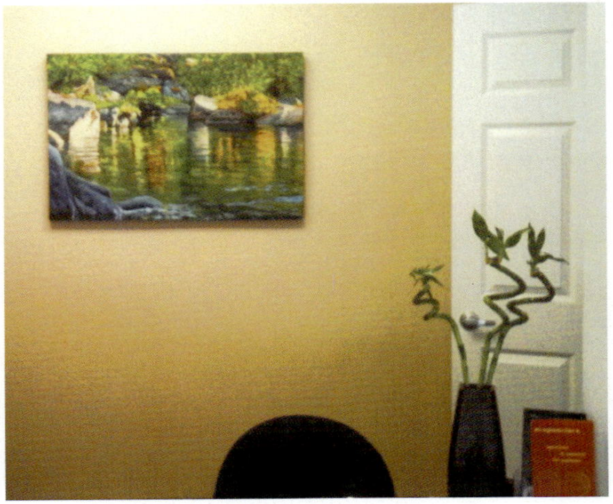

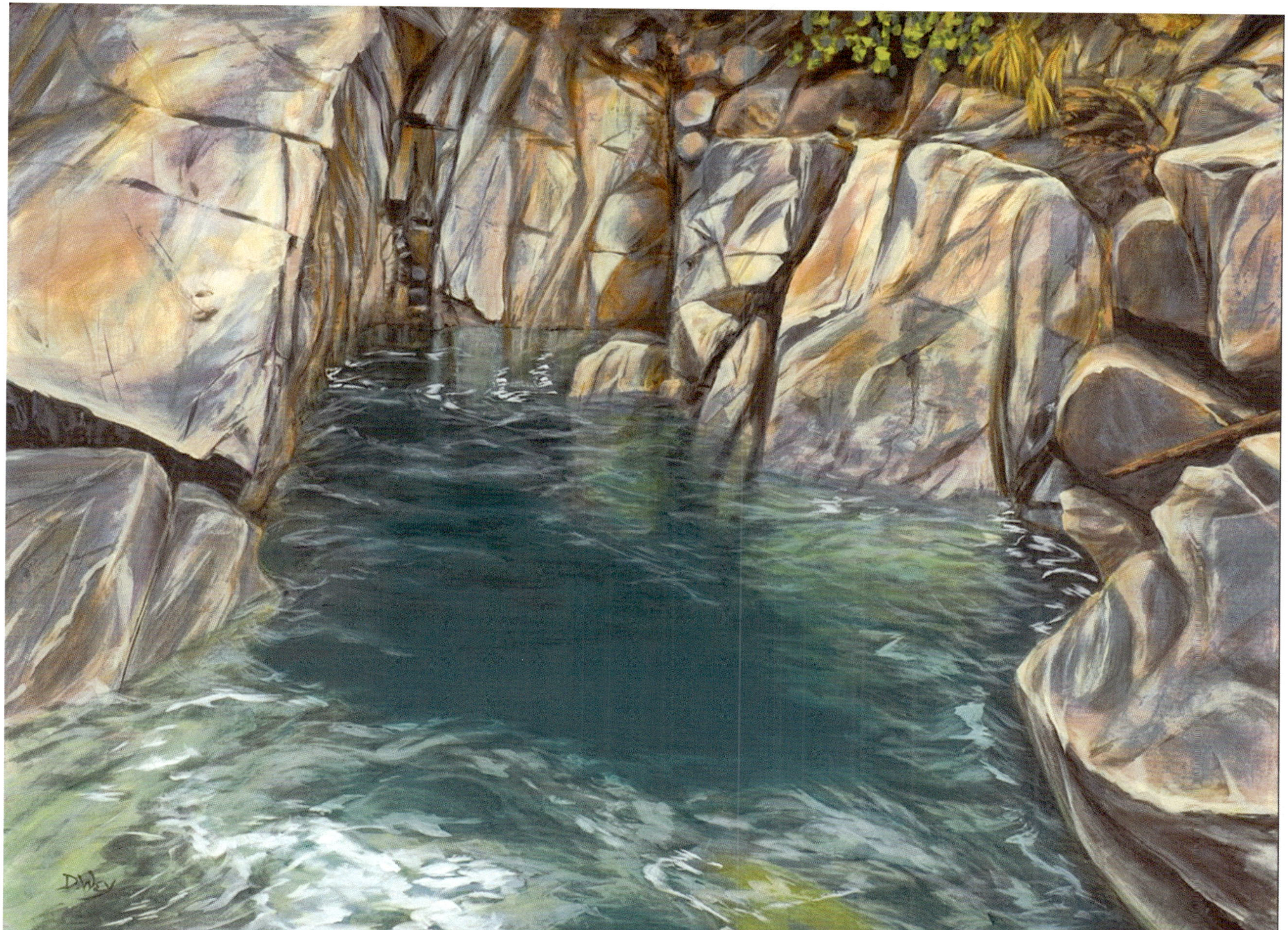

River Music, #060, 36″ x 48″, acrylic on canvas, private collection

River Necklace was a breakthrough for me because the painting seemed to vibrate with presence throughout its emergence. I began this diptych on my birthday, February 20, 2014. I laid in my value under-painting and really liked the loose qualities that happened. However, the painting seemed to communicate to let it be…to be careful and go slow. As a result, I felt unsure of my next step. So I flagged down some help from another artist who kindly came to the rescue. Her suggestions were sound, and I was able to move on. This painting sort of rolled out to completion with very little effort and still holds a special place in my heart.

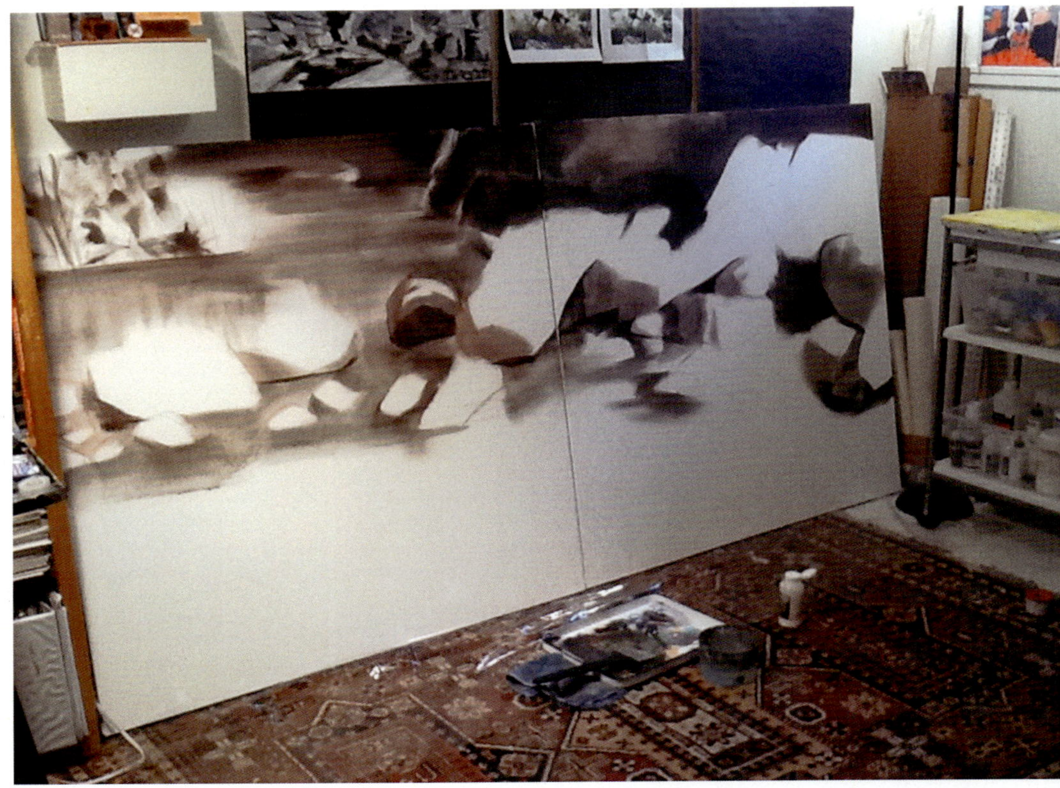

River Necklace
in progress, first layer

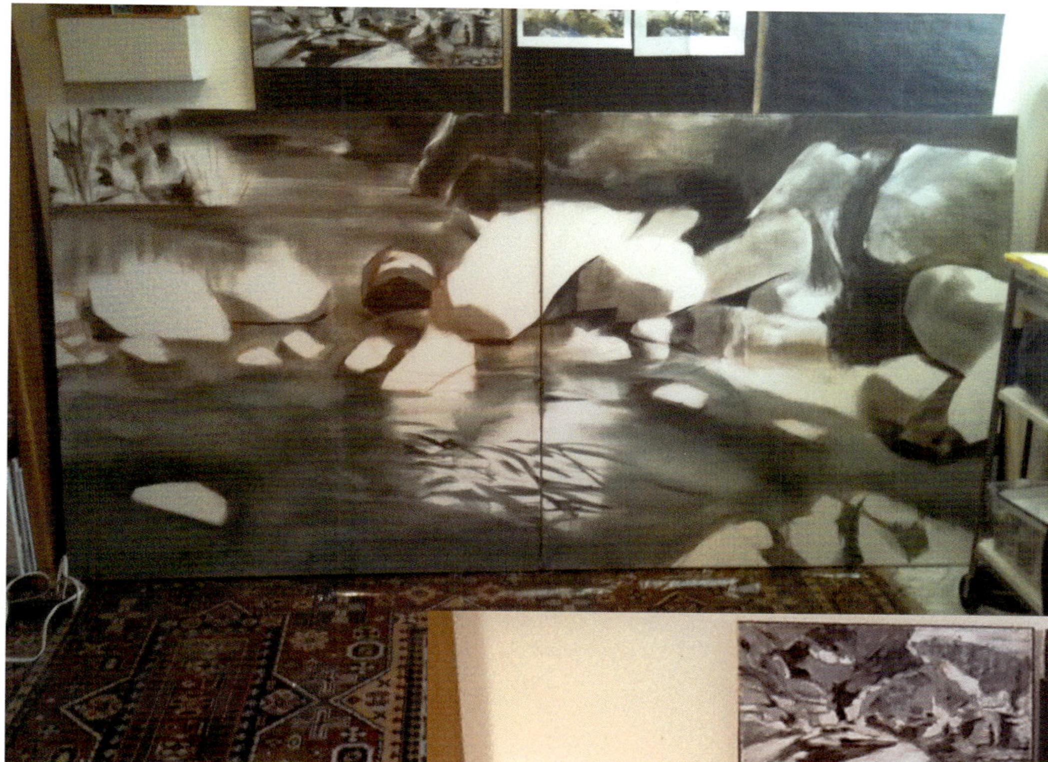

River Necklace
in progress, second layer

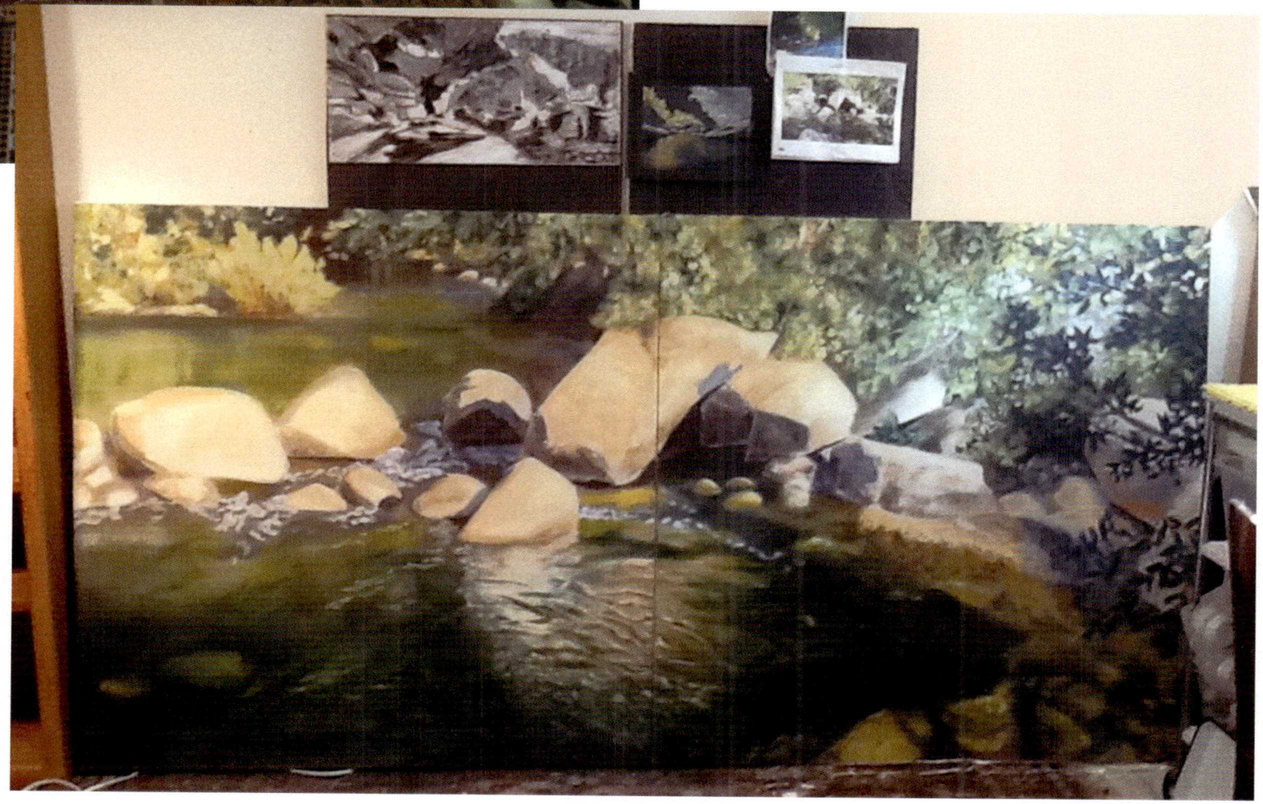

River Necklace
in progress,
many layers later

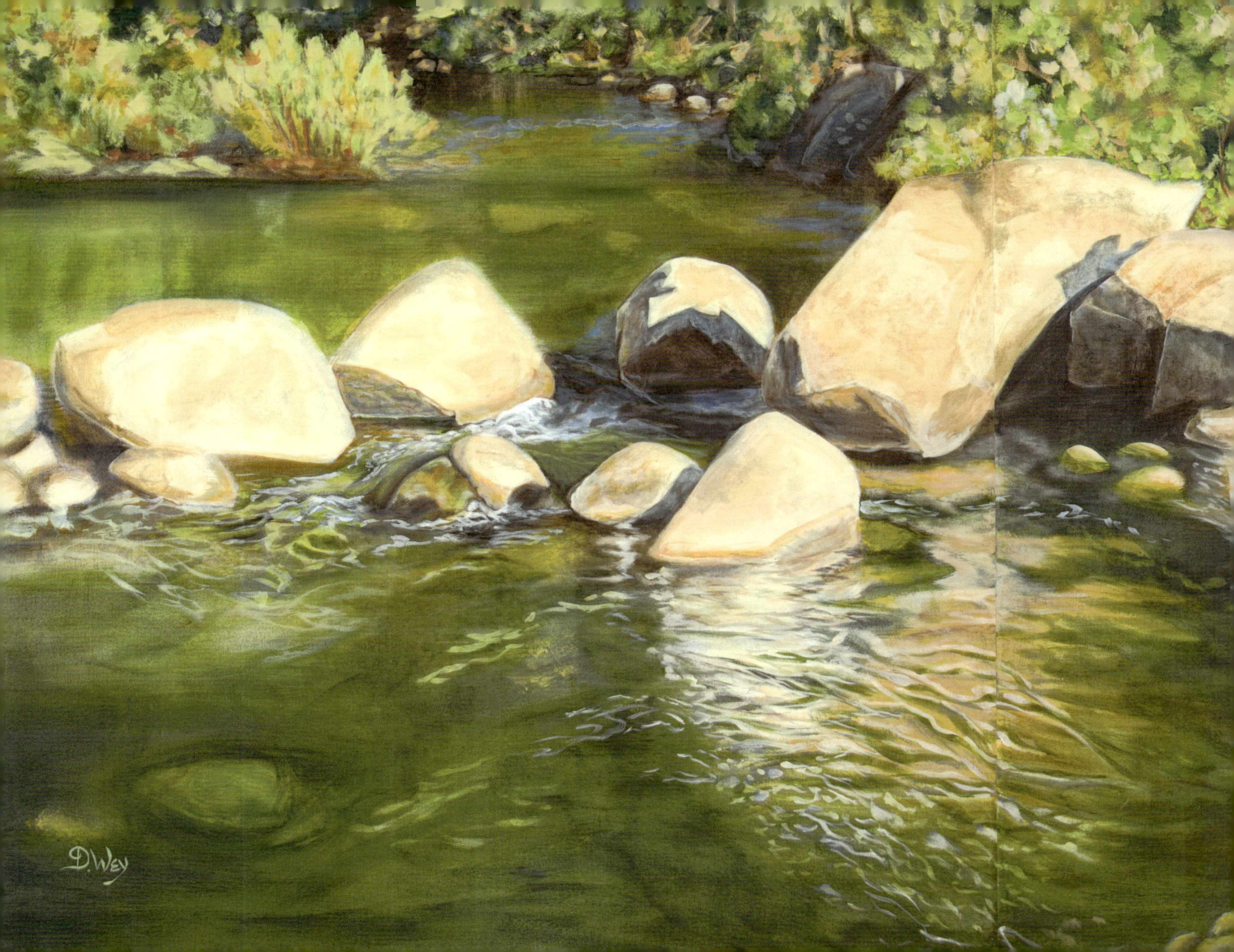
D.Wey

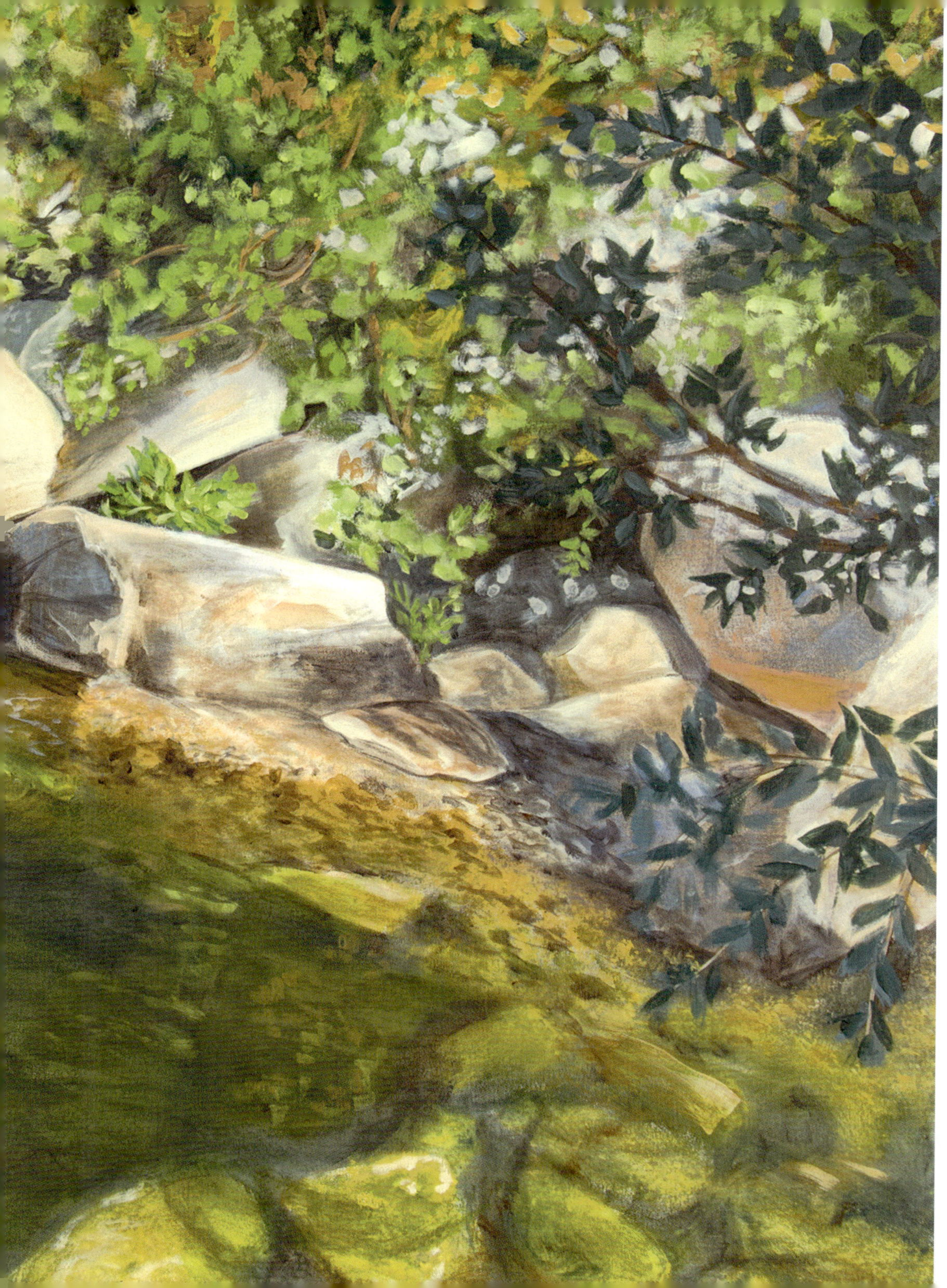

River Necklace, #042 & #043
48″ x 96″, diptych
acrylic on canvas
private collection

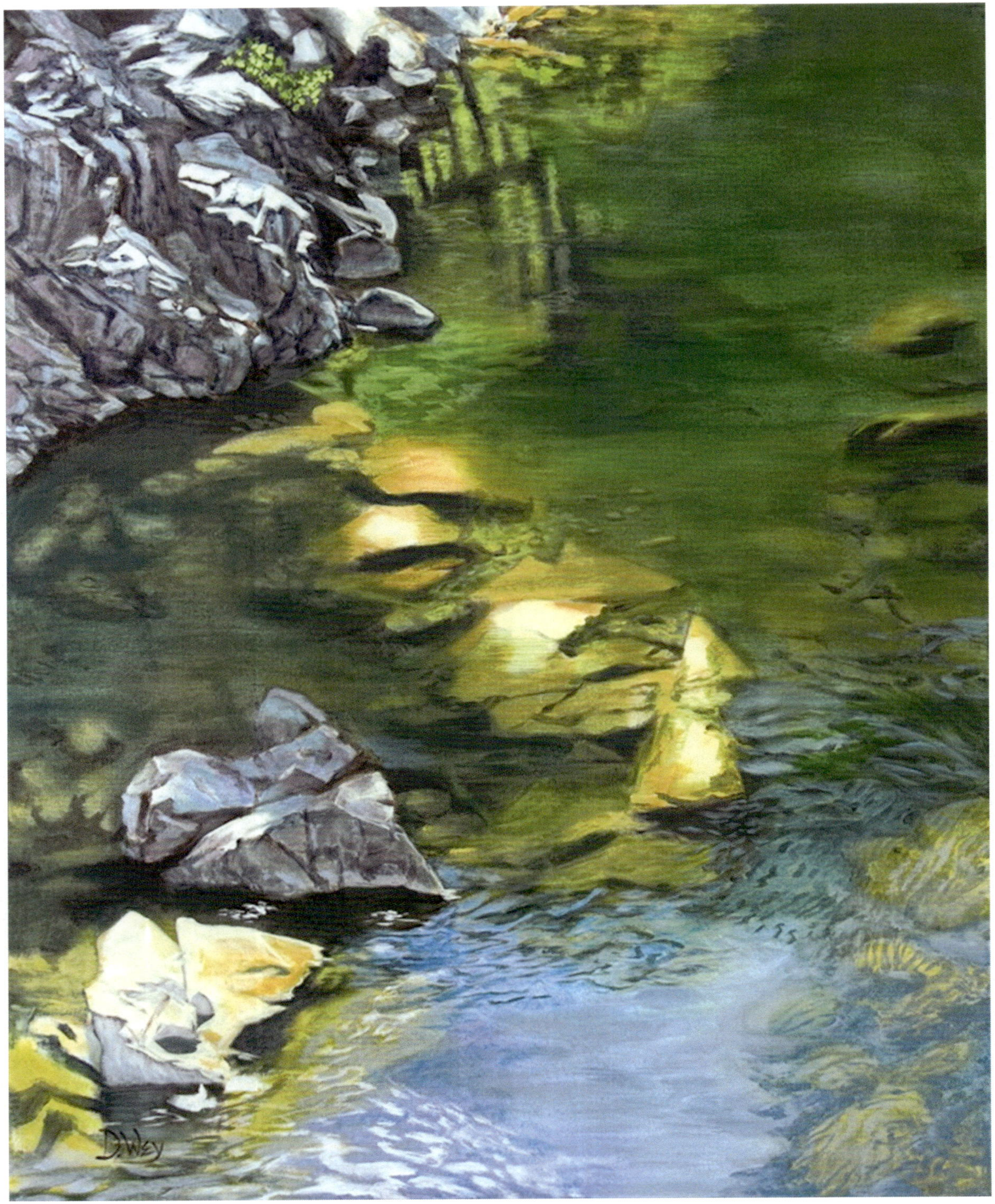

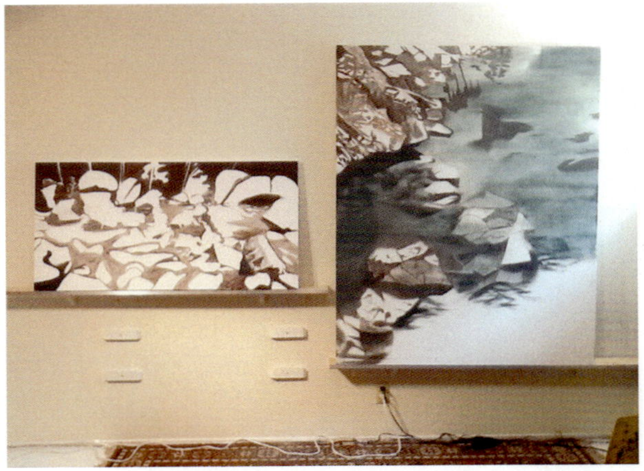

Two Swimmers and Emerald Waters: values laid in here.

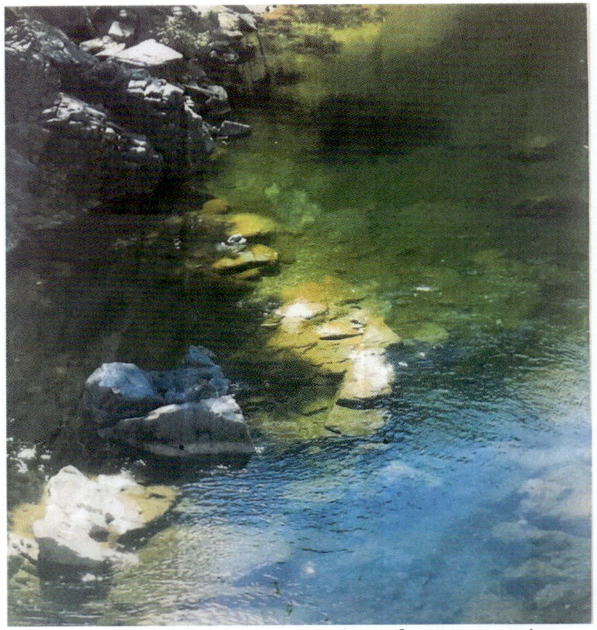

reference photo

Emerald Waters, #047
60" x 48"
acrylic on canvas
private collection

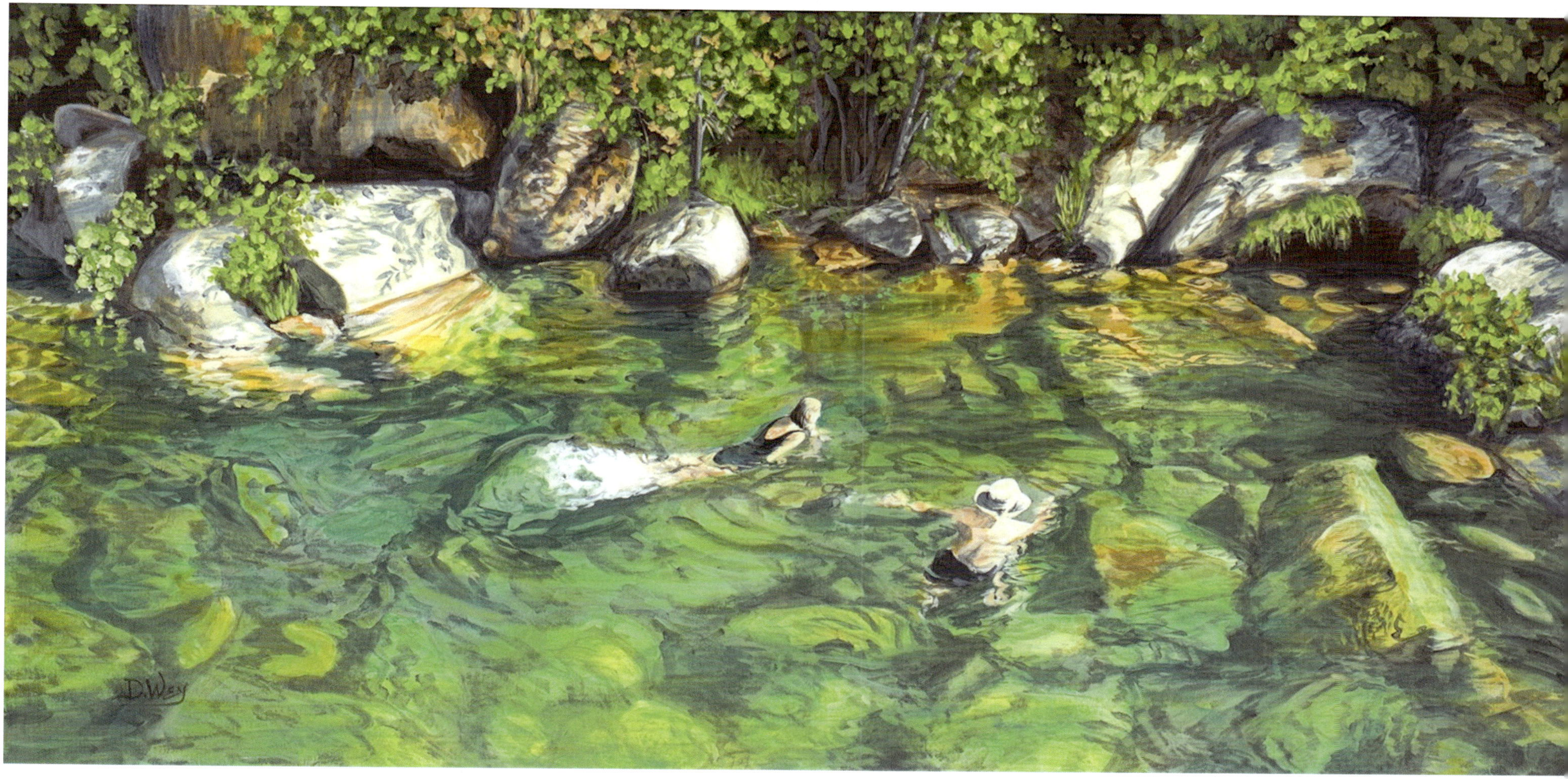

Two Swimmers, #046, 24″ x 48″, acrylic on canvas, private collection

It was pure painting pleasure to work on Emerald Waters. It was a 60″ x 48″ canvas and I used large brushes and lots of paint. Painting it was a dance and took no time or maybe it just felt that way! I love the perspective from on high looking down.

At the same time I began Two Swimmers. It's rare that my paintings of the river are populated with humans but this was an exception for some reason. I enjoyed painting them, too!

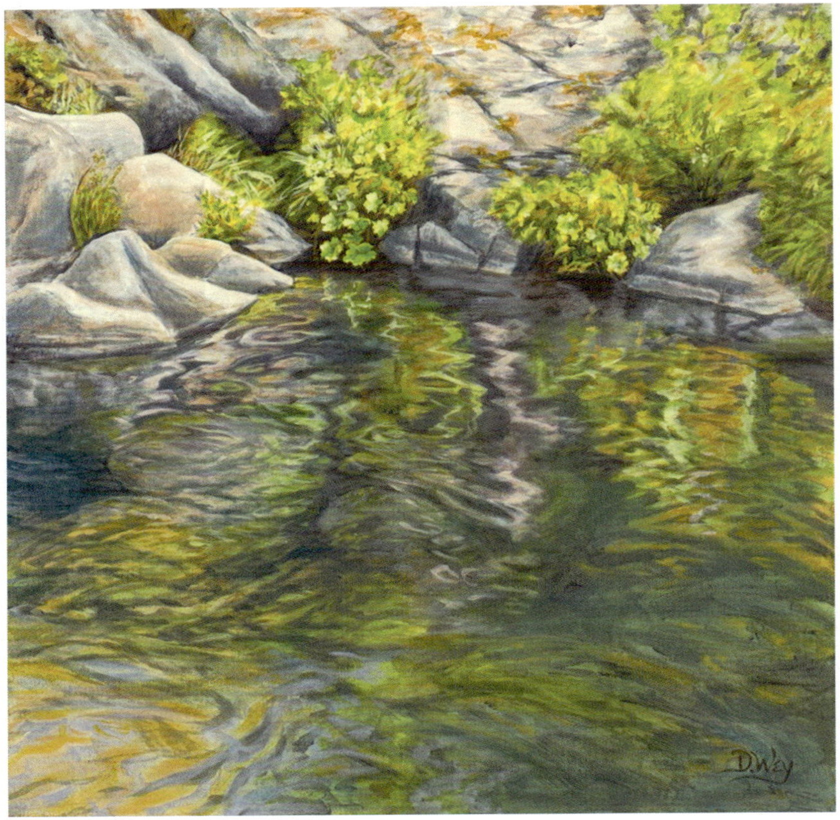

Summer River, #045
36″ x 36″
acrylic on canvas
private collection

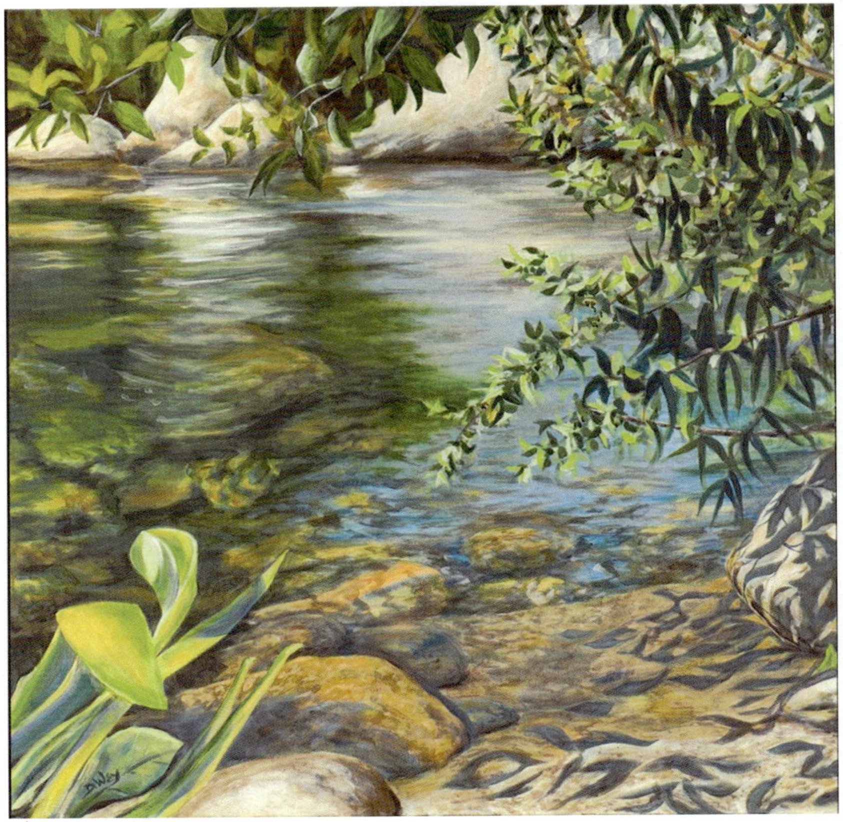

River Sanctuary, #062
36″ x 36″
acrylic on canvas

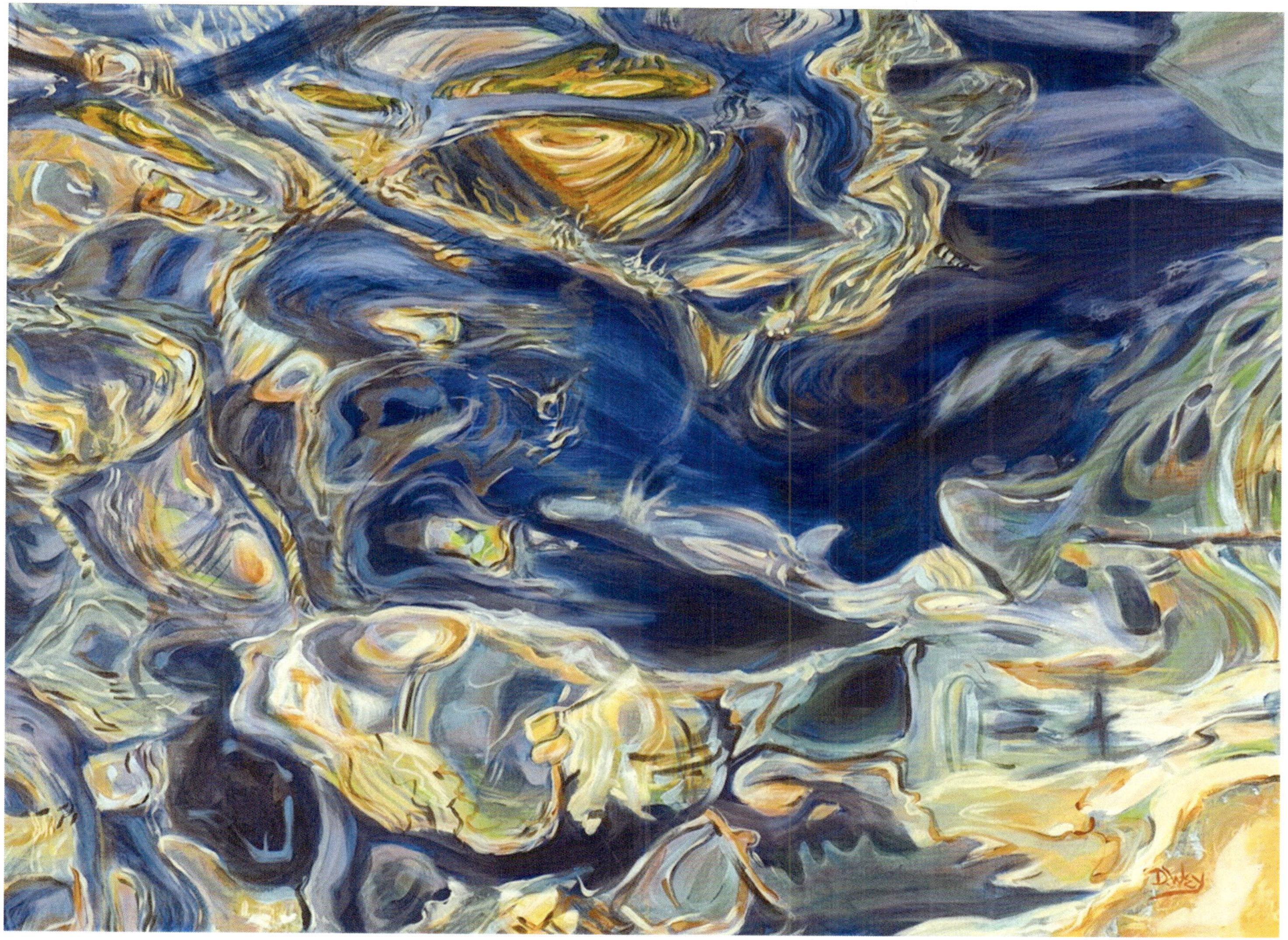

River Dreaming, #061, 36″ x 48″, acrylic on canvas

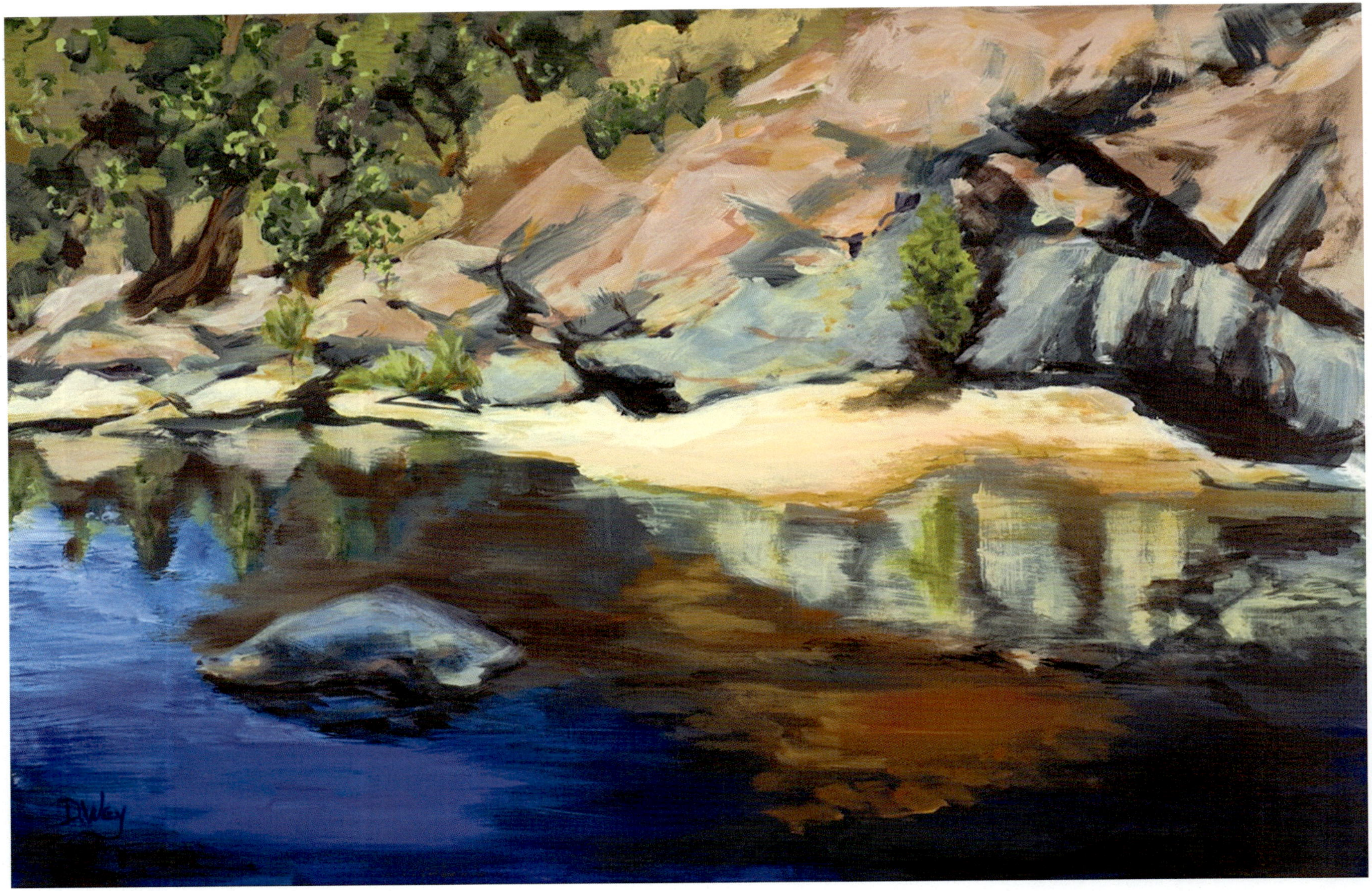

Spring Yuba, #049, 24″ x 36″, acrylic on canvas, private collection

Spring Yuba was a painting demonstration at a Studio Tour and was simply painted from memory, using warm and cool colors.

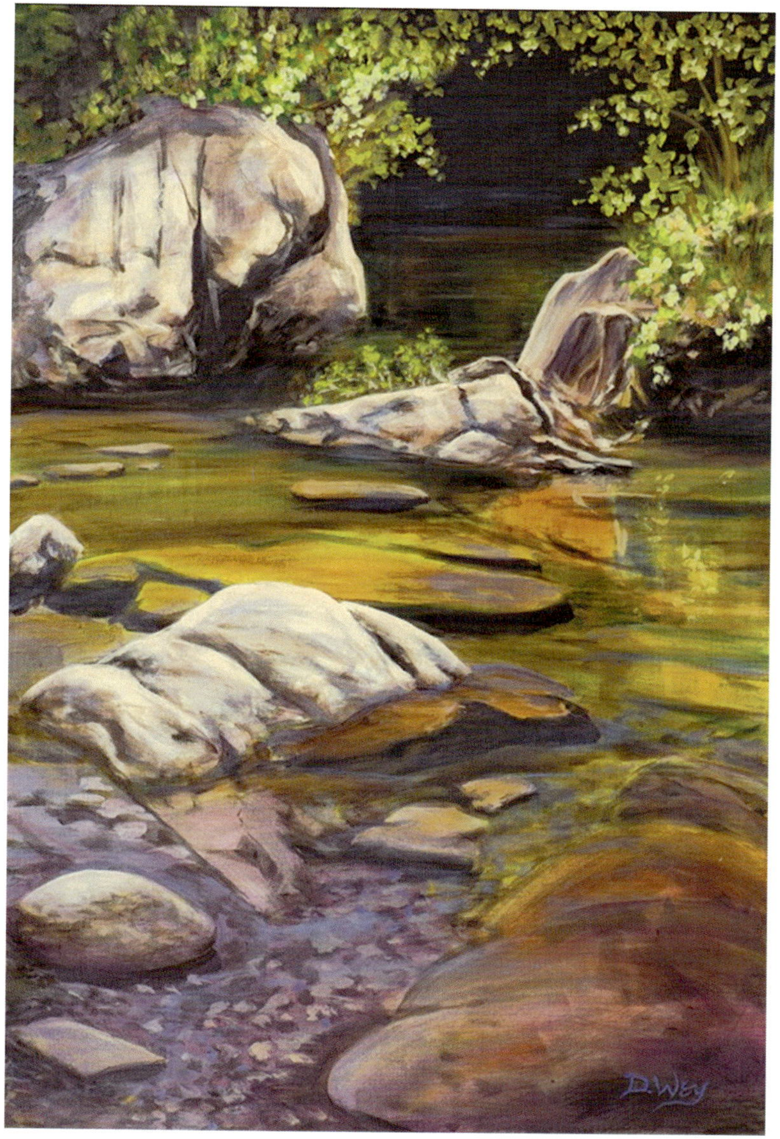

Washington, CA, #054, 36″ x 24″
acrylic on canvas, private collection

Washington CA was an experiment in a color palette I don't usually use—complimentary purple and yellow.

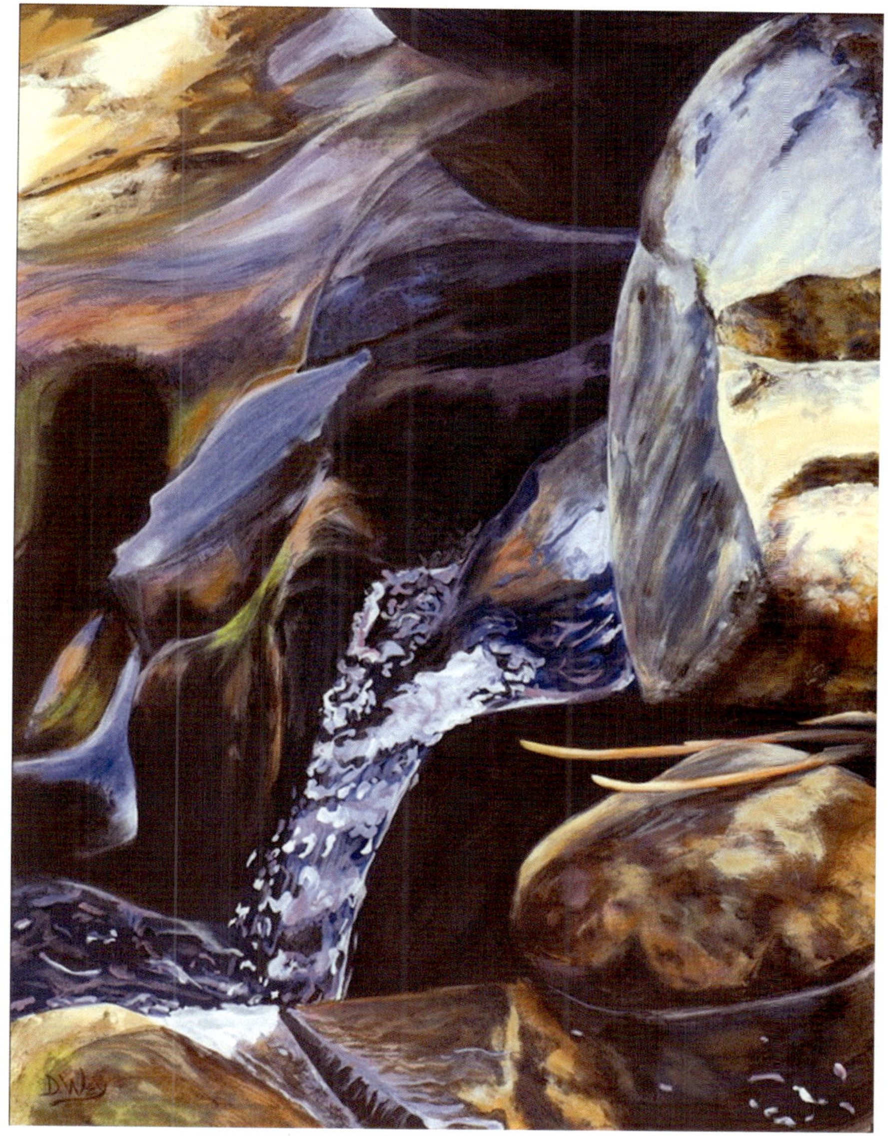

Yuba Blues, #050, 40″ x 30″, acrylic on canvas

The cool palette of Yuba Blues is imbued with the mystical powers of Nature, doing what She does when no one is watching.

Oregon Creek is easy access for when you just need a river fix fast! It has great swimming in crystal clear waters and lush trees along the river.

Oregon Creek, #051
24″ x 48″
acrylic on canvas
private collection

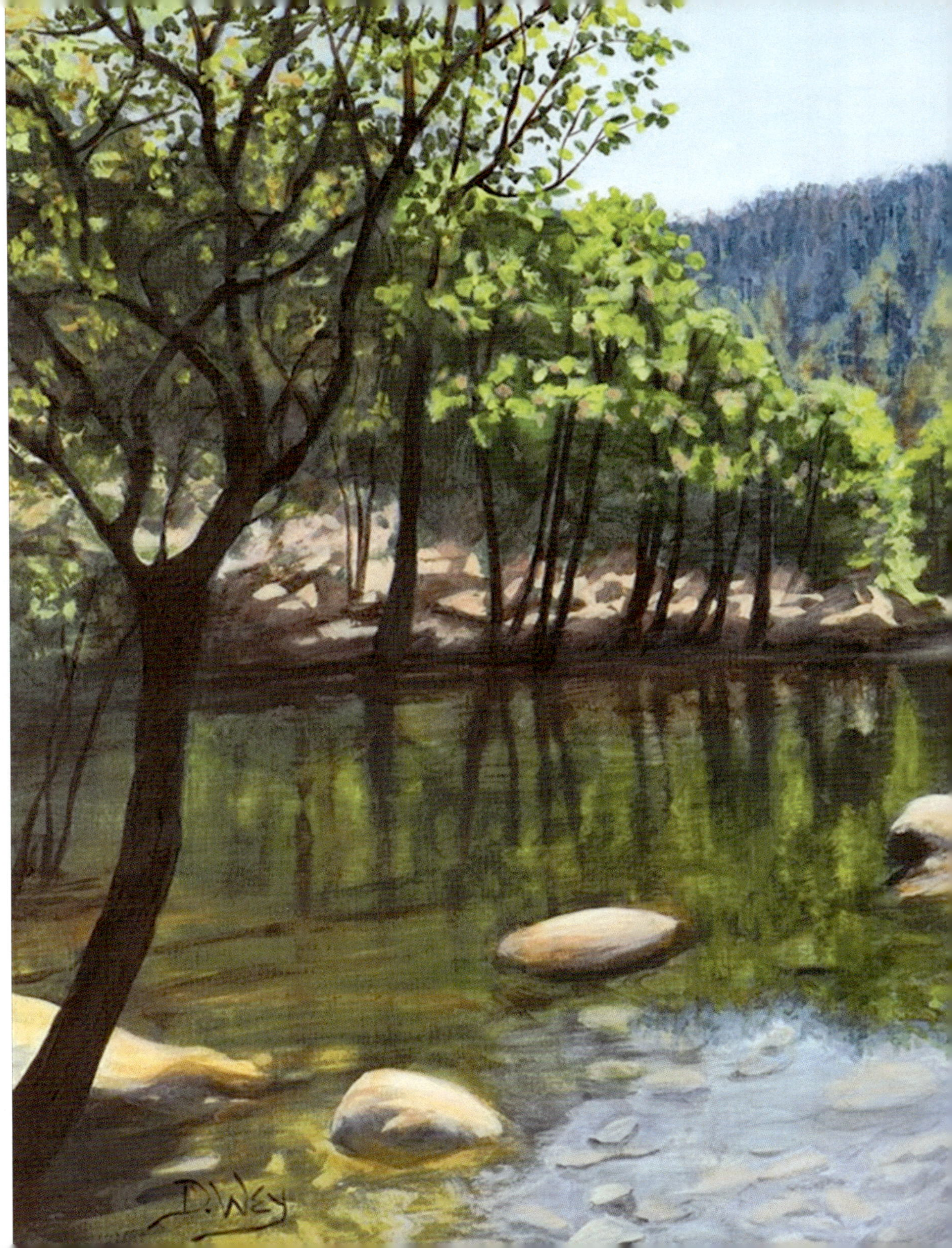

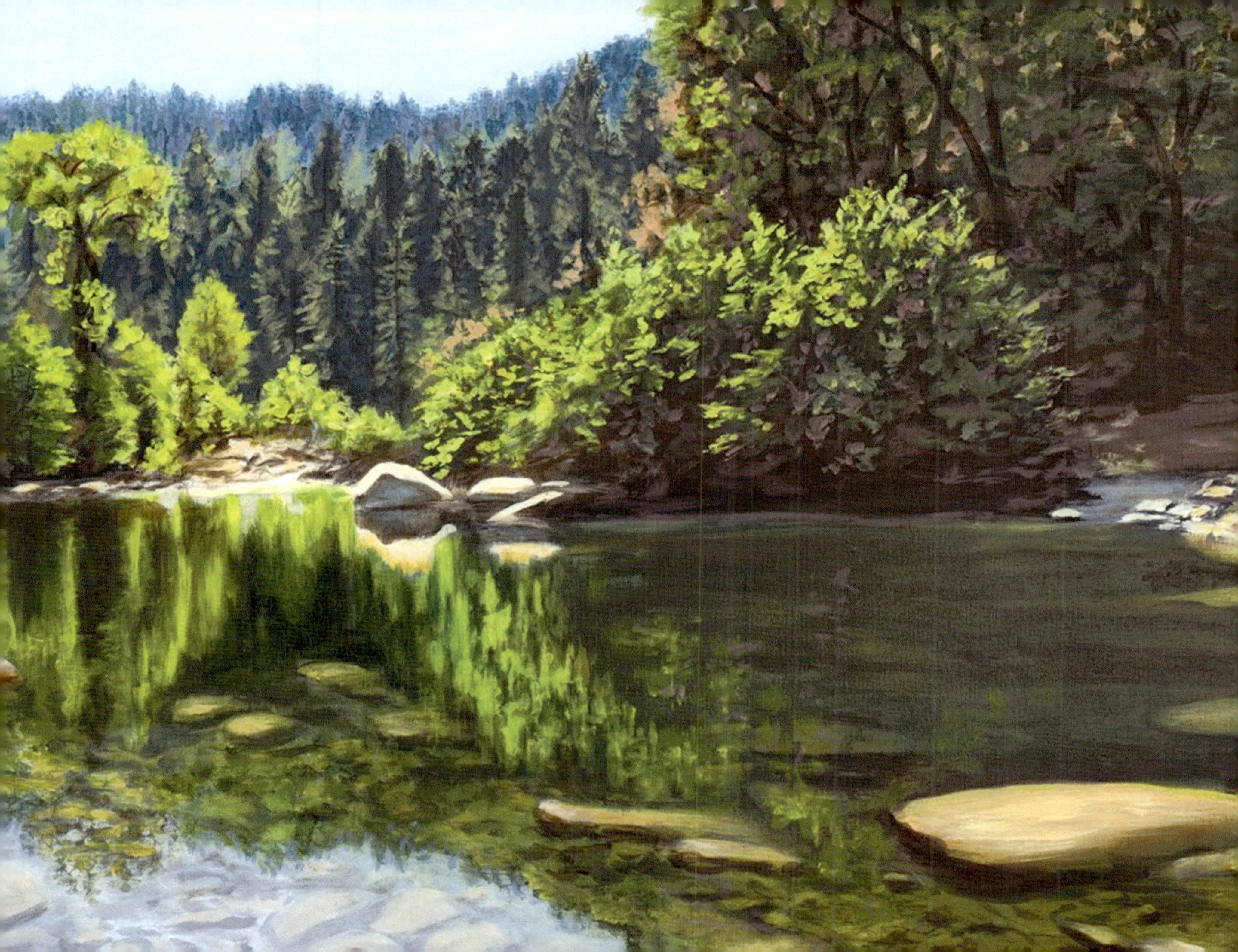

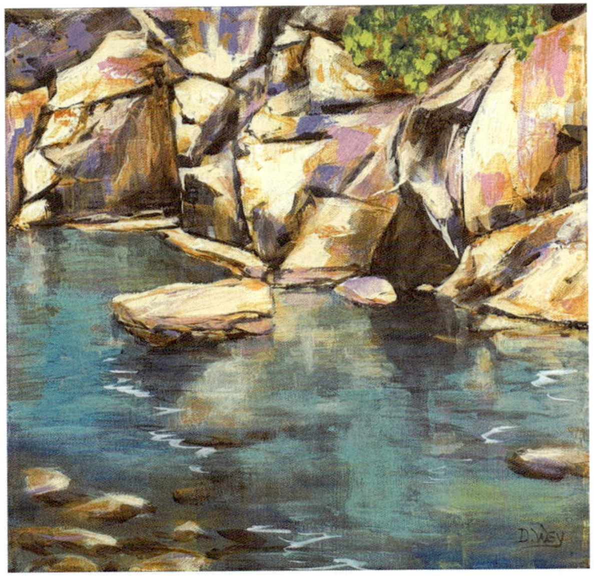

Yuba Swimming Pool #065, 12″ x 12″
acrylic on canvas, private collection

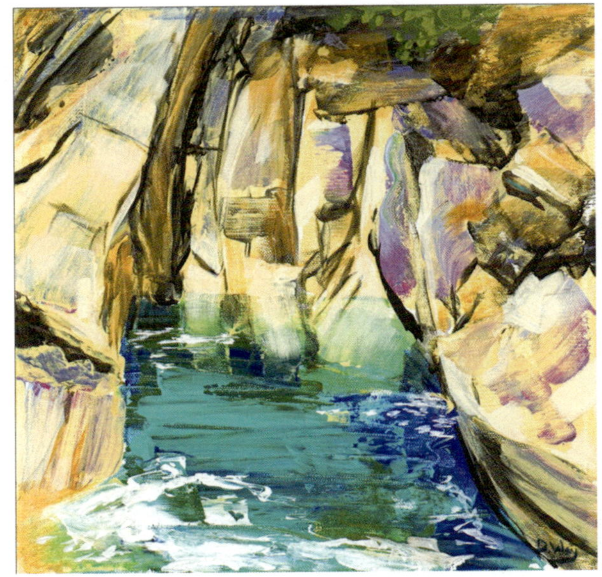

Yuba Rocks, #055, 12″ x 12″
acrylic on canvas, private collection

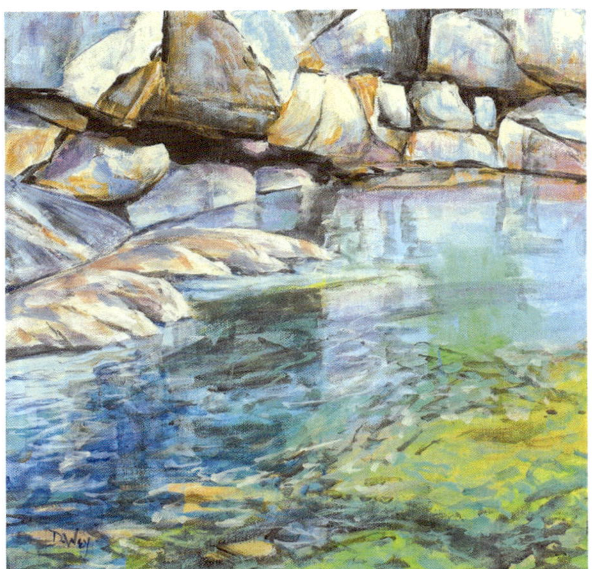

Bouldered Shoreline, #064, 12″ x 12″
acrylic on canvas, private collection

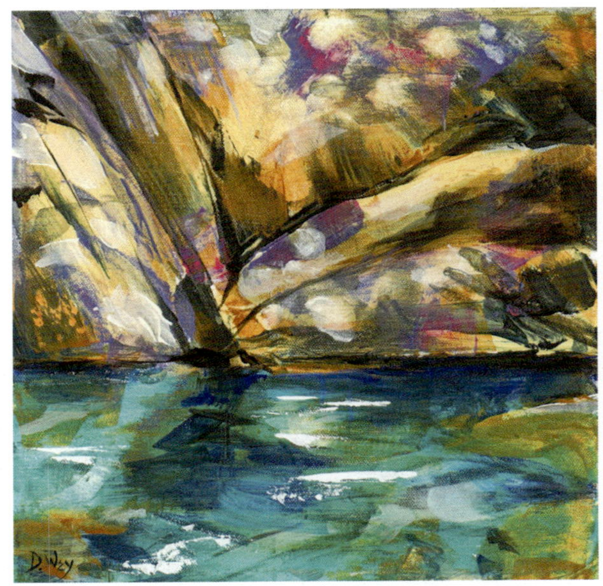

Sunlit River, #056, 12″ x 12″
acrylic on canvas, private collection

My one attempt at palette knife painting, a series of 12x12 canvases, was exciting. I thought I might keep it up as I liked having less control but went back to my brush habit. I just love a brush in the hand!

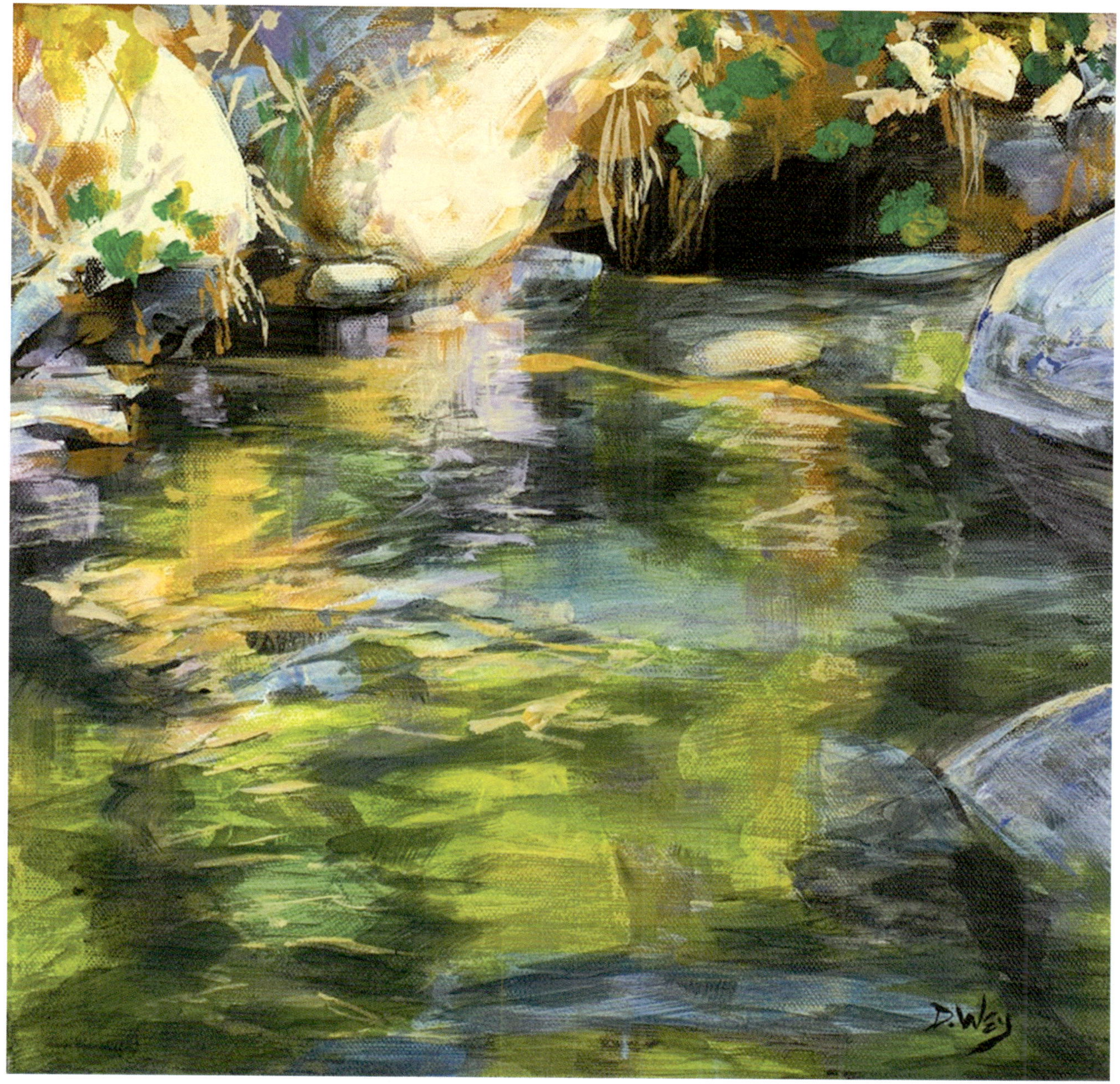

River Song, N. CA, #057, 12" x 12", acrylic on canvas, private collection

Chapter Four: 2016 - 2018

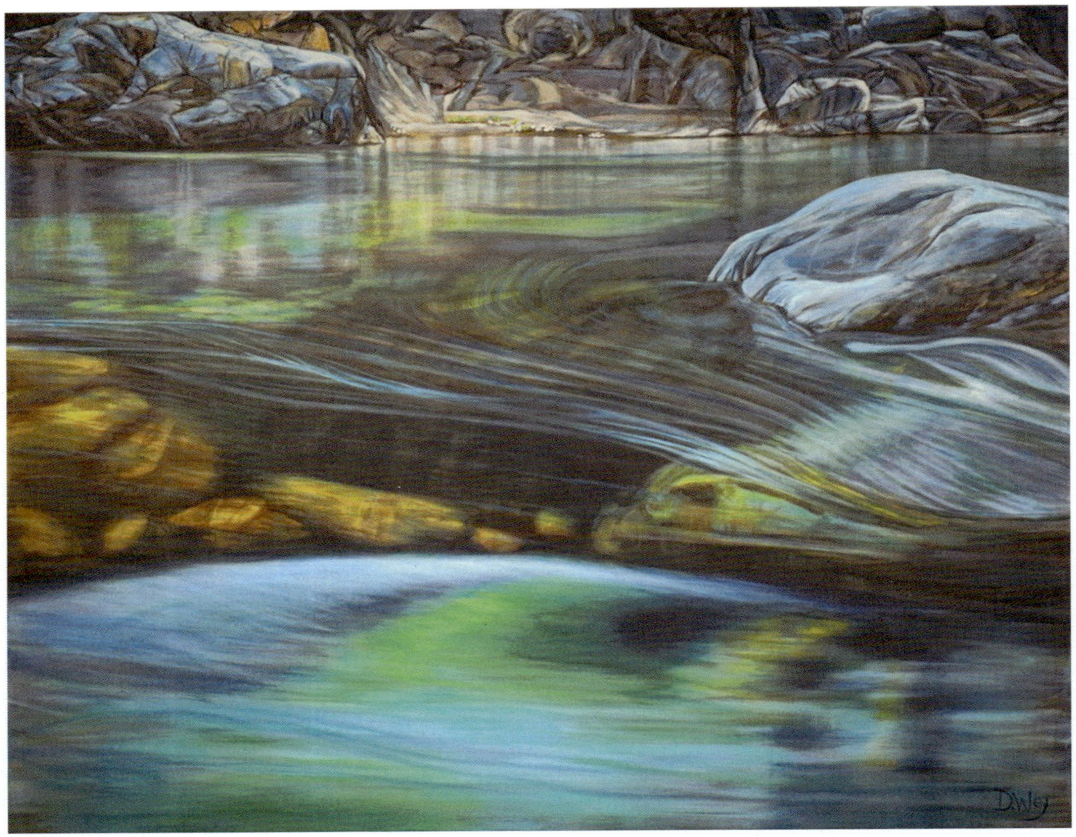

River of Light, #074, 60" x 48", acrylic on canvas, private collection

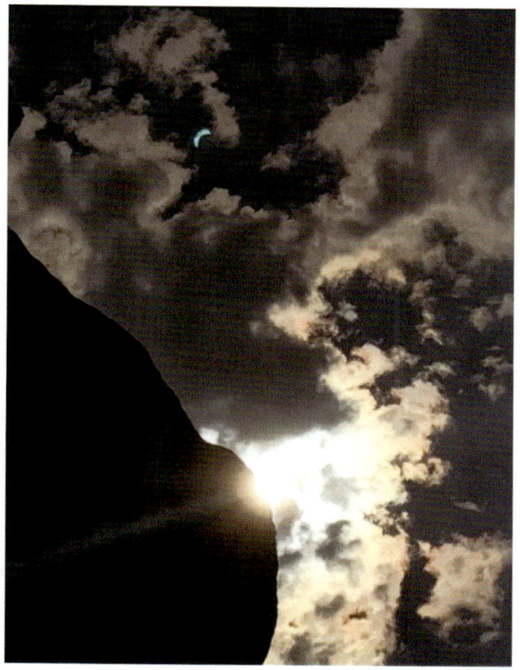

solar eclipse,
photo credit: Lil McGill

The morning of the eclipse --

the morning
of the eclipse
we took a retreat
at the river
my friends
let me be
for awhile
tucked in the shade
thanking the spirits
of rock water air
earth sun moon
going inward
to restore balance
to wonder,
here the change
was gentle, as if
no more than a cloud
had passed over
the exclamations
of young people
swimming in the
cooling shadows
and then the
quiet after,
the hush

words by Lil McGill

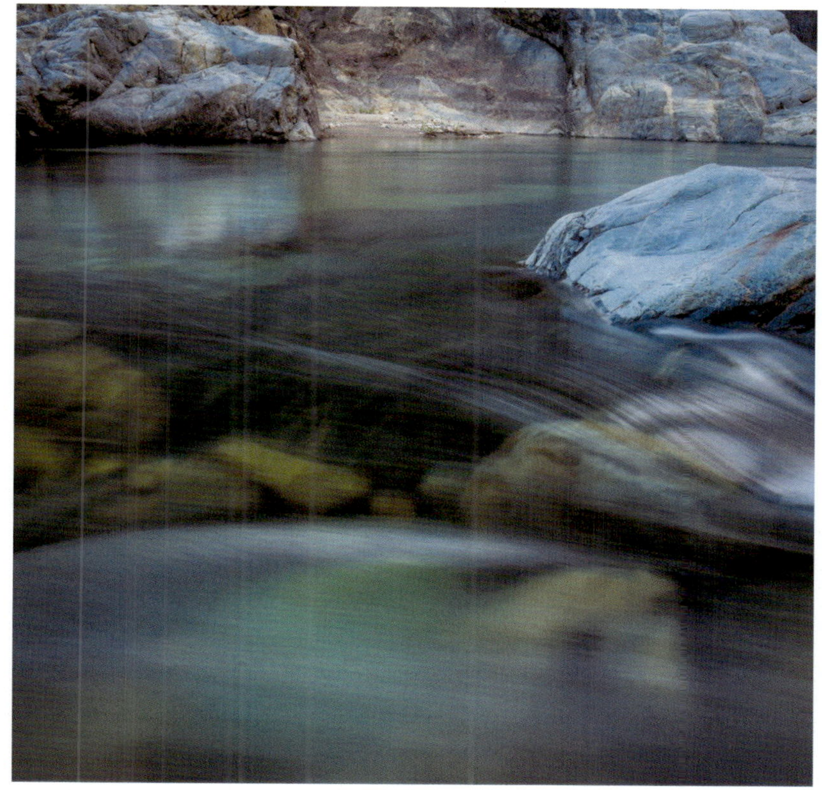

photo credit:
Matthias Schossig

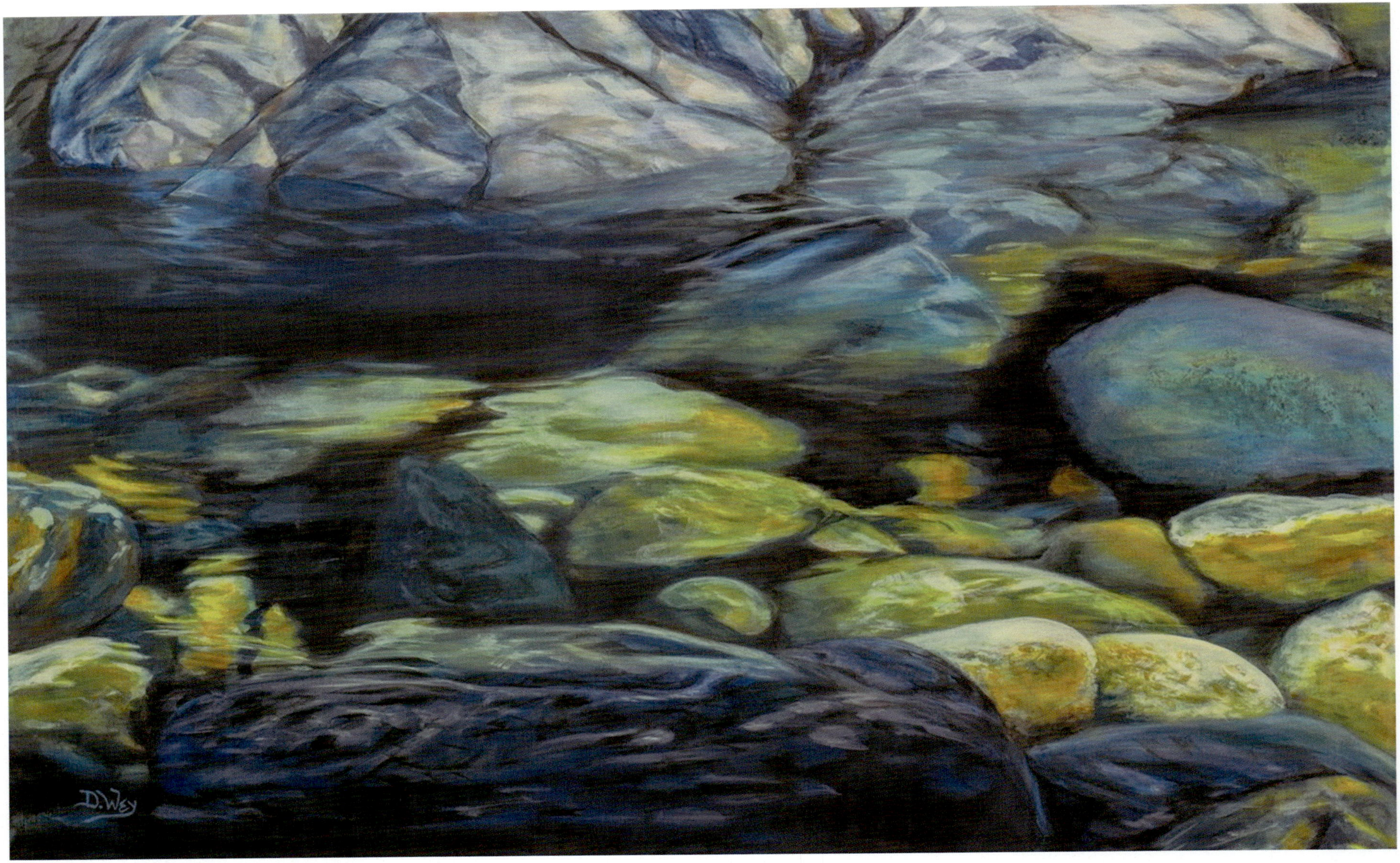

Yuba Love, Morning Whispers on the Yuba, #099**,** 30″ x 48″ acrylic on canvas

photo credit
Melinda Vienna Saari

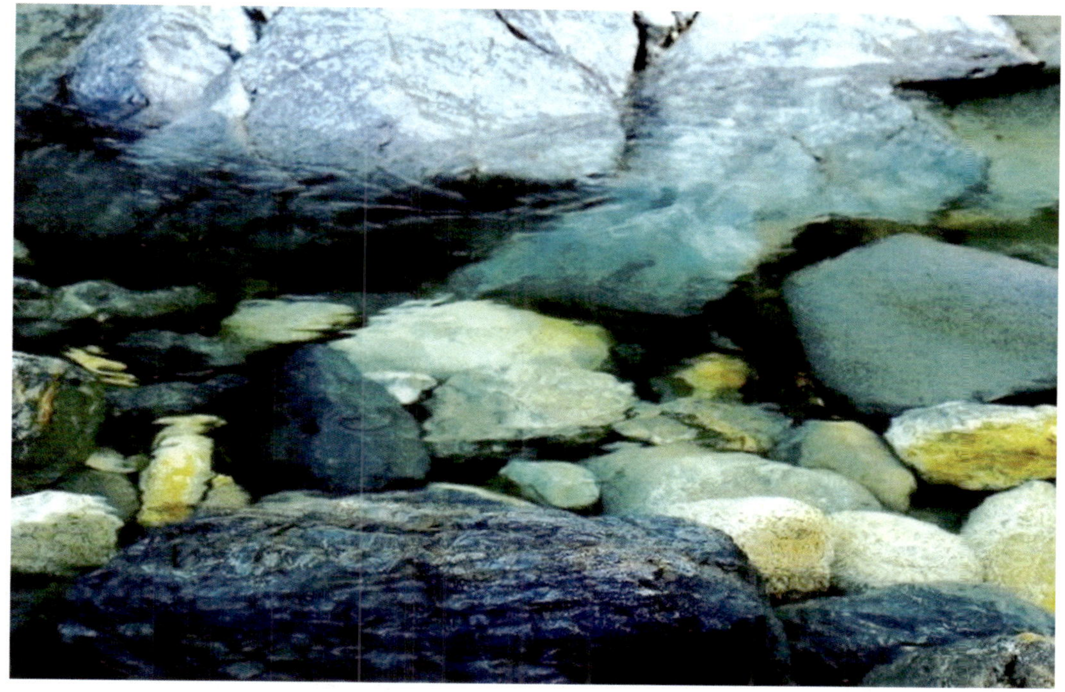

An interesting conversation with a fellow artist during one of the Open Studio Tours yielded much to think about in regard to my own art journey.

He said that in his art group, some of the artists were also musicians and in one of their meetings, they likened learning music to learning painting: "In music, you crunched a part of the song until you got it down and then went on to crunching another part (as in 'crunching' the numbers). Not in order, either: You might begin with the end of the song, for instance. Then when you've learned all the parts, you put it together and play the song. In painting, you crunch parts of the landscape: how to paint the sky, then maybe the foliage, the rocks after, etc. And you put them all together and you've painted a song!" I love this analogy!

These were the years I crunched both rock texture and white water. I have much gratitude for a commission to paint *Twin Flames*, which helped me dive into a series of whitewater pieces. Painting the variety of flows from trickle to rapids was next on my journey.

Painting the close-up Daowaga rock paintings was an important lesson for me and directly influenced how I handled rocks afterwards in subsequent paintings; the *Hoyt's Crossing* series, for instance.

I made a decision to retire from my clay art and teaching to make room for more painting. This chapter in time was both useful and rewarding and I loved the mood and direction of the new work.

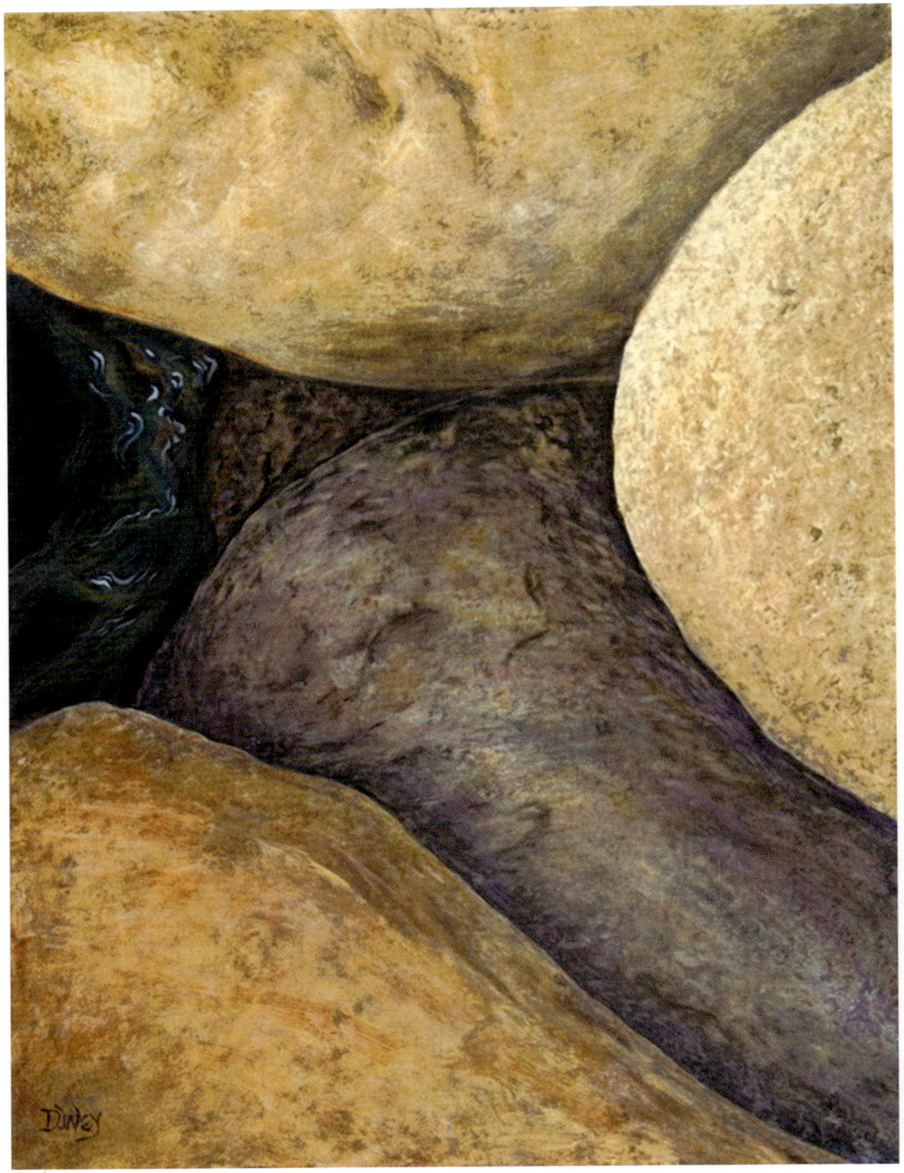

Daowaga II, #070
30″ x 40″
acrylic on canvas

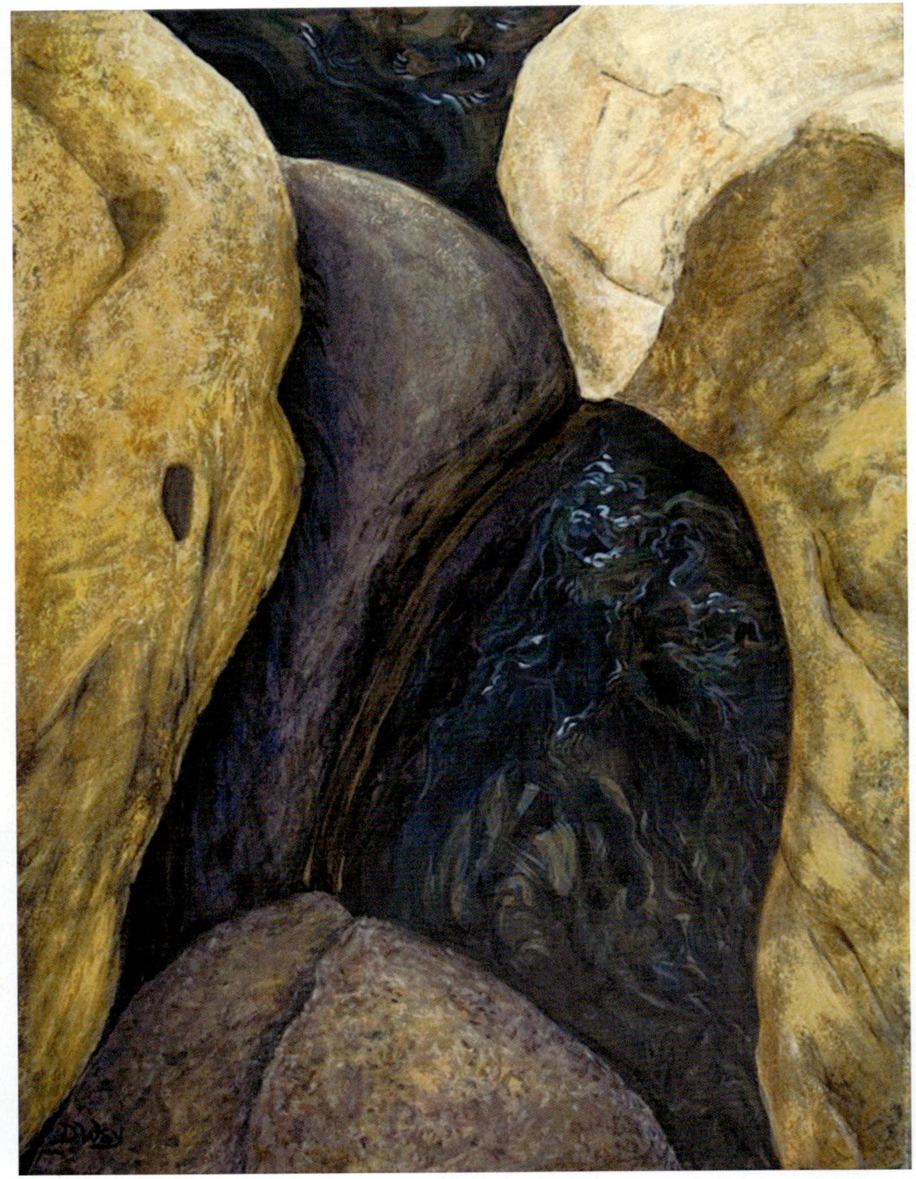

Daowaga I, #069
30″ x 40″
acrylic on canvas

in situ

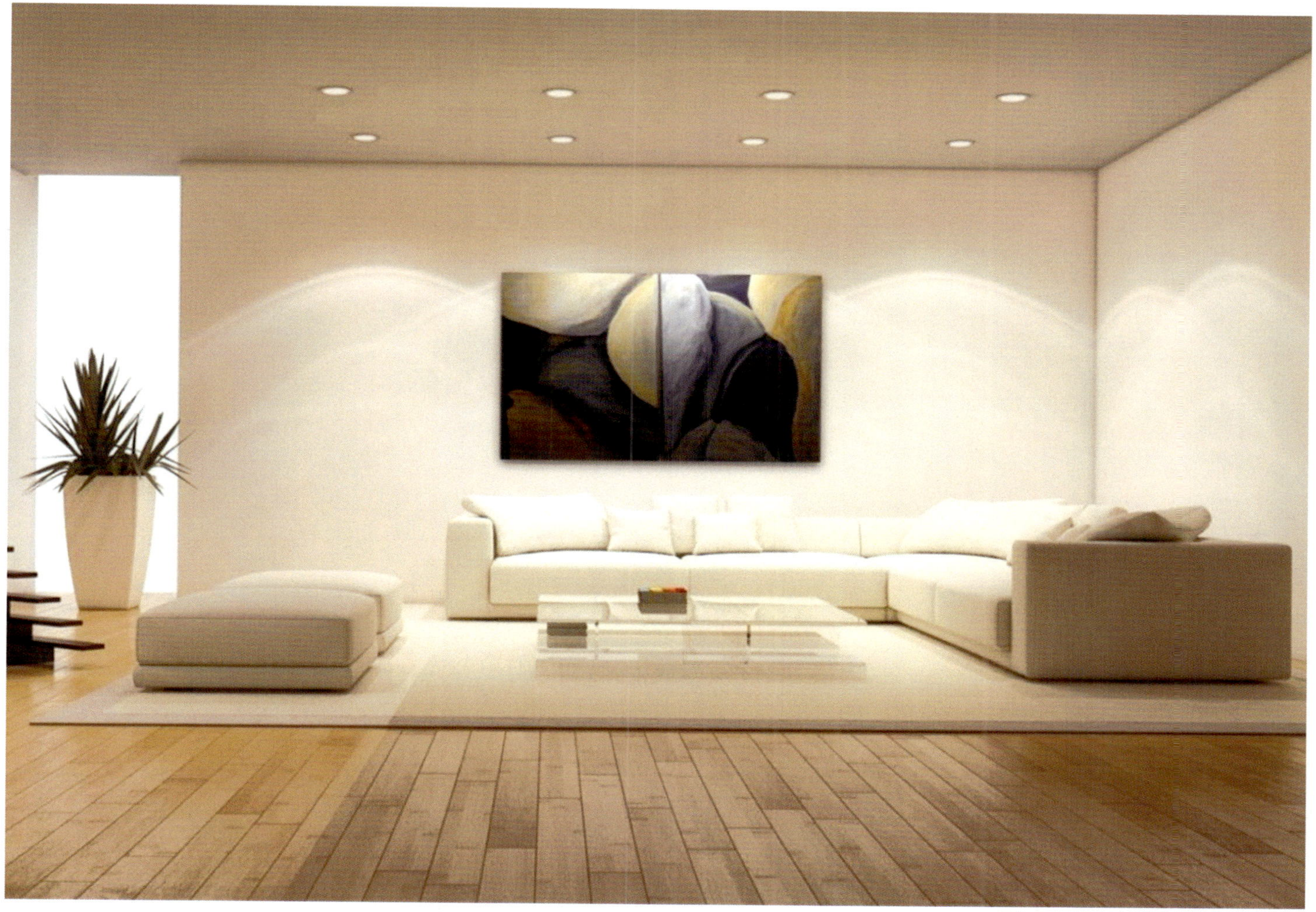

Daowaga I & II

I got close-up and personal with the texture on my large rocks by visiting Lake Tahoe and doing a set of 40" x 30"s titled Daowaga I & II. The name translates as "the shores of the lake" and is what Tahoe is referred to by the indigenous Washoe people. My first round of the under-painting on these huge rock formations was very soft and had an O'Keeffe feel. I liked that direction but liked the rough surface of the rocks in the reference photos and got caught up in a puzzle of trying to figure out how to describe that texture in a subtle way.

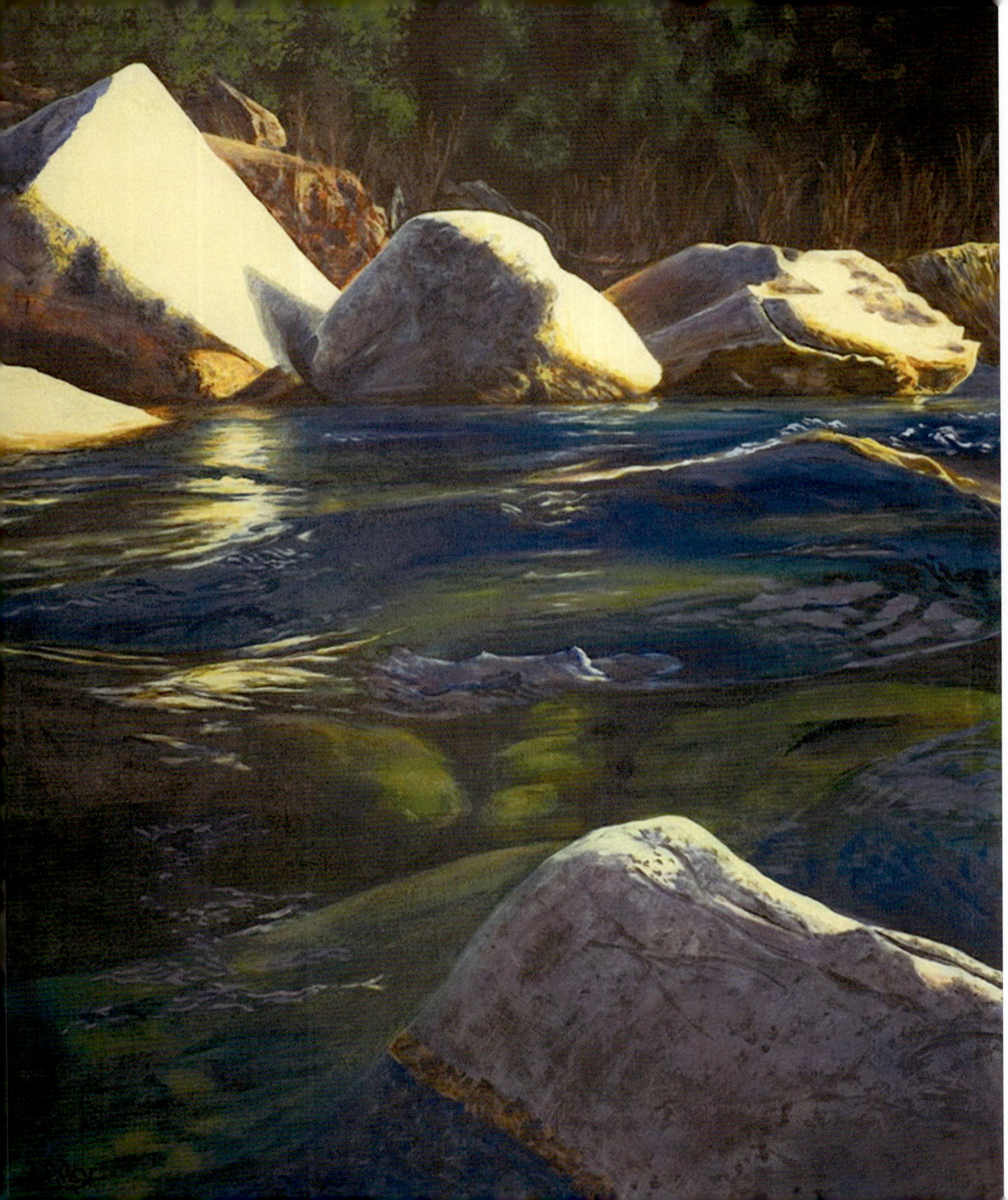

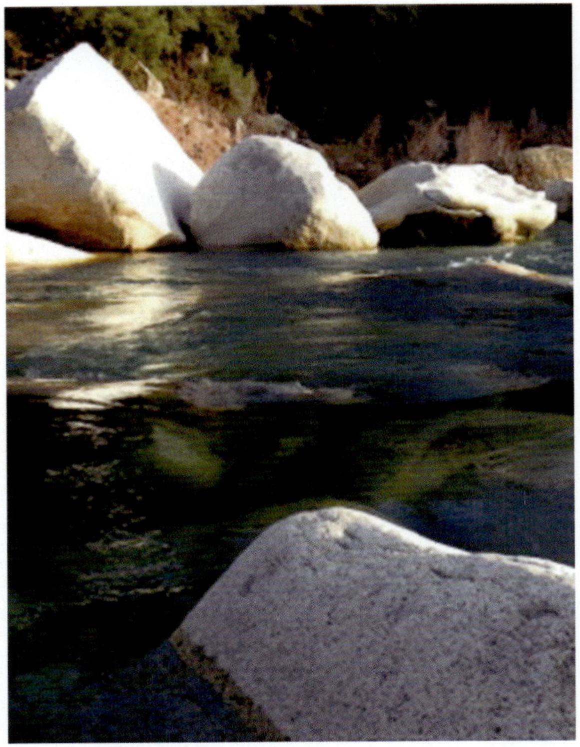

photo credit: Lil McGill

When I saw my friend's photo, it was all I could do to get through my week so I could begin this painting! It came through easy and fast and it was one that was hard to let go of, when it finally found its home. It began the Hoyt's Crossing series.

Hoyt's Crossing, #071
48" x 60"
acrylic on canvas
private collection

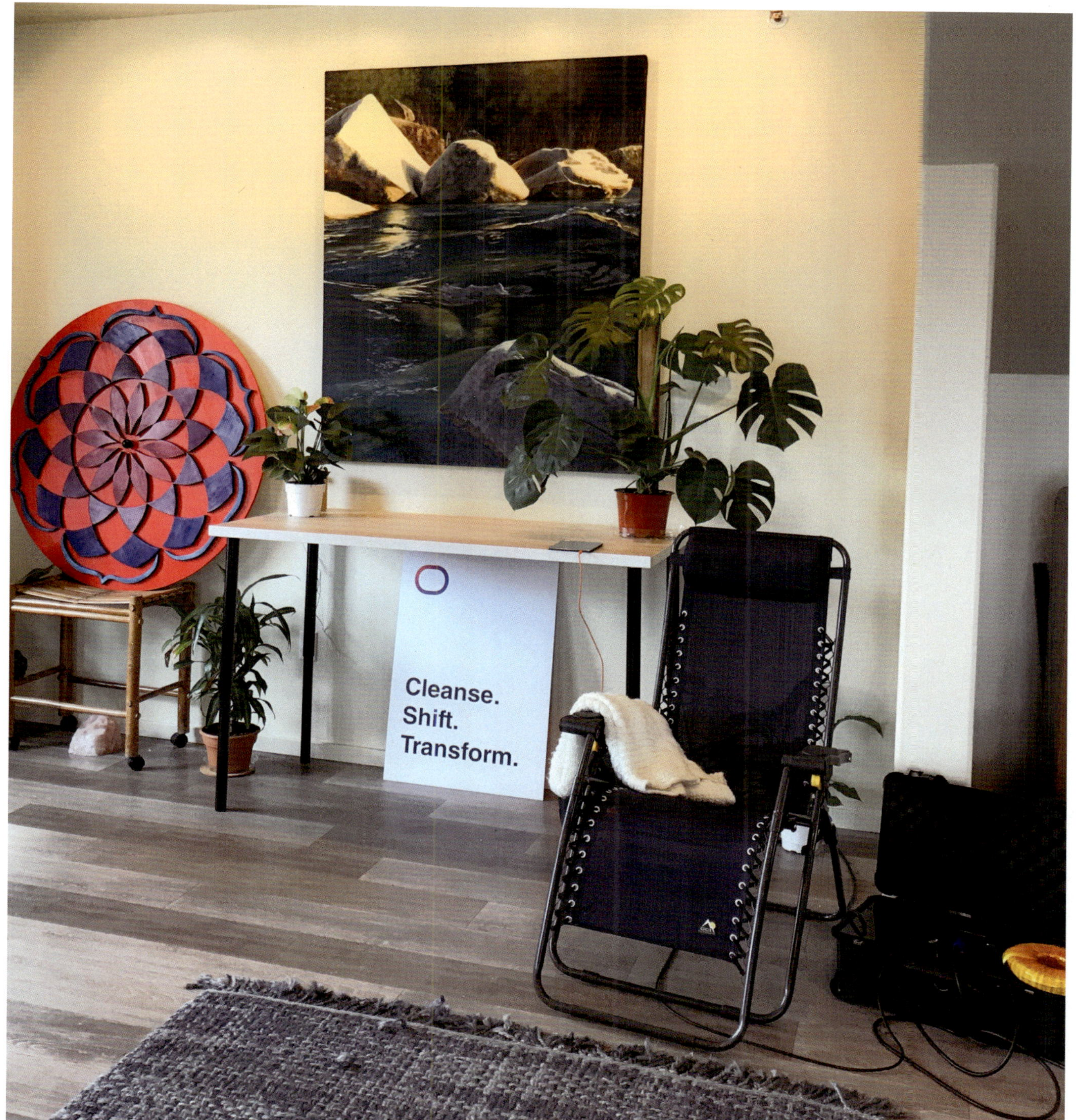

in situ

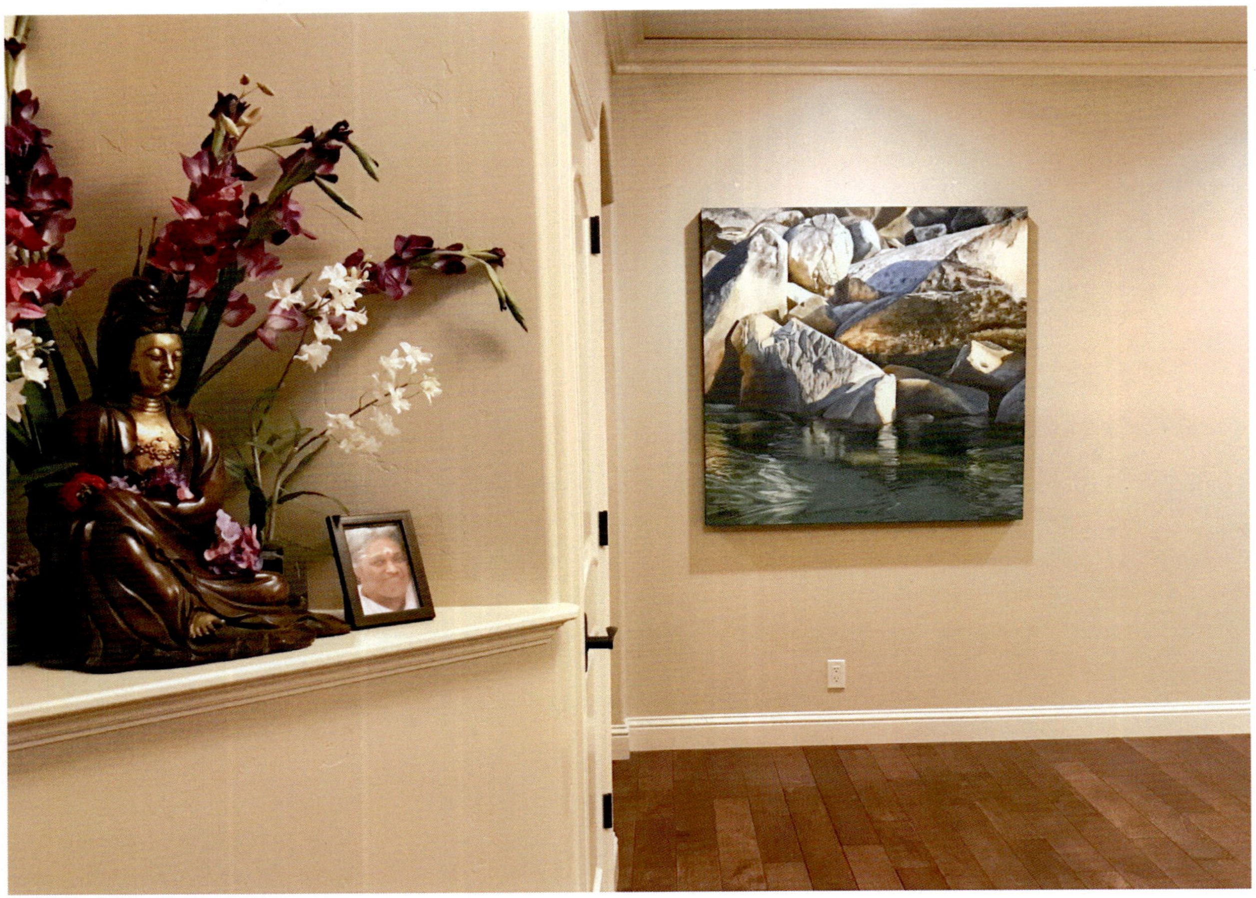

in situ

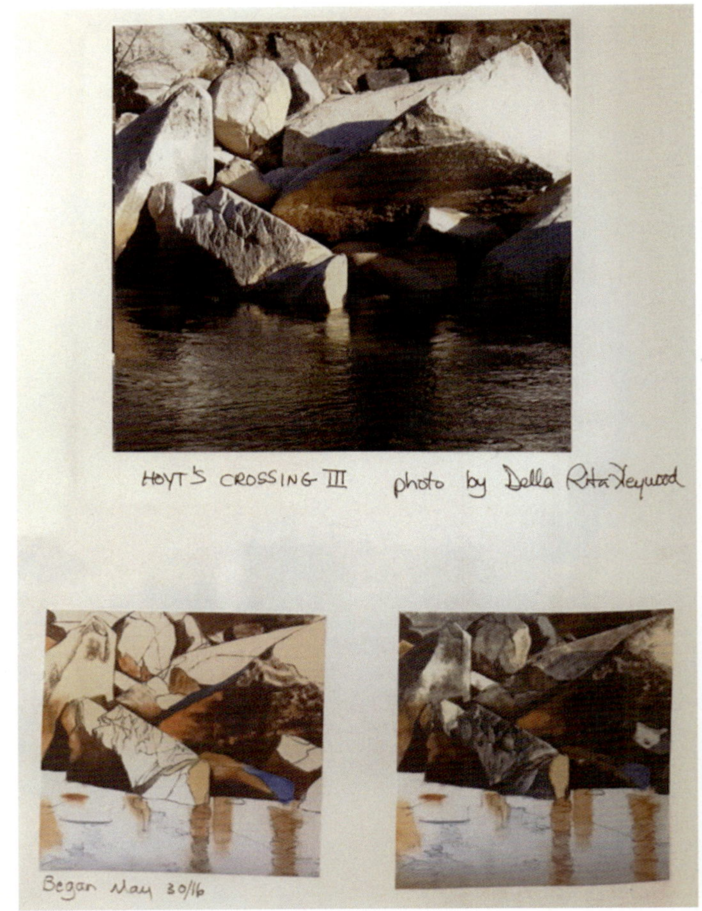

A page from my Yuba River paintings scrapbook, which I use to keep track of my process in the framework of a sort of timeline. Here you can see the reference photo of Hoyt's III and the second and third layers applied to the painting.

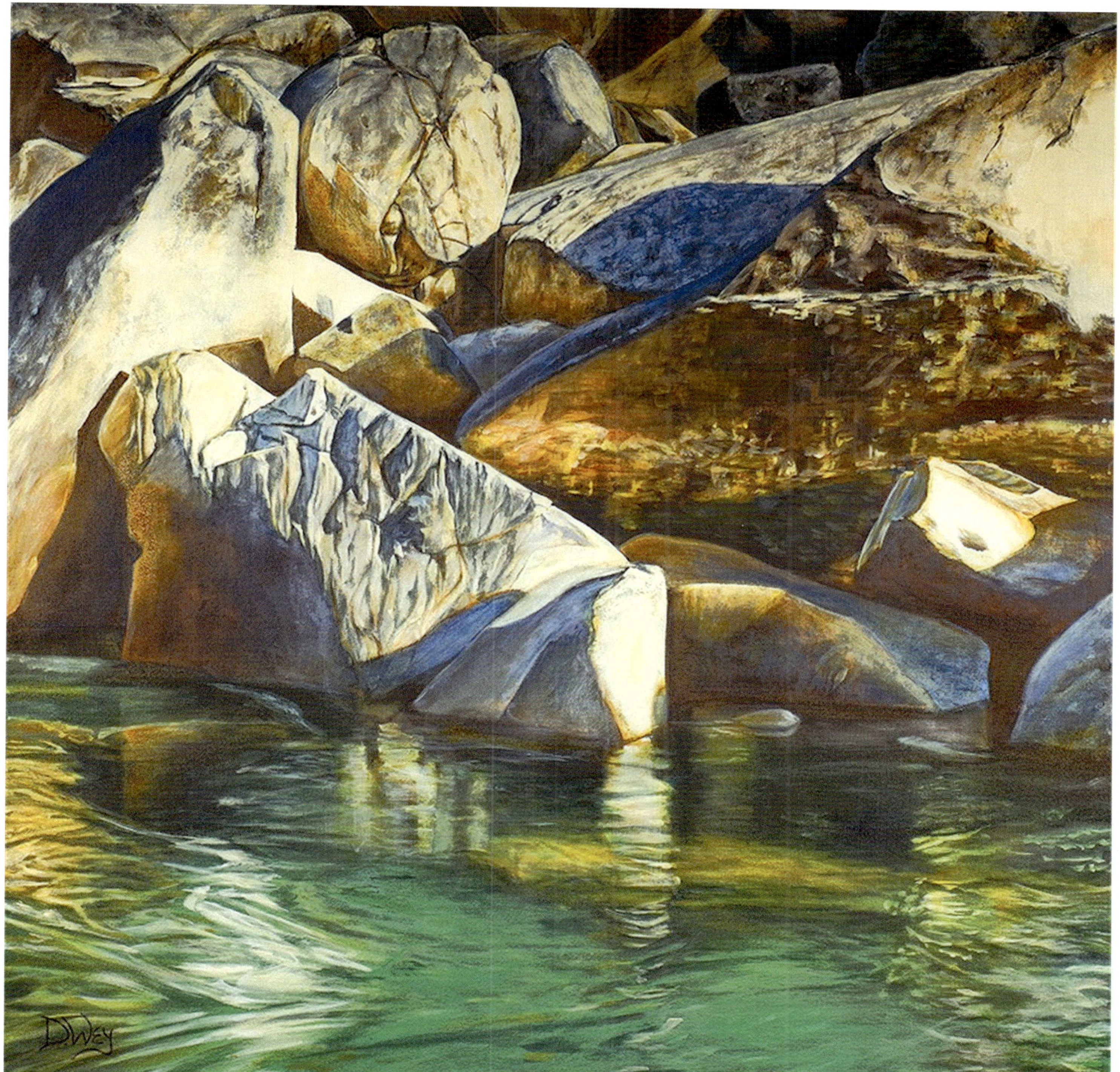

Hoyt's Crossing III, #073
48″ x 48″
acrylic on canvas
private collection

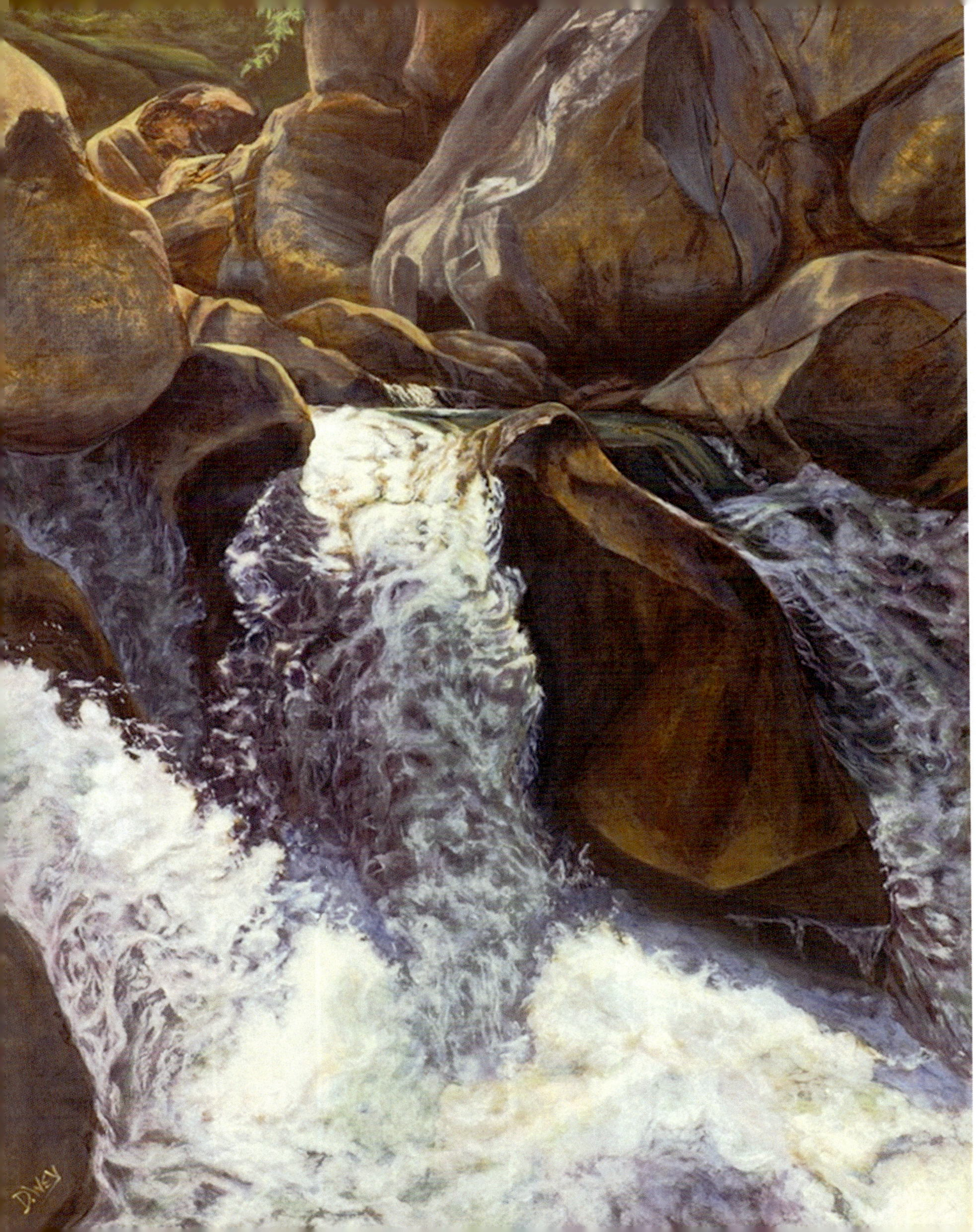

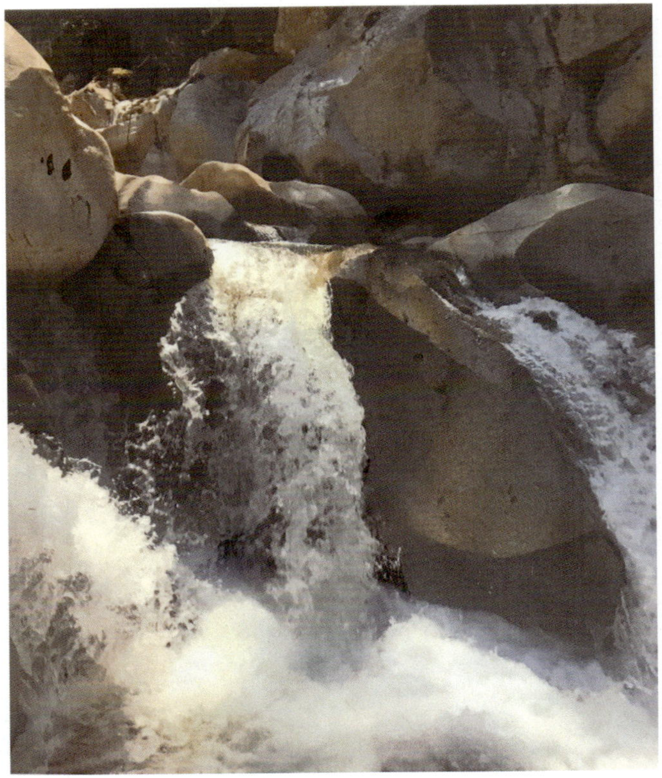

photo credit: Ivy Brott

Deer Creek, #083
48″ x 36″
acrylic on canvas
private collection

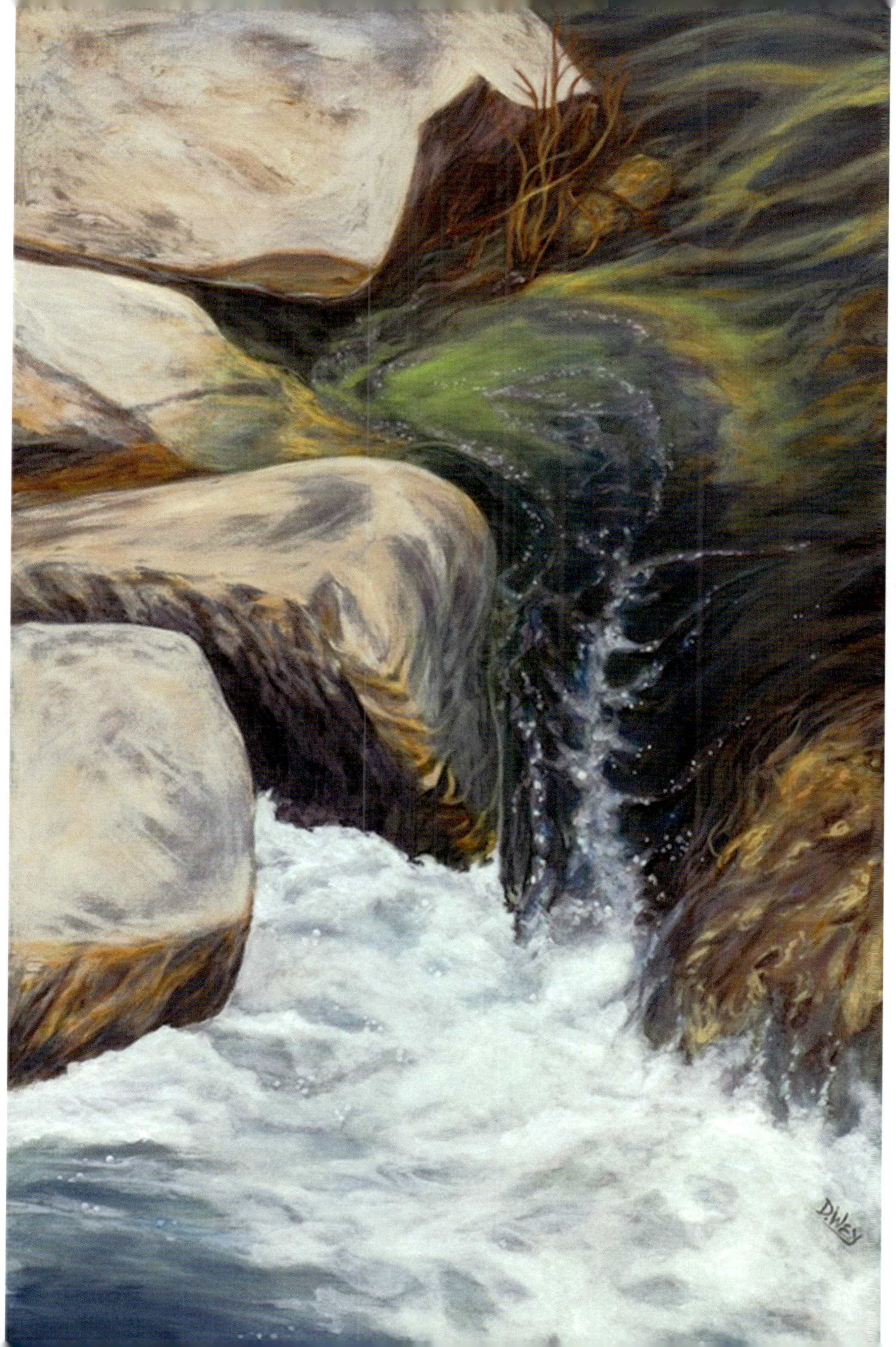

Yuba Flows, #085
48″ x 30″
acrylic on canvas,

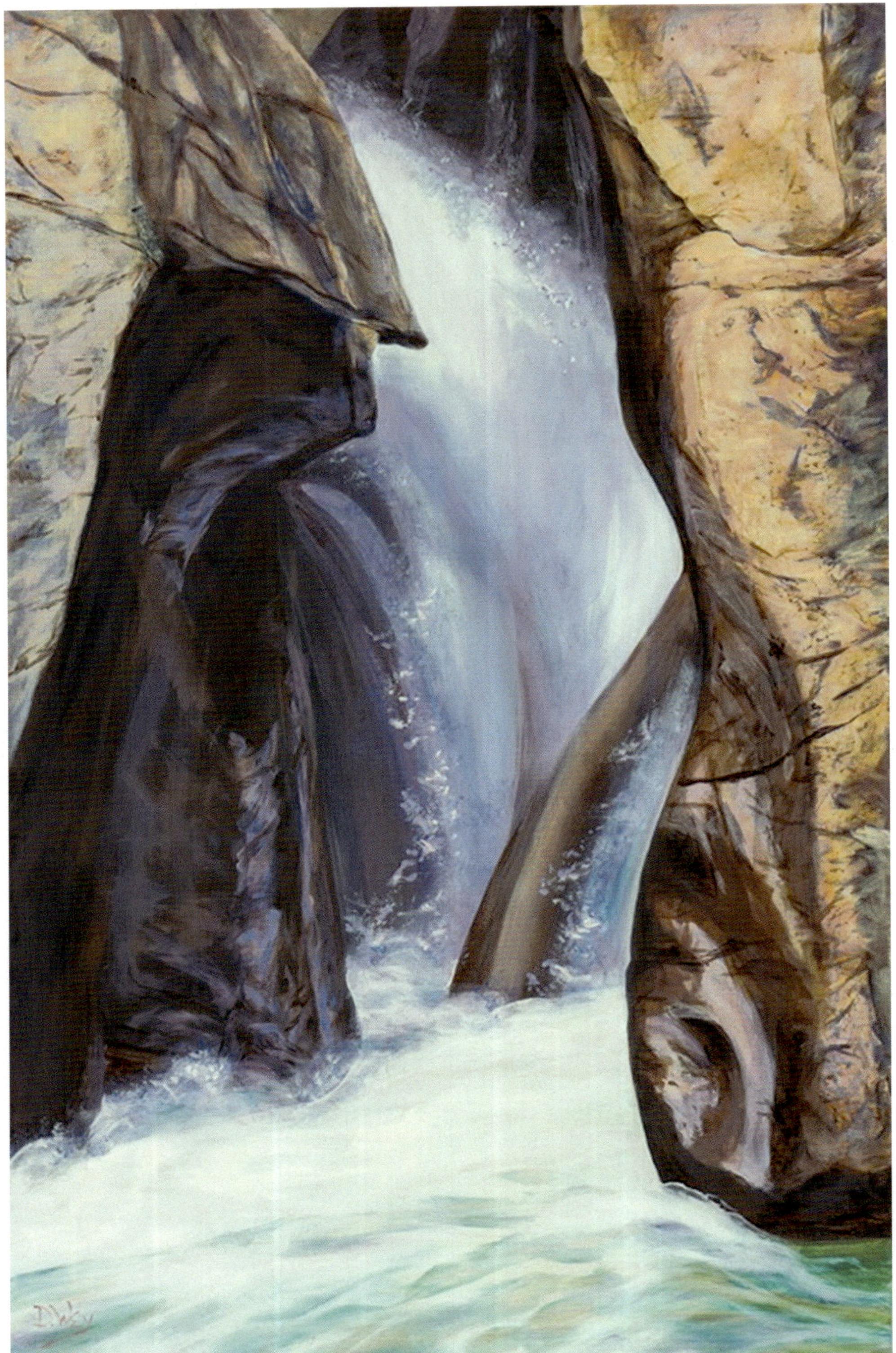

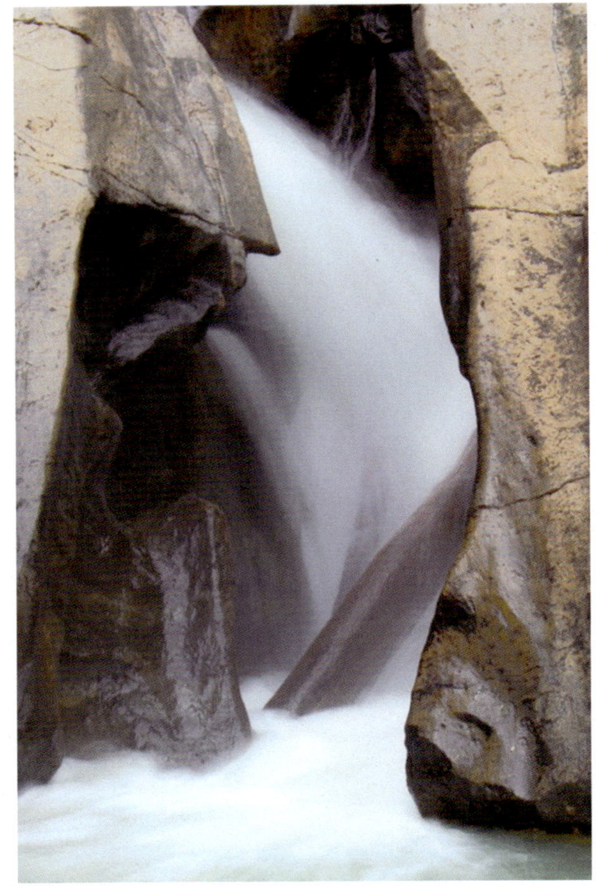

Humbug Trail Waterfall
photo credit: Doug Greene Media

River Dance, #098
48″ x 30″
acrylic on canvas
private collection

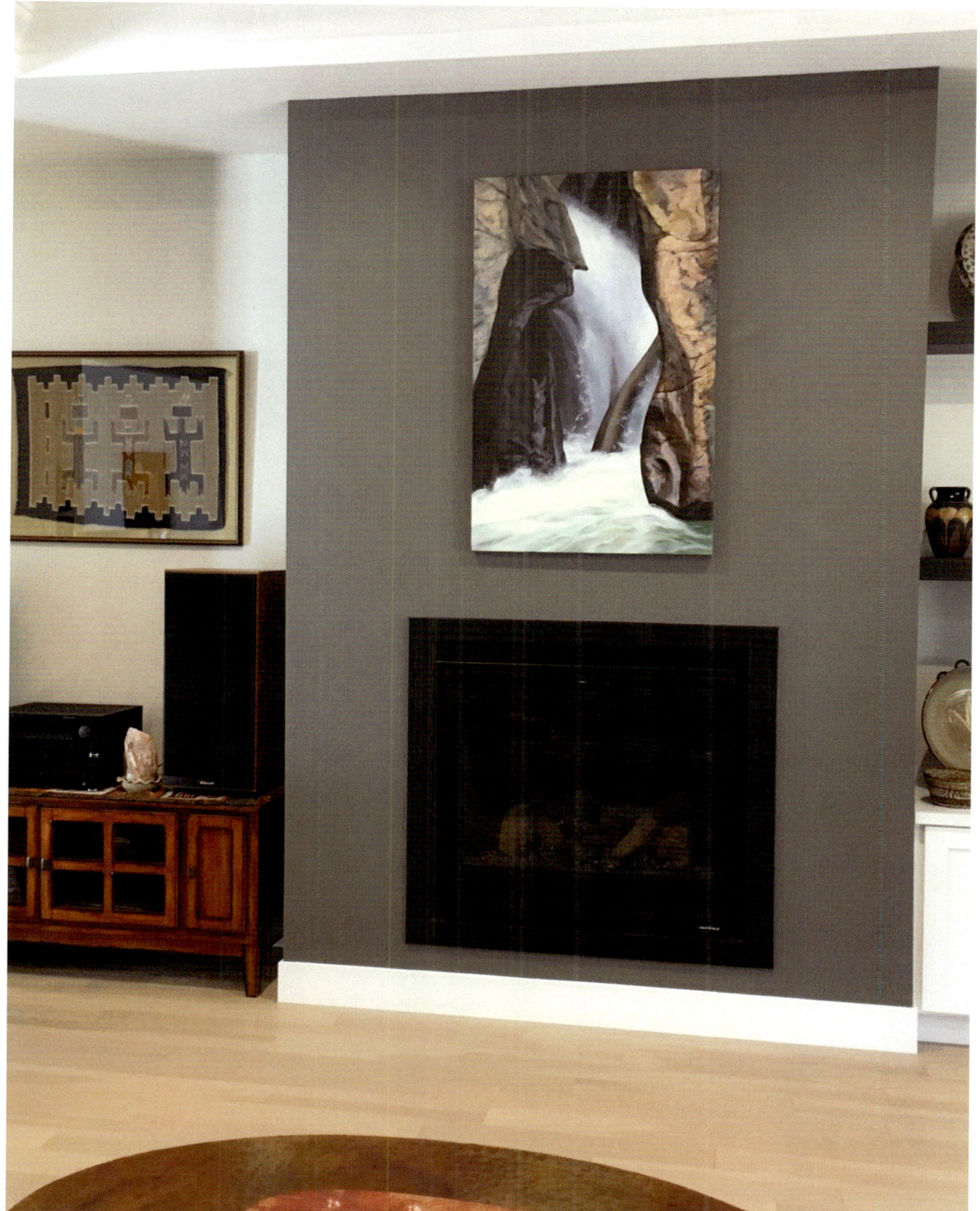

in situ

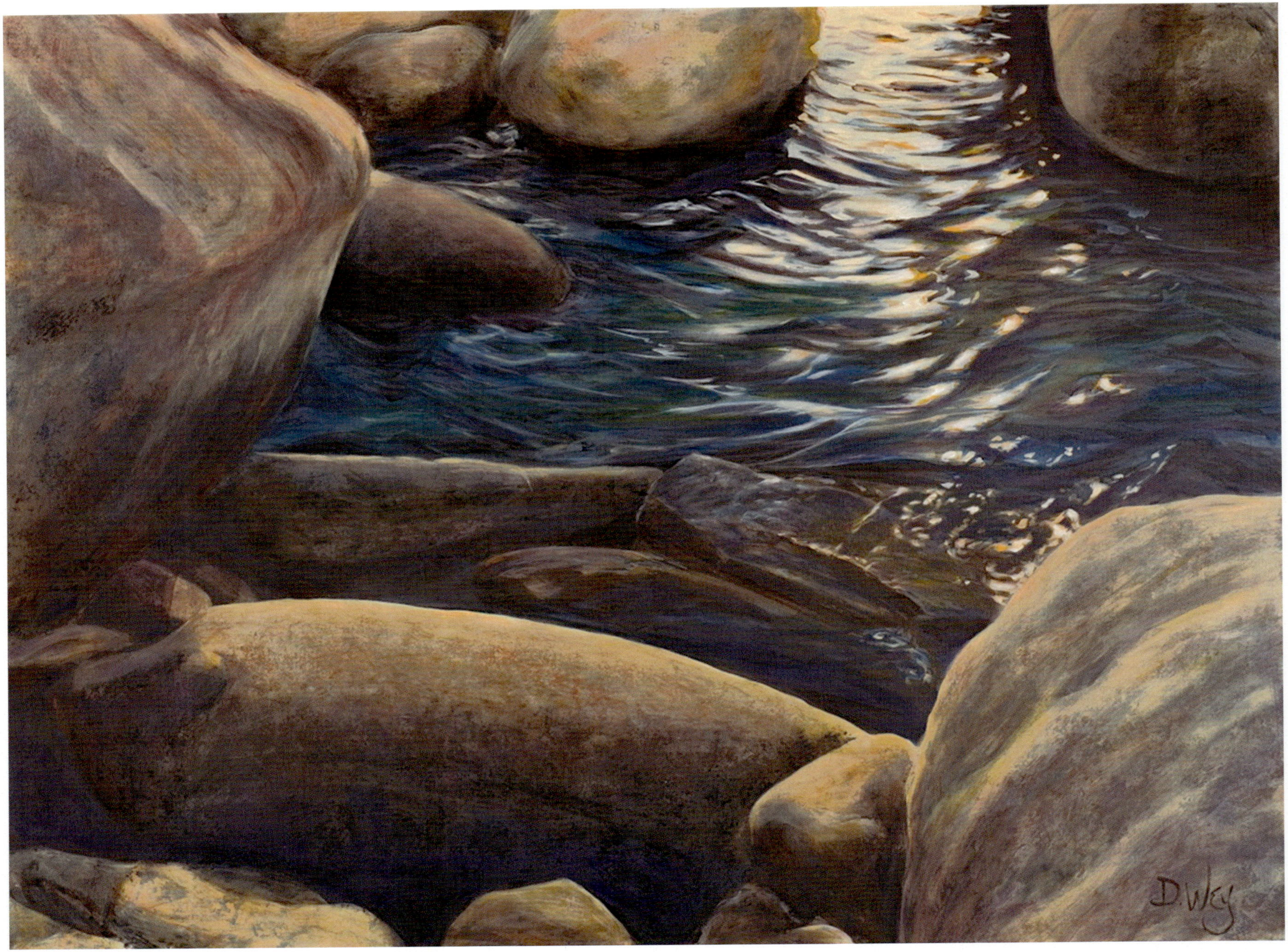

The Lake, #075, 48″ x 36″, acrylic on canvas, private collection

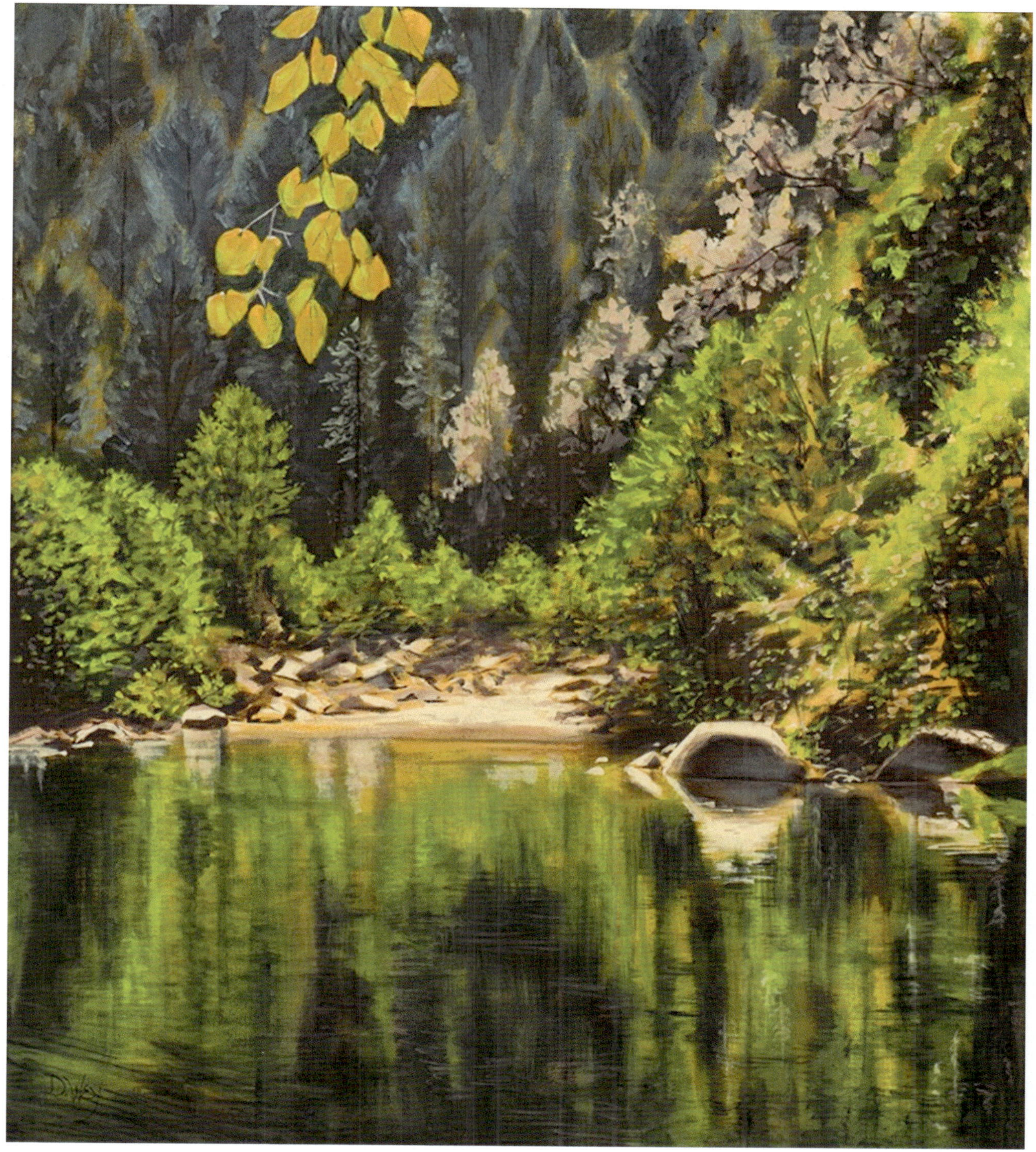

High Sierra, #076, 28″ x 32″
acrylic on canvas, private collection

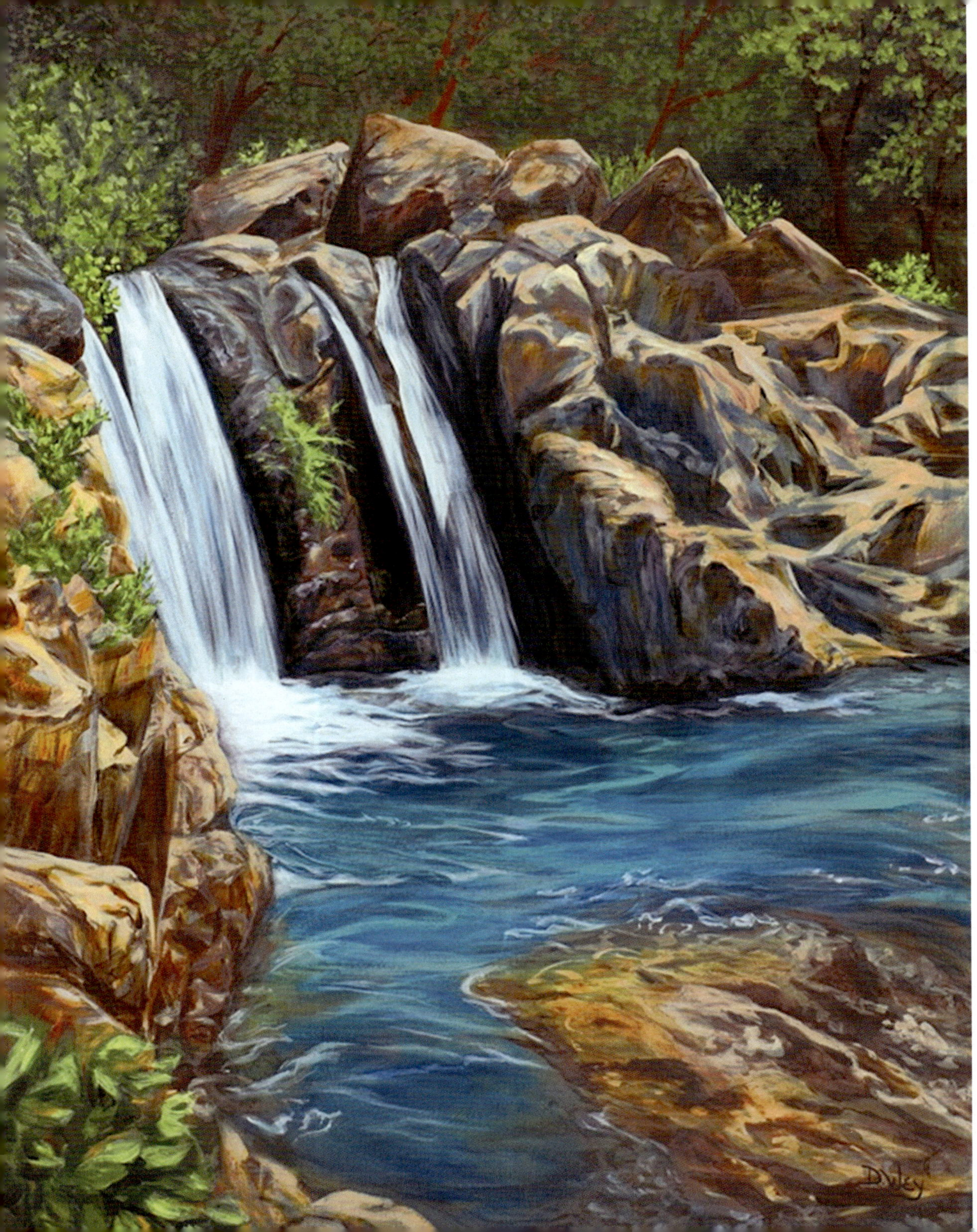

Twin Flames, #078
48″ x 36″
acrylic on canvas
private collection

Twin Falls, #081
36″ x 48″
acrylic on canvas
private collection

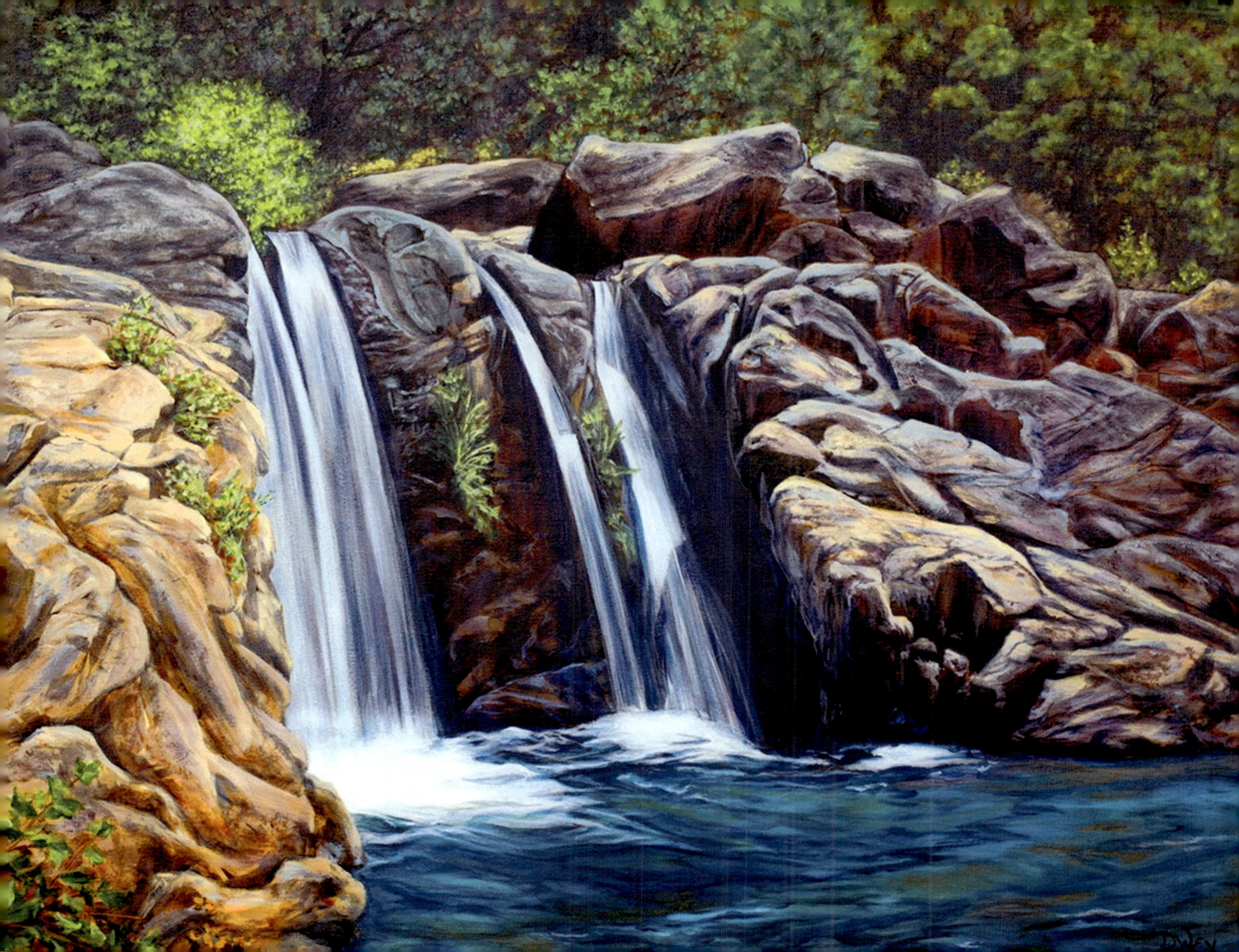

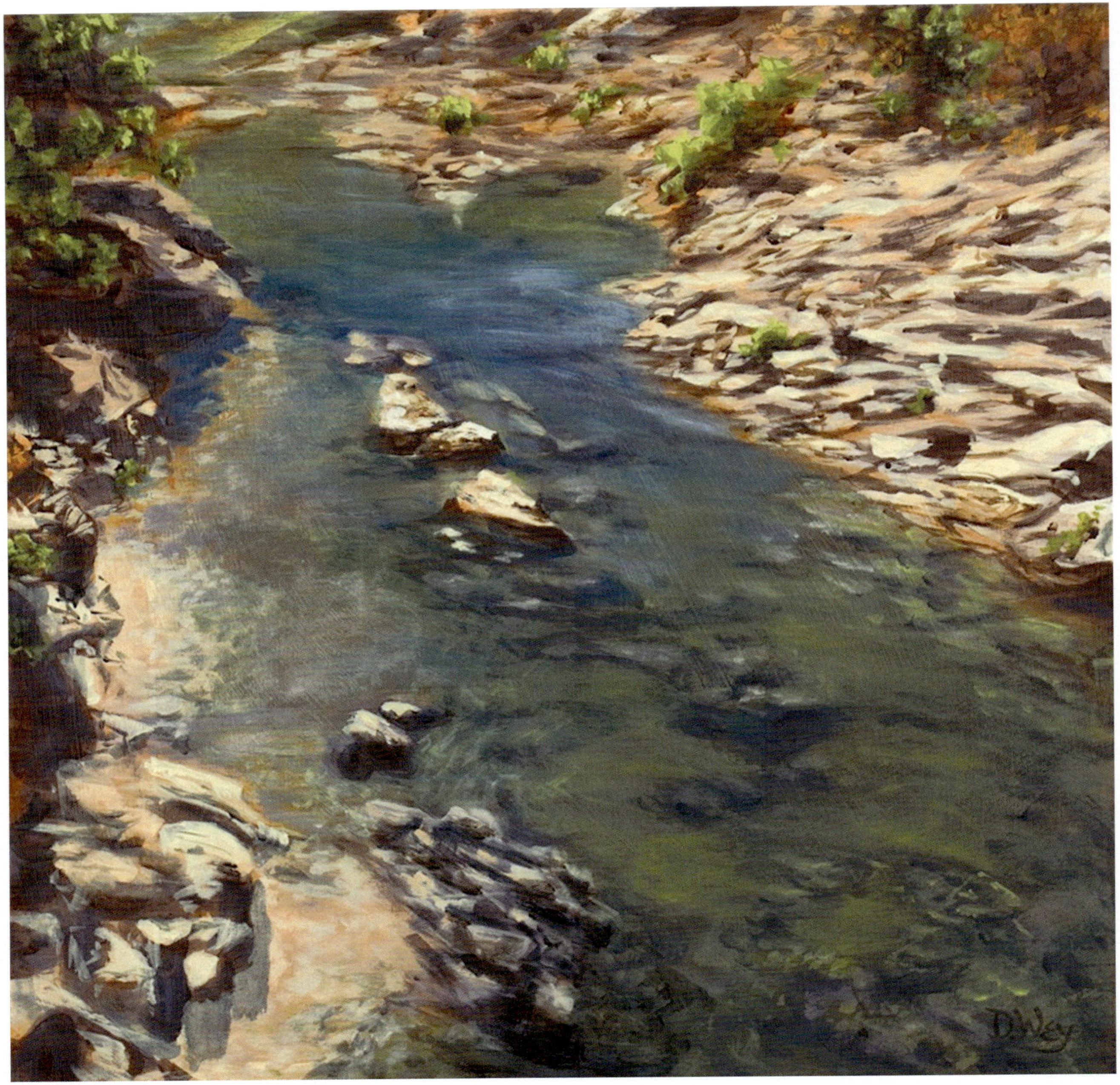

Eagle's View, #080, 18″ x 18″, acrylic on canvas, private collection

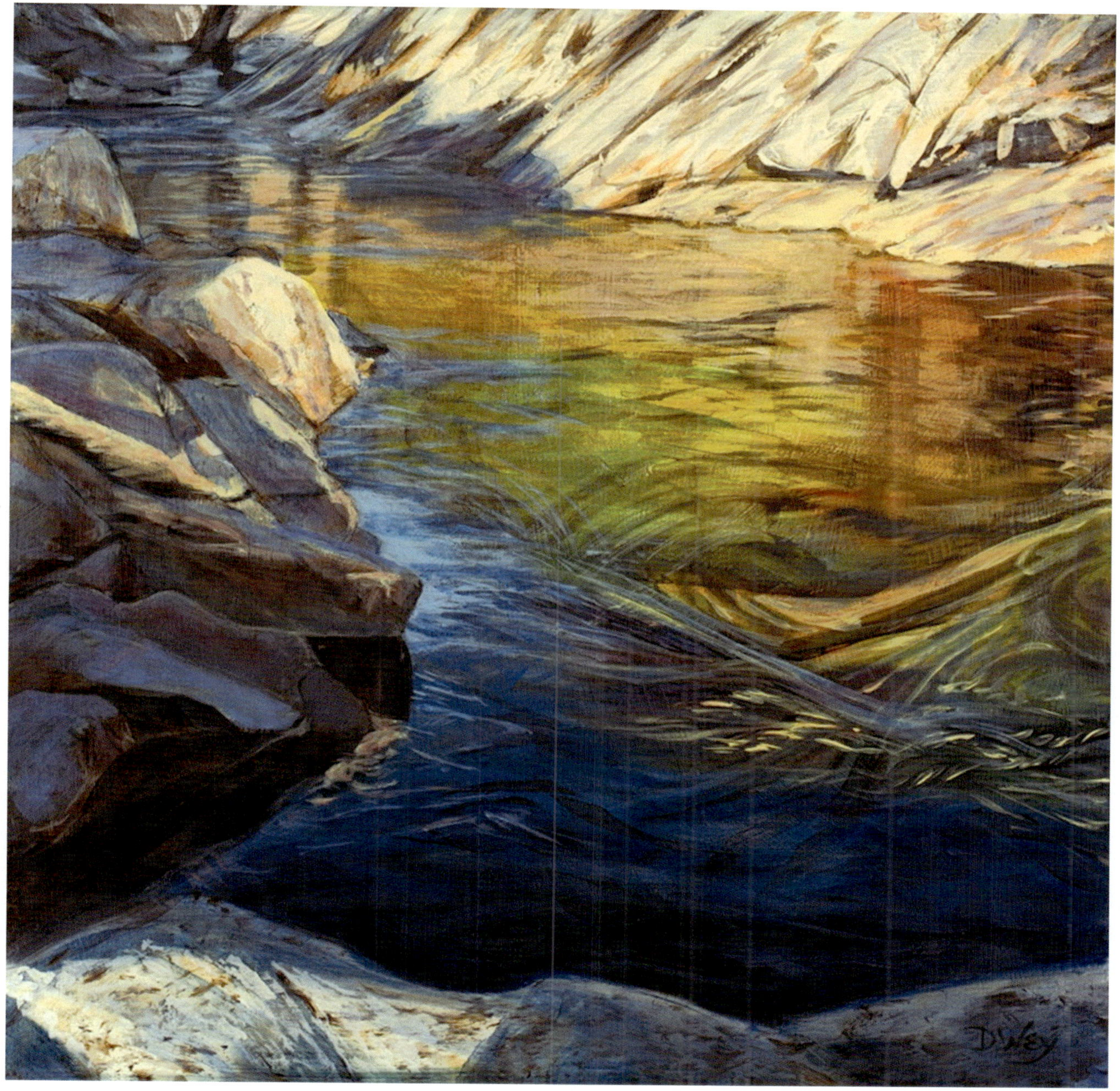

Hoyt's Crossing IV, #079, 18"x 18", acrylic on canvas, private collection

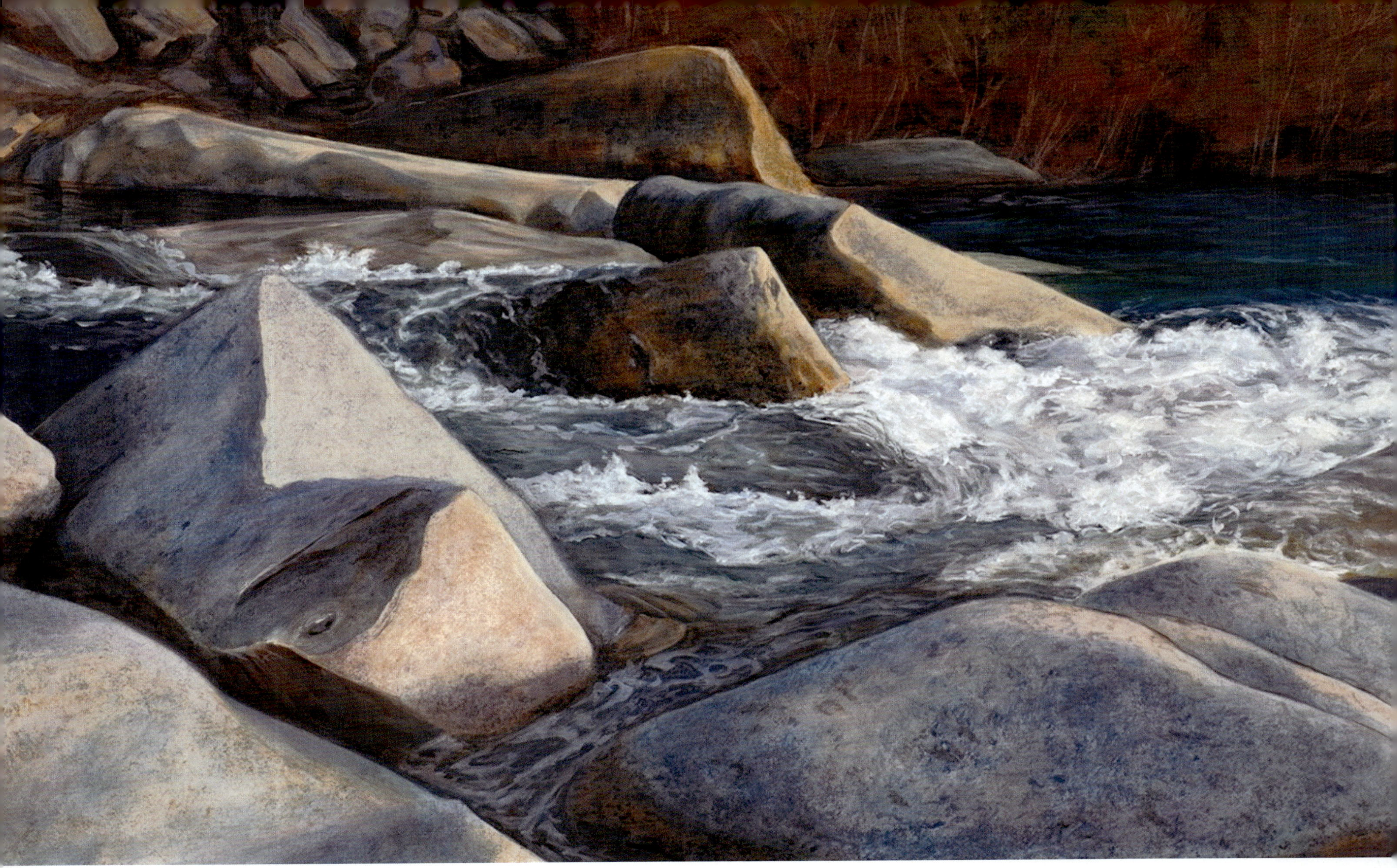

River's Journey, #082, 48" x 24", acrylic on canvas, private collection

This painting came into being relatively smoothly and I made a mental note to use the palette of earthy complementaries because I liked the zen-mind quality of mood.

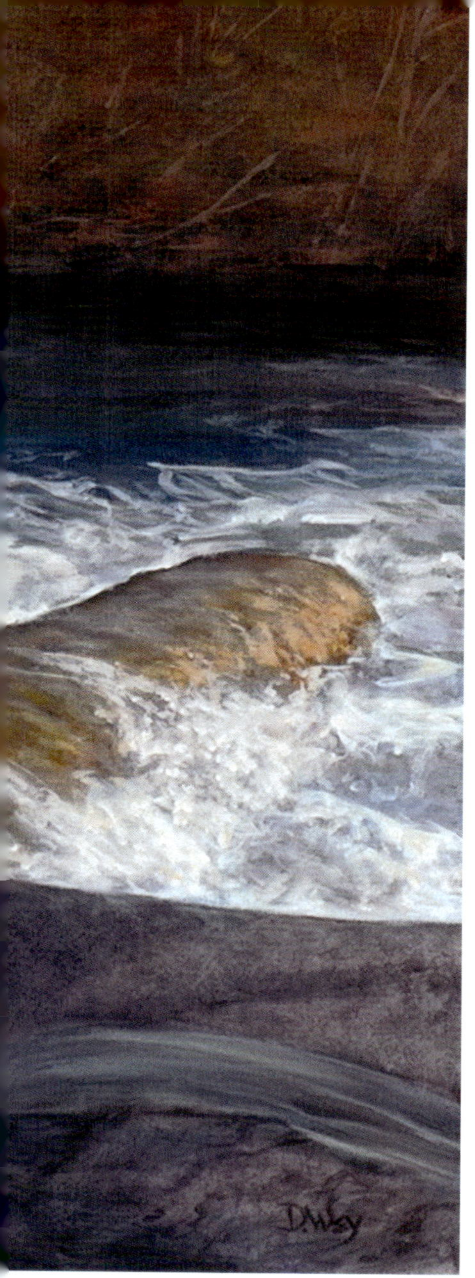

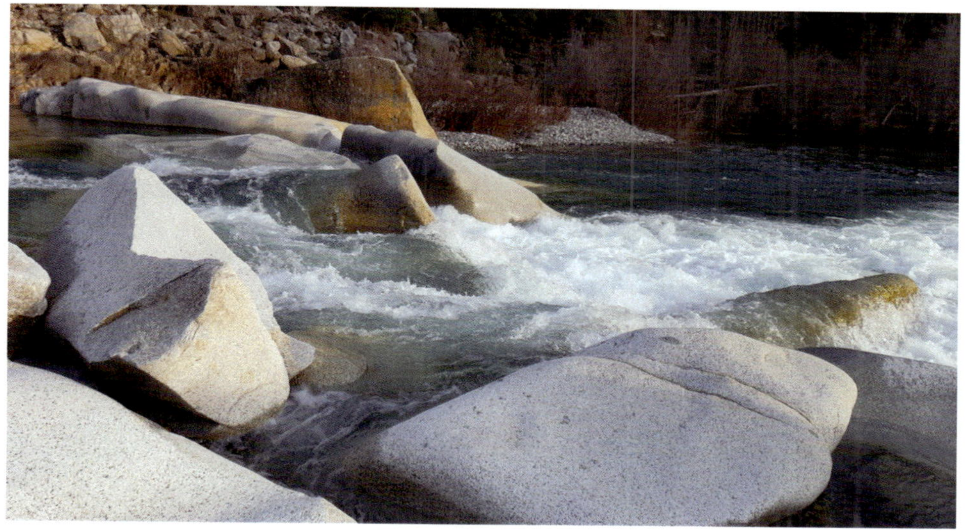

photo credit:
Della Heywood

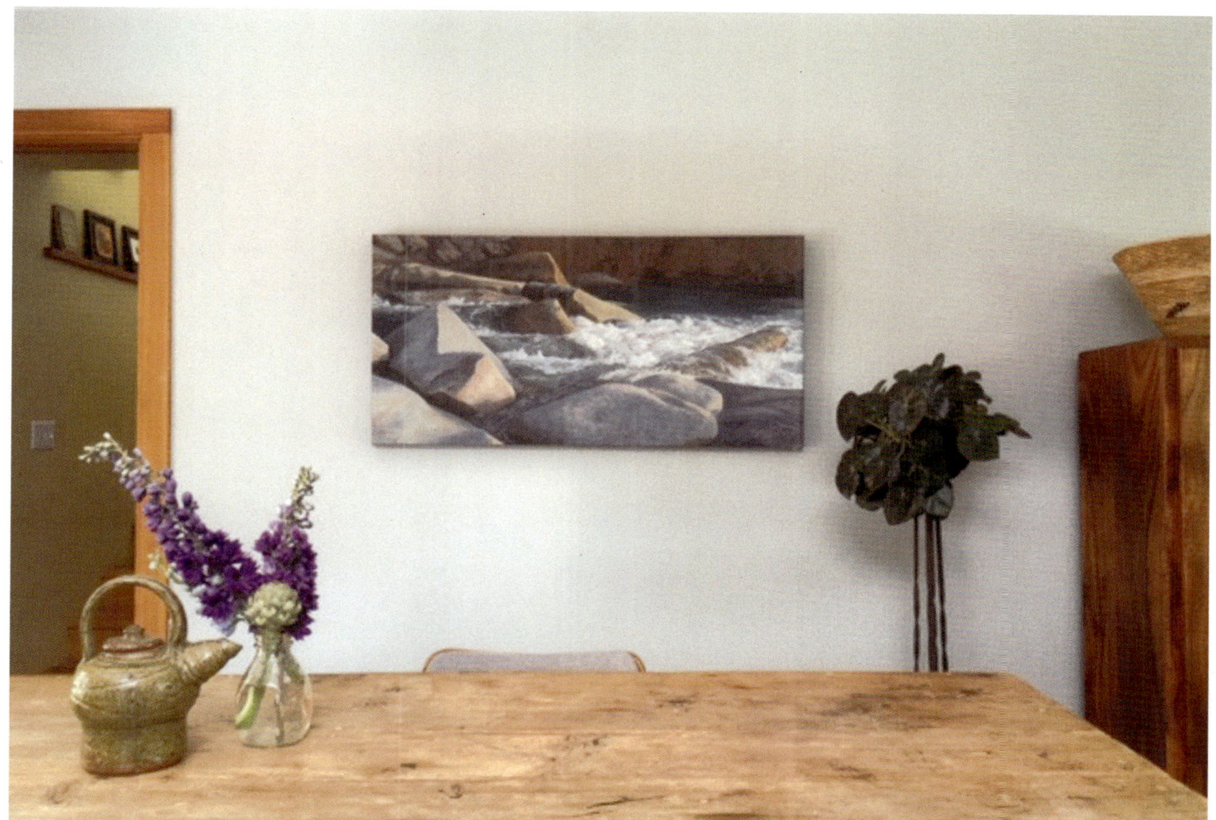

in situ

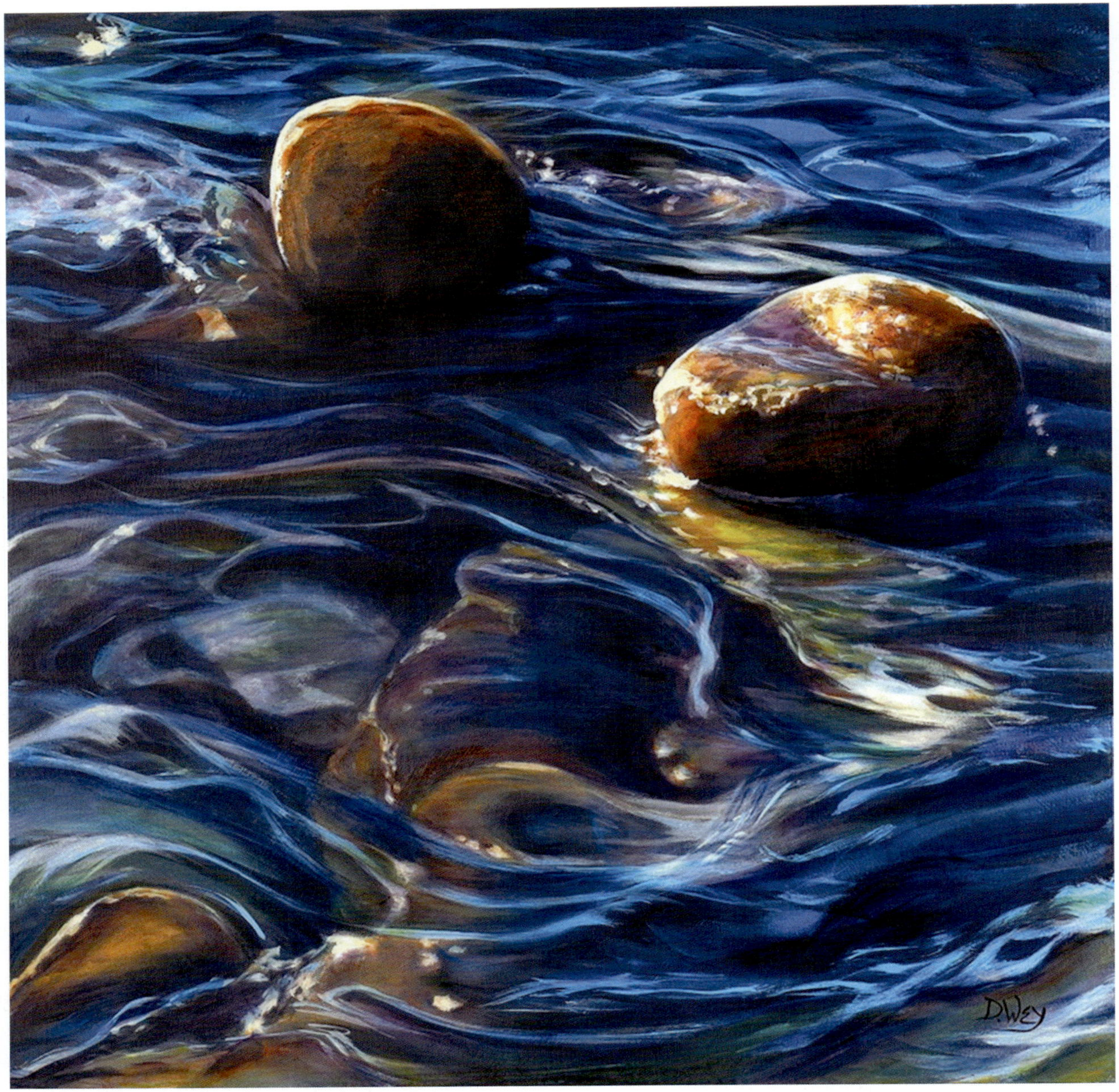

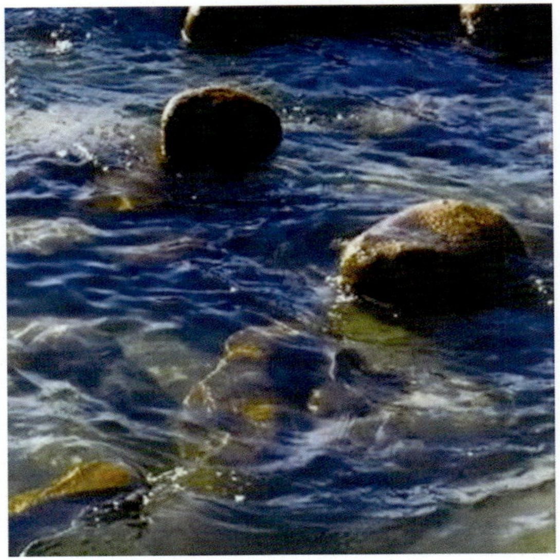

photo reference

The River Meditation series created another palette I love—deep prussian blues and golds!

River Meditation, #087
36" x 36"
acrylic on canvas
private collection

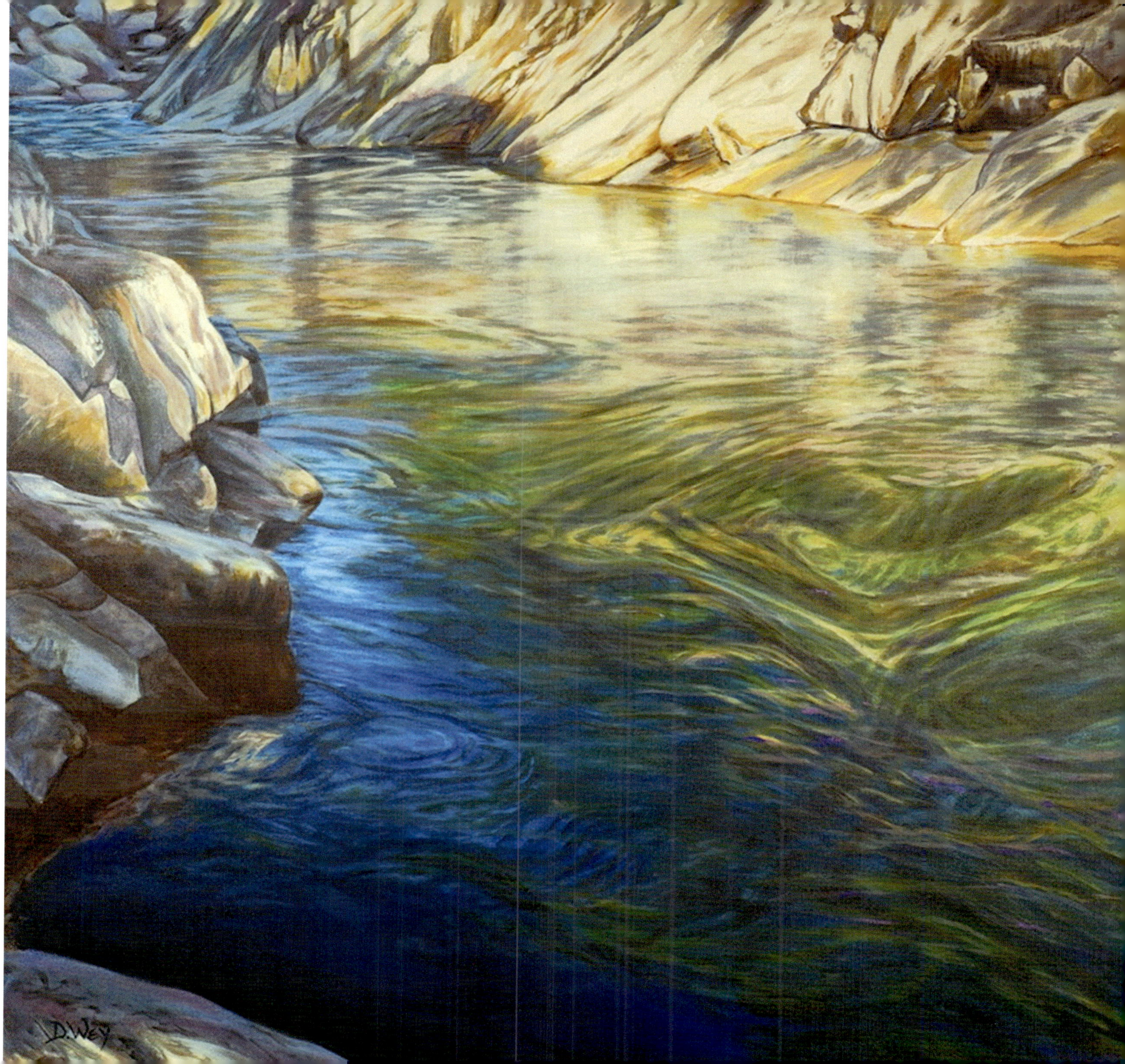

Hoyt's Crossing II, #072
48″ x 48″
acrylic on canvas
private collection

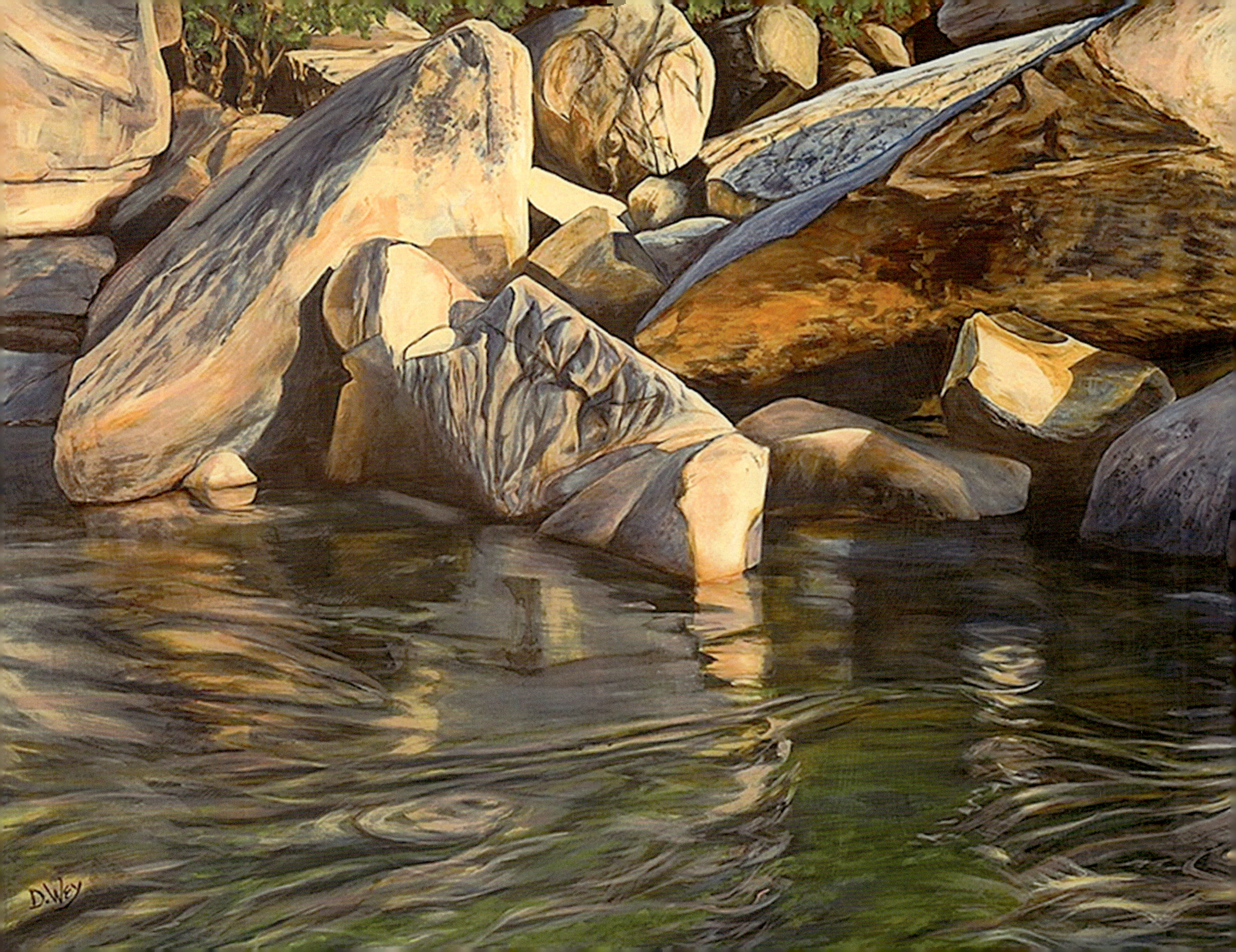
D.Wey

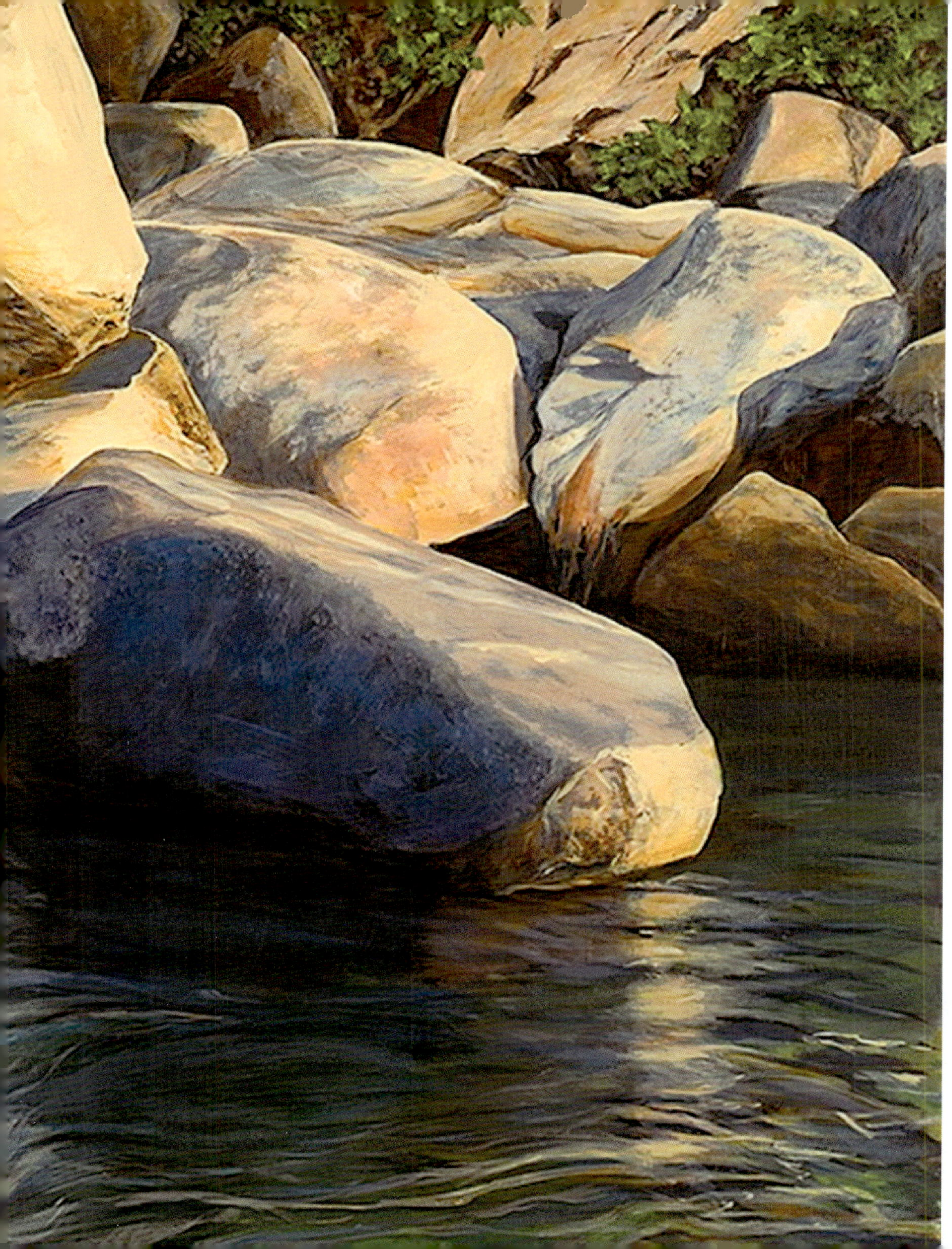

Magic Rocks at Hoyt's Crossing, #036
48″ x 96″
acrylic on canvas
private collection

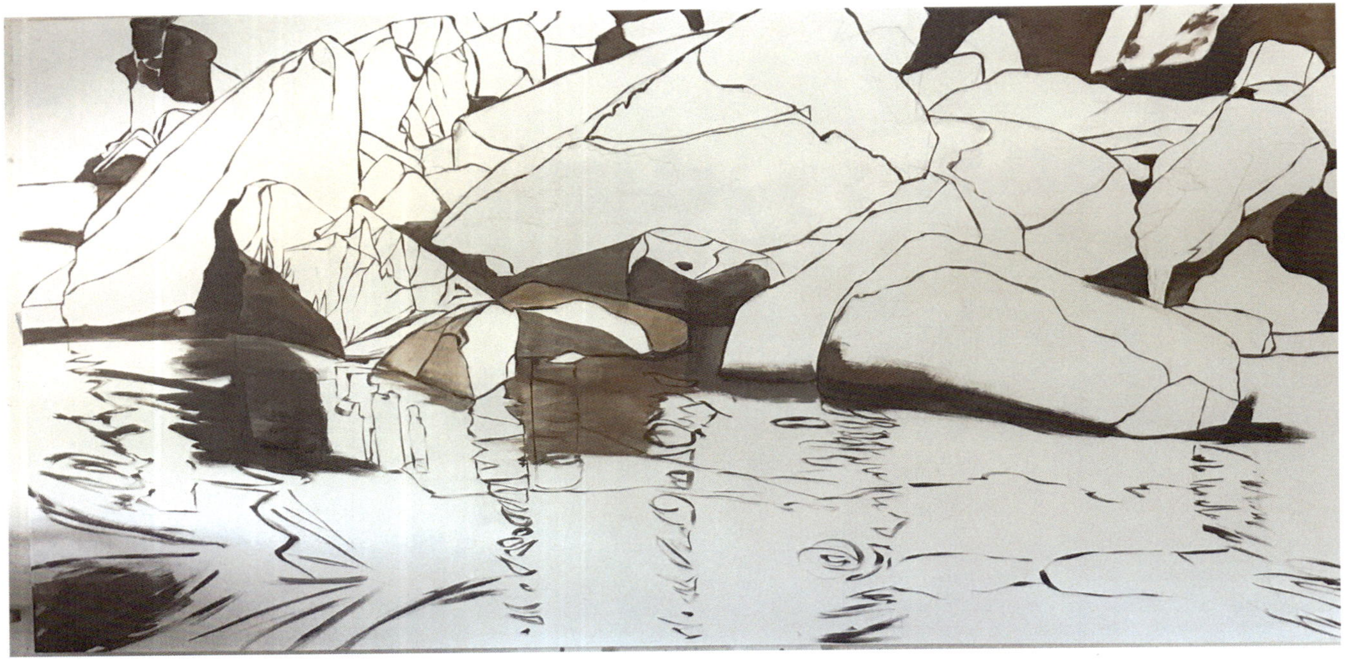

Magic Rocks, dark tones rendered onto panel

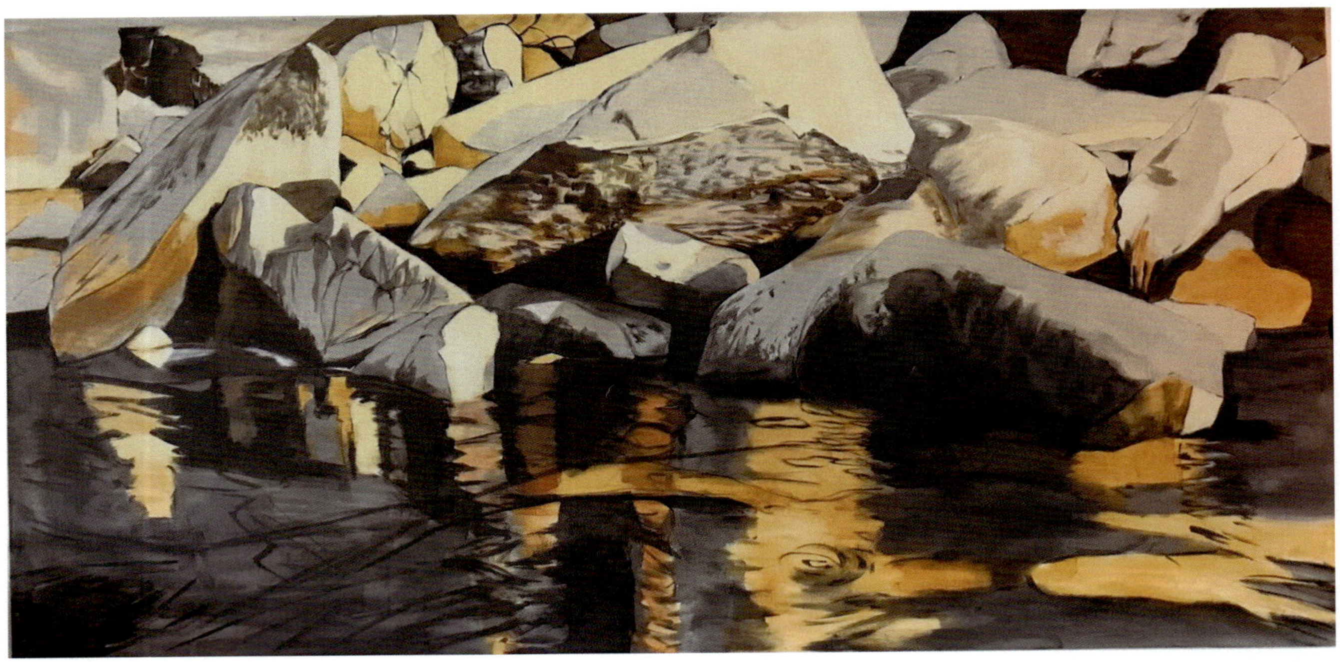

Magic Rocks, fourth layer of lights and shadows

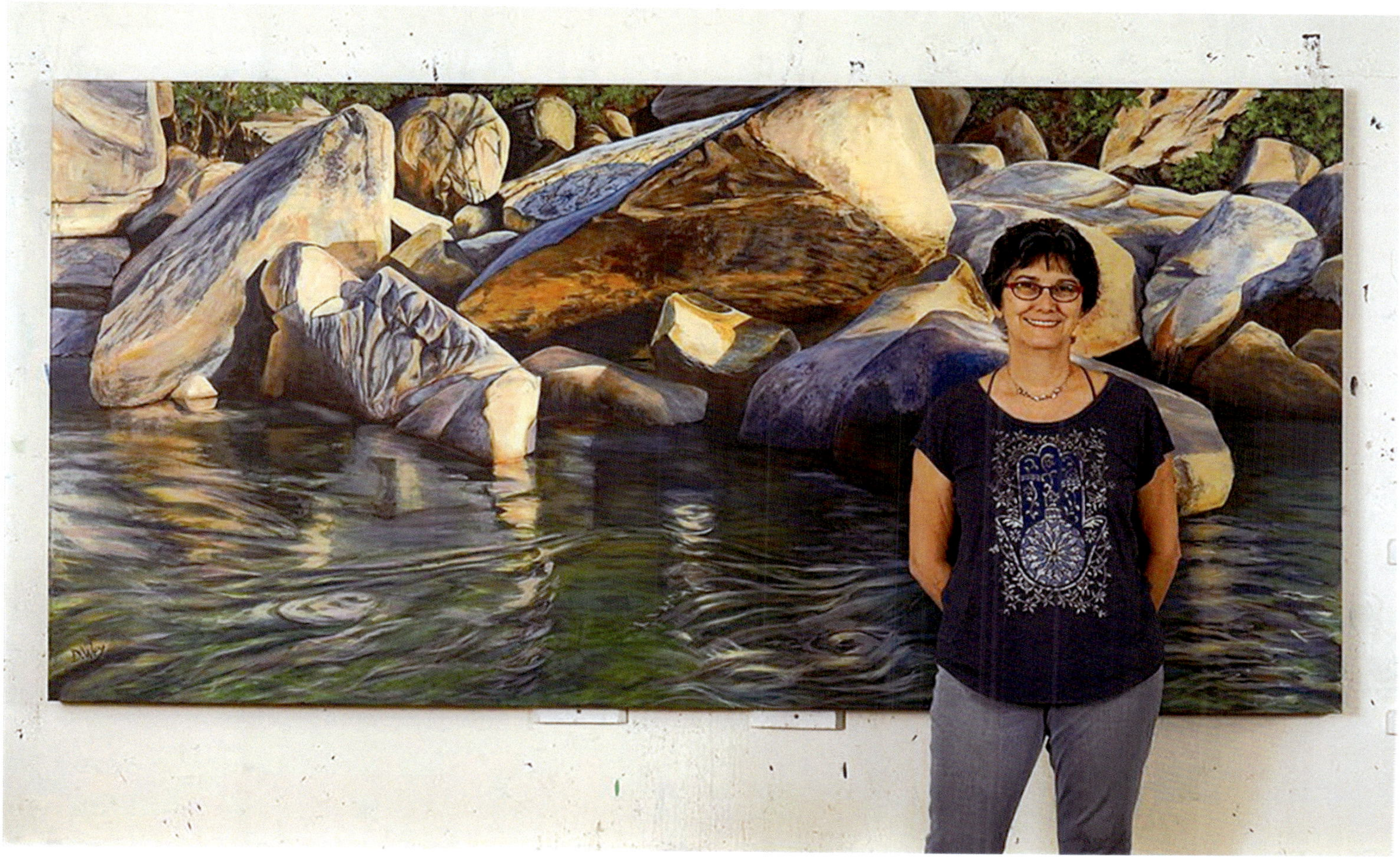

Magic Rocks photo credit: David McKay Photography

Here is another commission I'm grateful for, which materialized this very large painting on birch panel. You can see the rendering (page 90) where the first layer of values had just begun and next, another in-progress photo a few layers further on. The photo of me in front of the finished work was taken while the painting was still hanging on my studio wall.

Chapter Five: 2019 - 2020

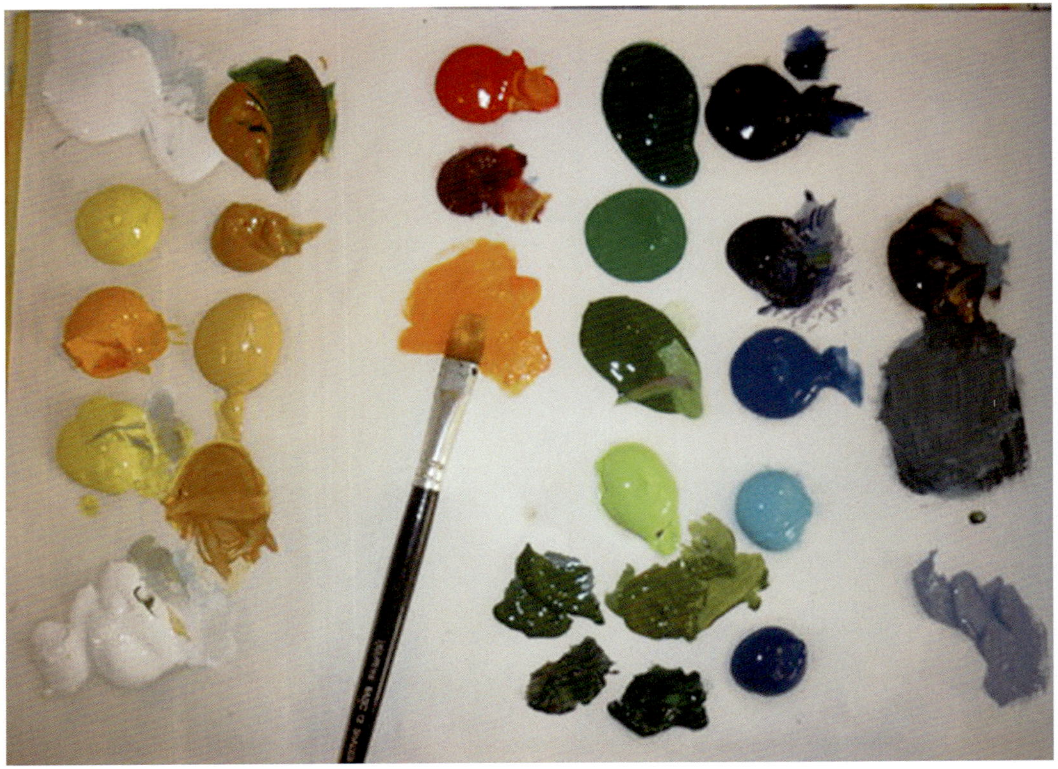

Denise's palette of colors

Yuba Rendezvous

about once a year
we take half a day
at the river
and after a long
winter silence
return to
the deep green
rock sun stillness
recounting the last
many months
how we are
restoring our
energies
divine threads
of art and song
weaving through
grief rising in layers
things that must end
how to be brave
enough to tell
the whole story
love of our families
inner life
artistic breakthrough
our toes dipping
into snowmelt
as we step forward
out of the shadows

—Lil McGill

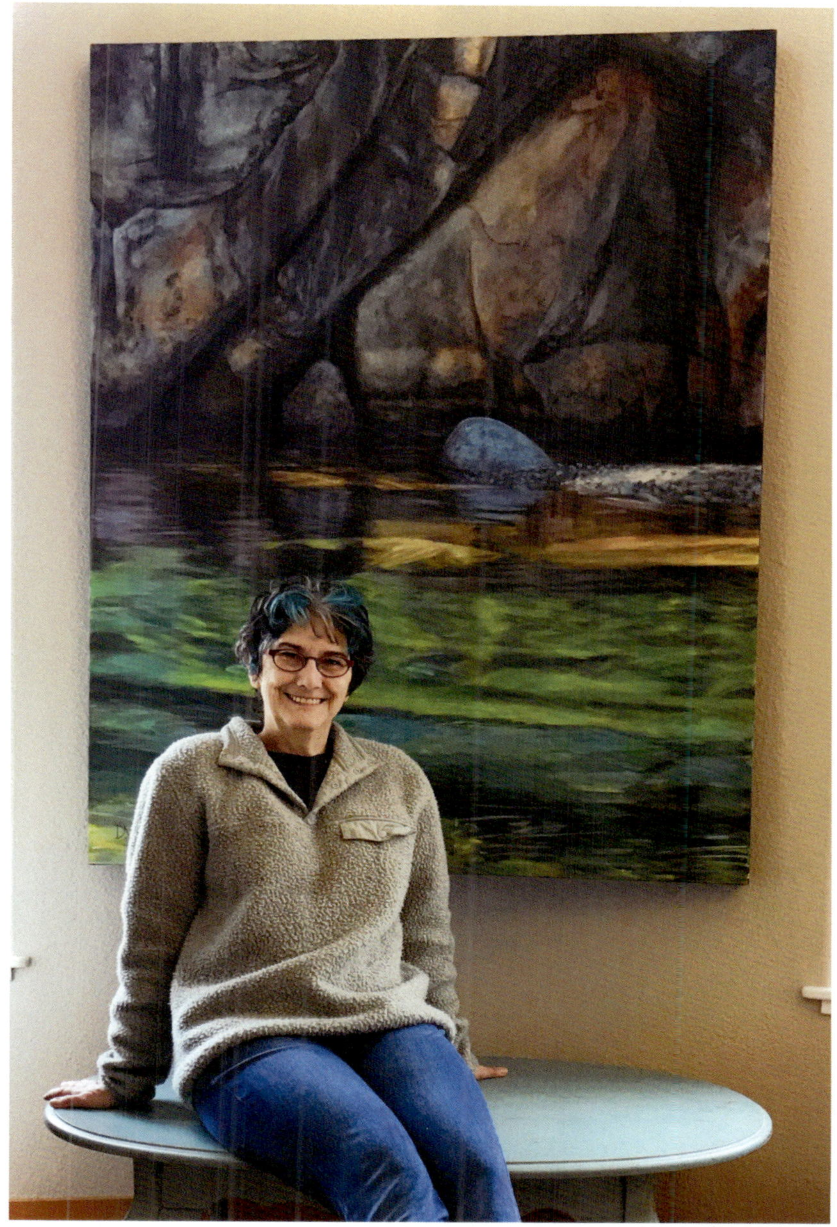

Earth Meditation
60″ x 48″
acrylic on canvas
private collection

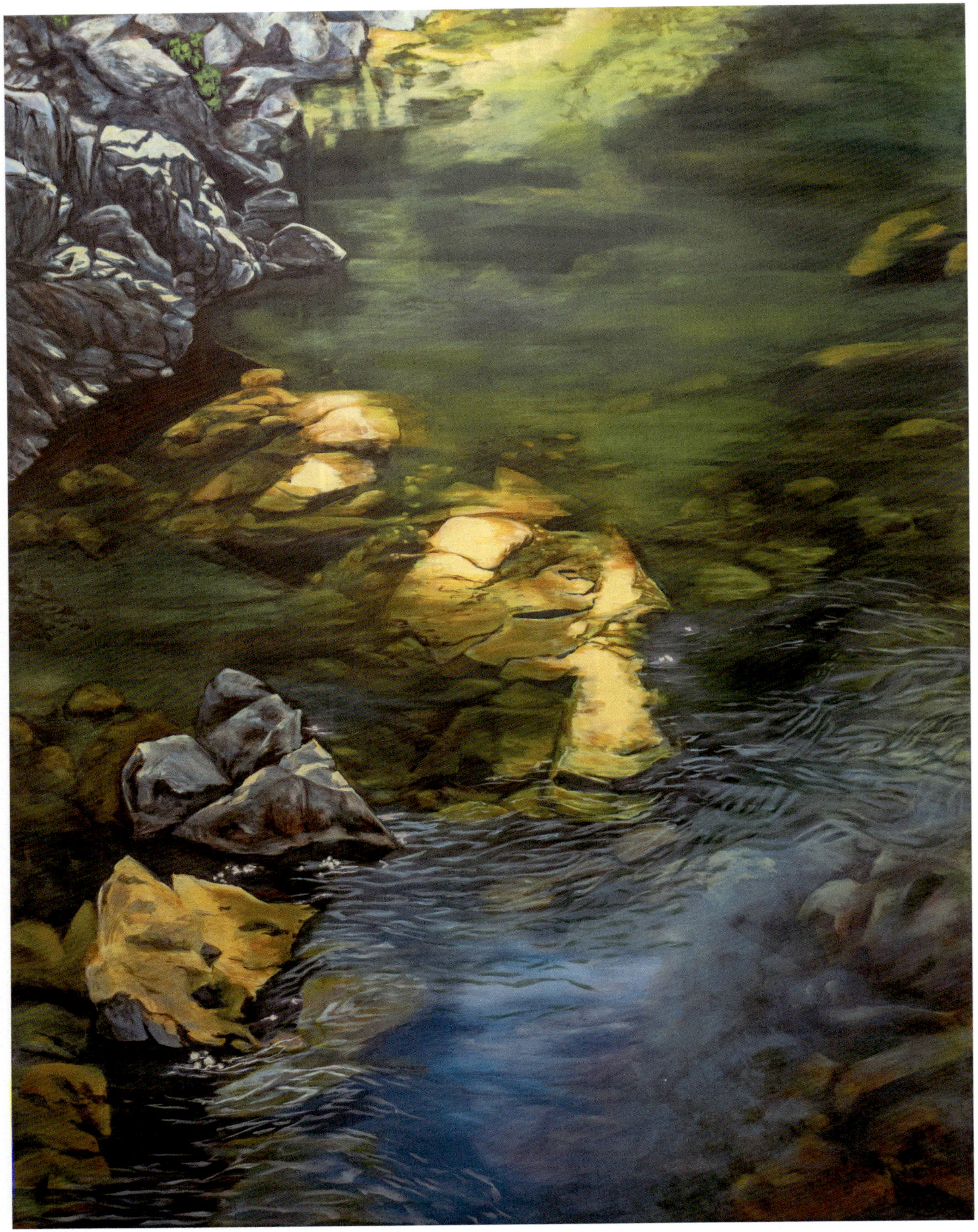

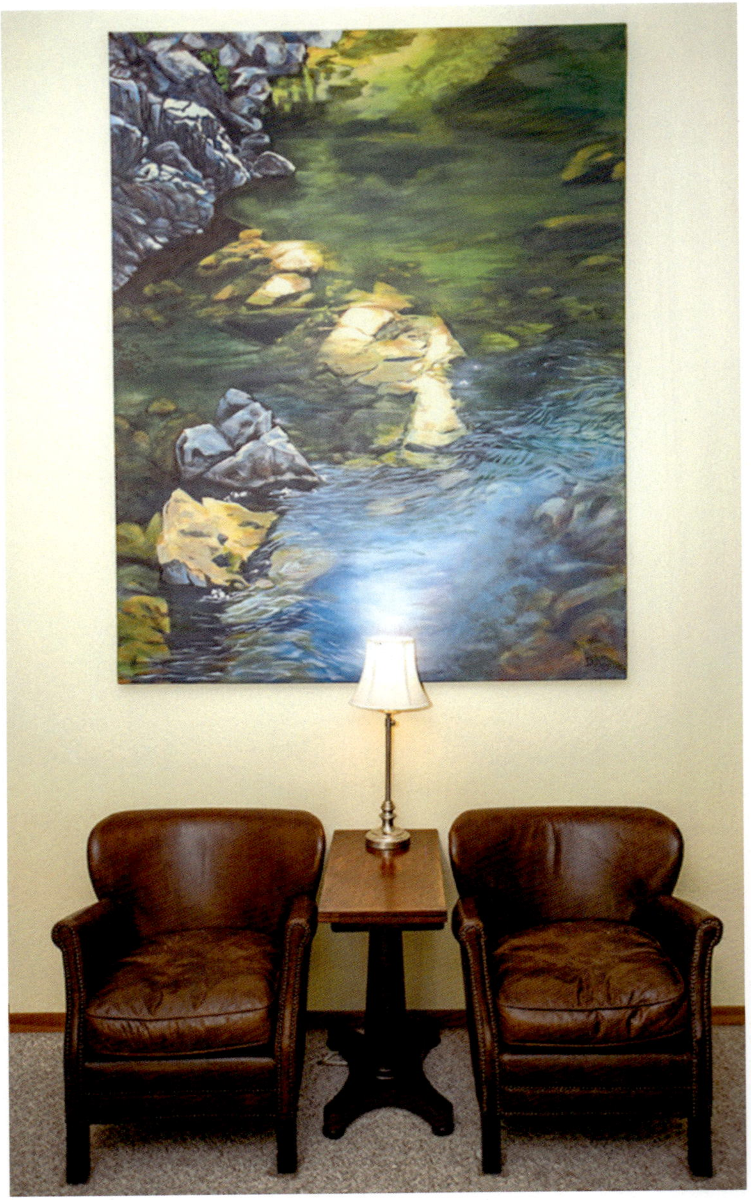

in situ

Amber and Emeralds, #105
78″ x 60″
acrylic on birch panel
private collection

One's way of painting and what one paints is a work in progress that evolves as long as the artist lives and breathes. This is how I paint now.

The image is rendered onto the canvas with the spark of inspiration that comes at the beginning. Next, the first layer of light and shadows is brushed in. This is what artists refer to as value. Now the painting stands as a value underpainting which reveals the composition or structure of the painting. At this point you can see what it may become.

The painting comes into being layer by layer—each one taking several hours—each layer applied as if it were the last, meaning that if I didn't touch the painting again, it should look complete. This doesn't always happen but is true a lot of the time.

Keeping hold of the unity of the vision sustained as one unbroken thread of consciousness, layer by layer as it comes through, is the goal.

Color mixing is a delicate and refined process to arrive at just the right tone. There are so many colors in a painting and each must harmonize with the others. I use many transparent layers and glazes. Much time is spent getting the color harmonies just right. I also spend a lot of time looking at the paintings, sometimes with other artists, whose fresh eyes often provide insights.

Painting is available to everyone. However, if you take it up be prepared to push through some struggles. That it is a demanding journey is the challenge that makes the reward so much more exhilarating!

I never really know what will actually be produced and even though I may have an idea at the beginning of the painting, it may take another direction entirely. That's part of the fascination of painting and perhaps part of the alchemy of the process, also. There's some magic involved.

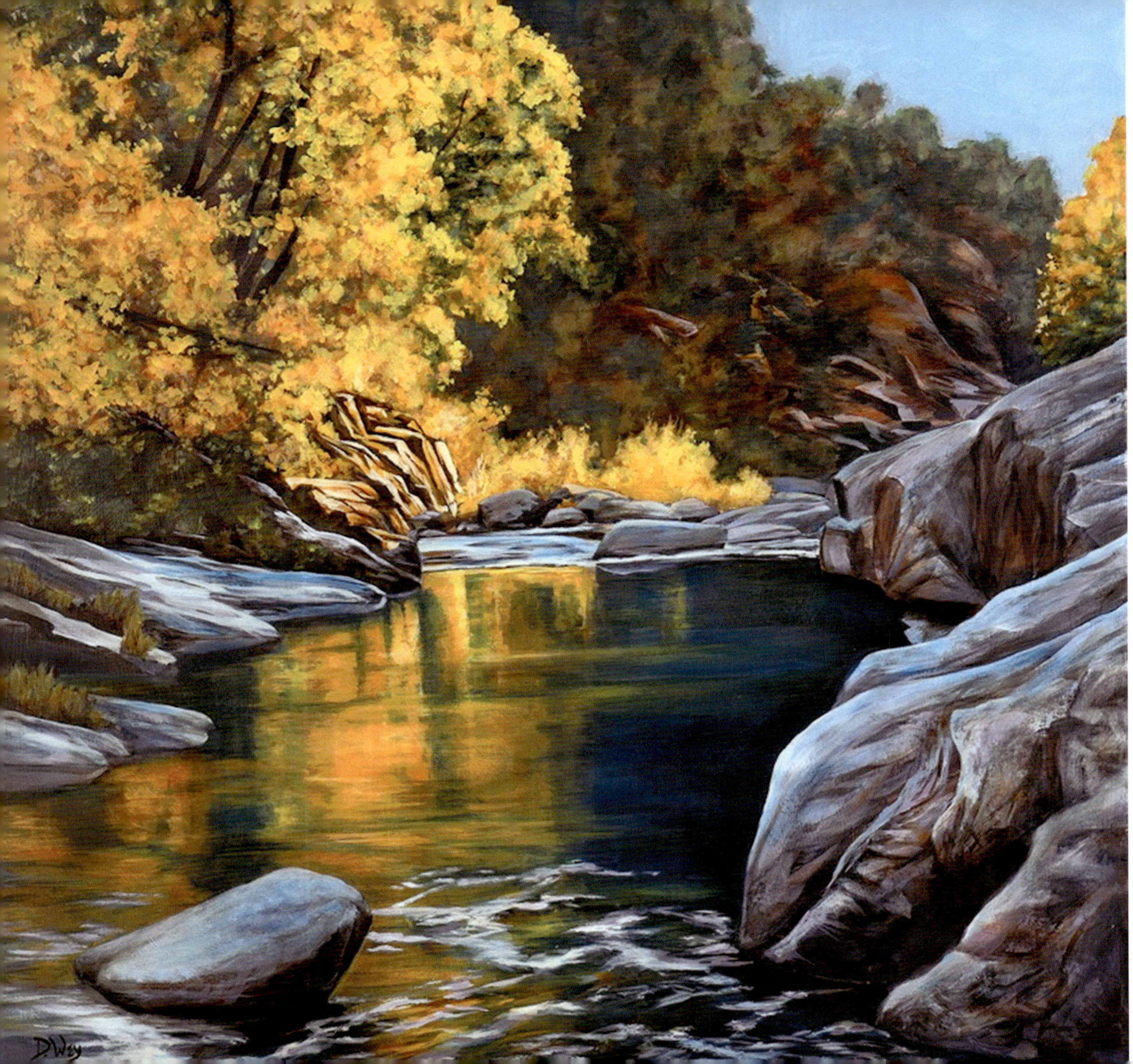

Serenity, #088
36″ x 36″
acrylic on panel
private collection

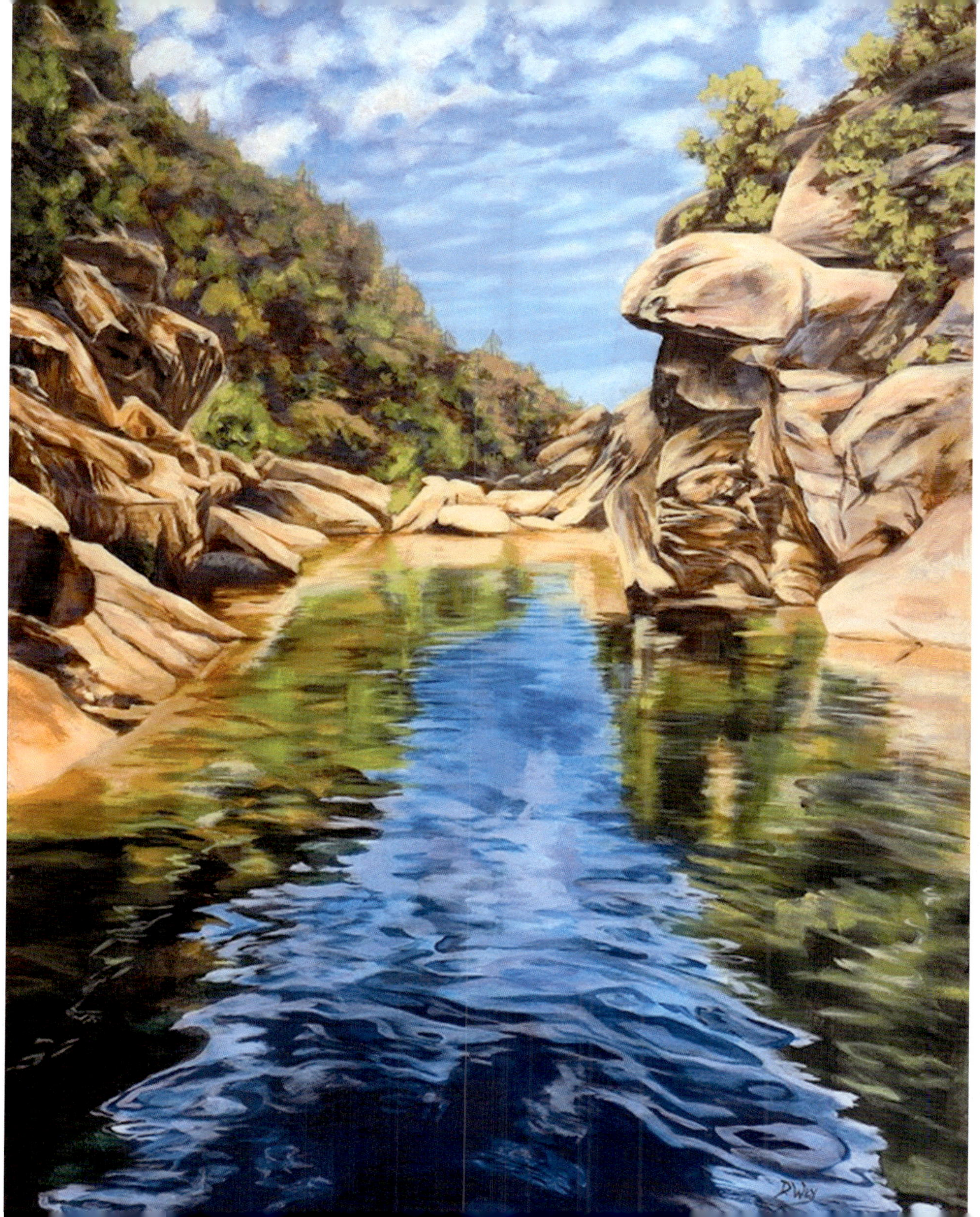

Ascend to Sky II, #089
40″ x 30″
acrylic on canvas

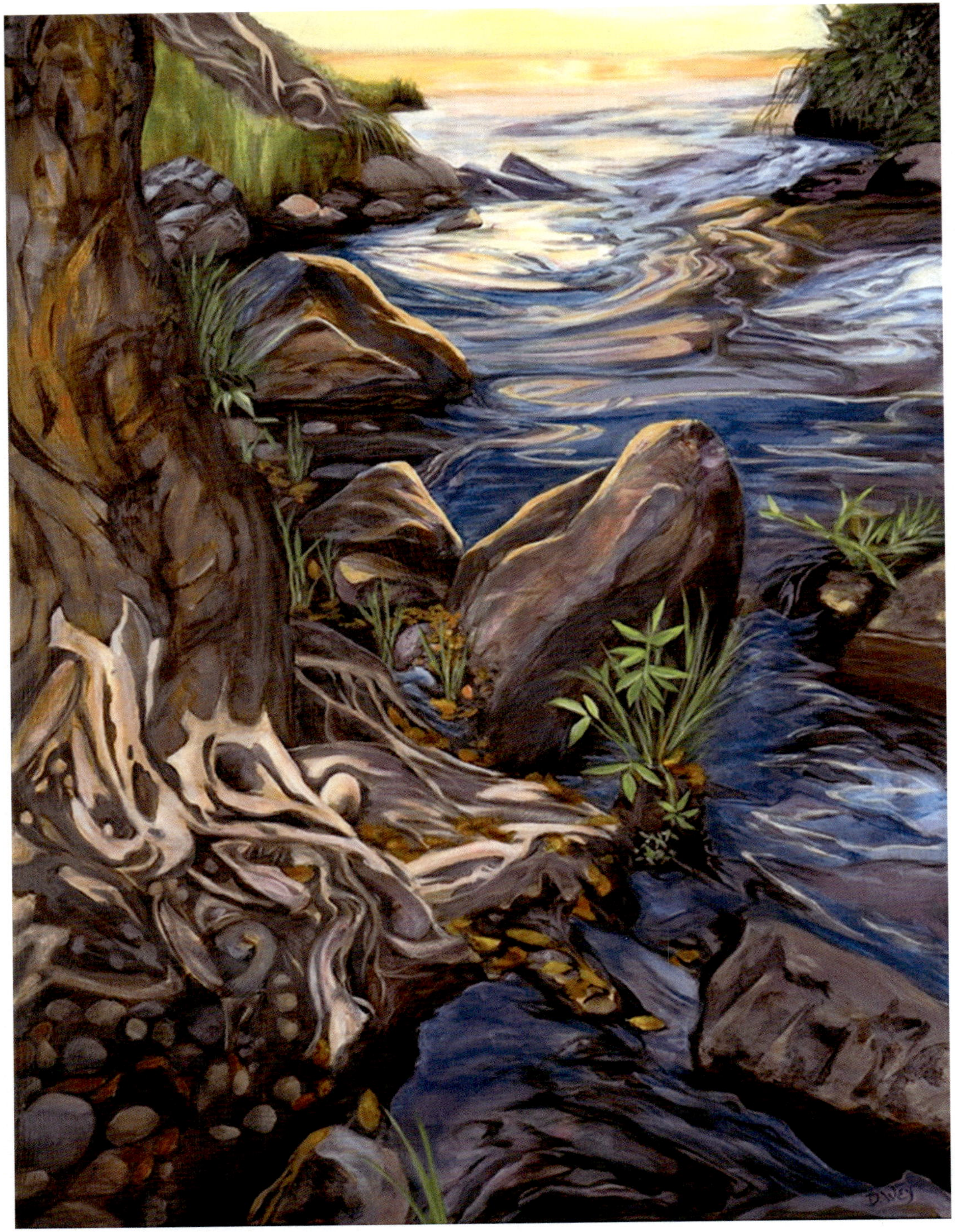

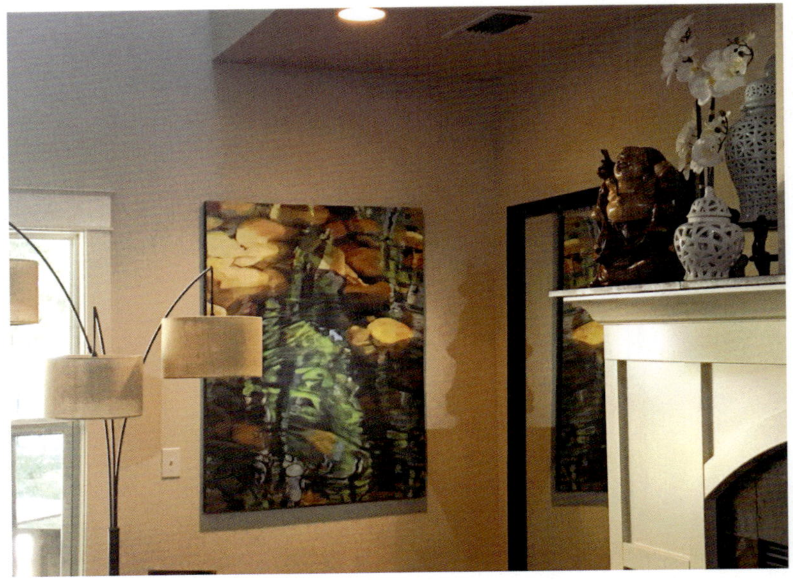

in situ

Fairy Village, #093
40″ x 30″
acrylic on canvas

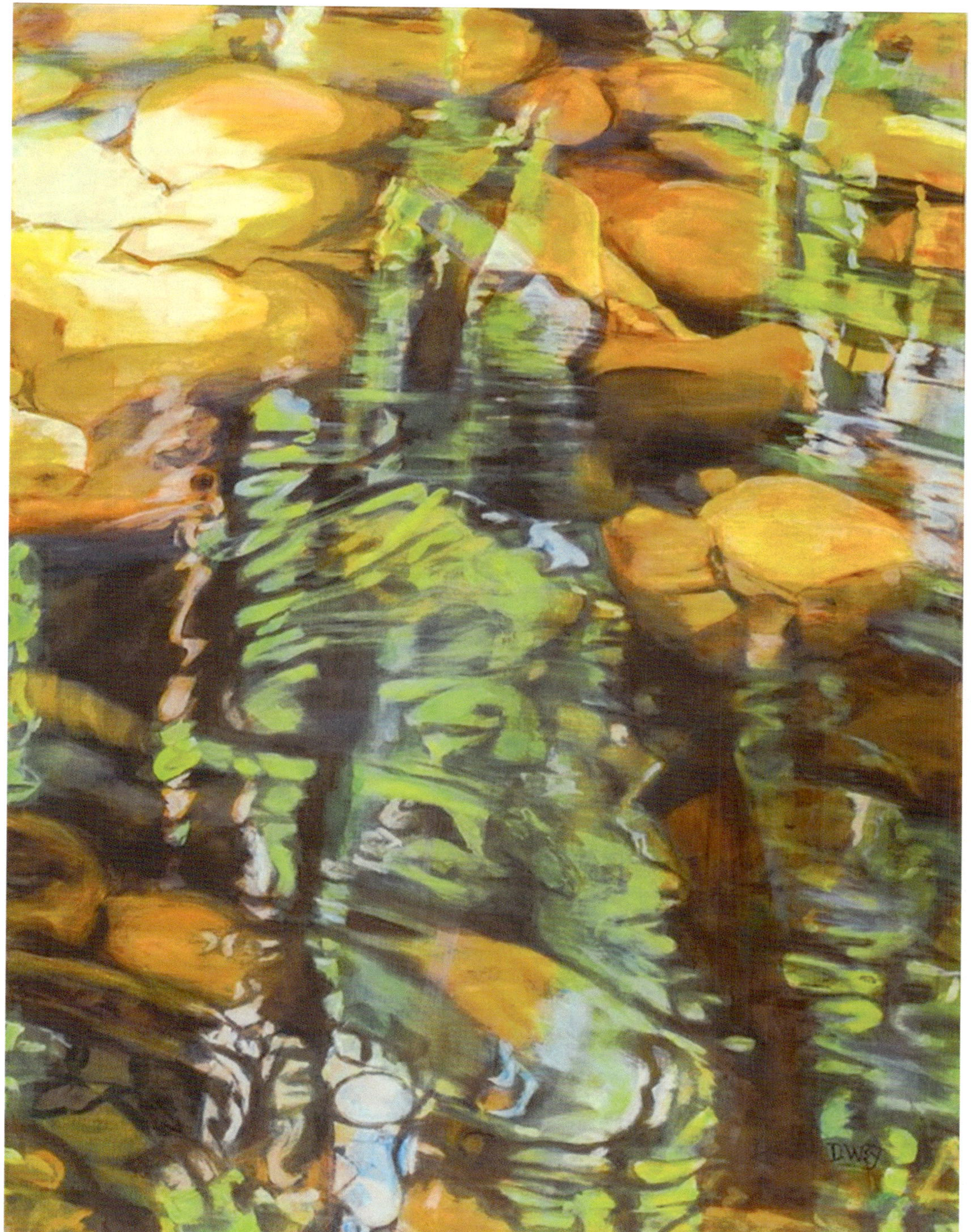

Cool Clear Water, #096
48″ x 36″
acrylic on canvas
private collection

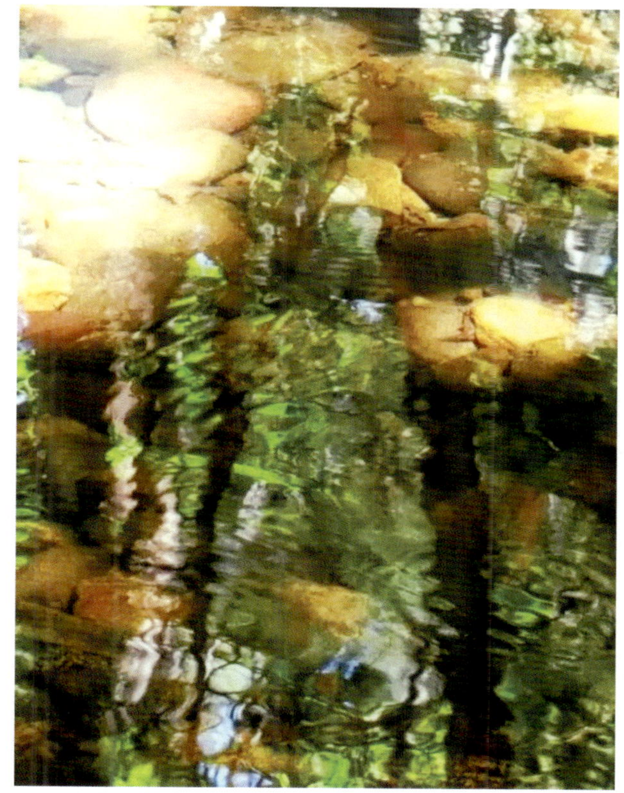

photo credit: Jill Stone

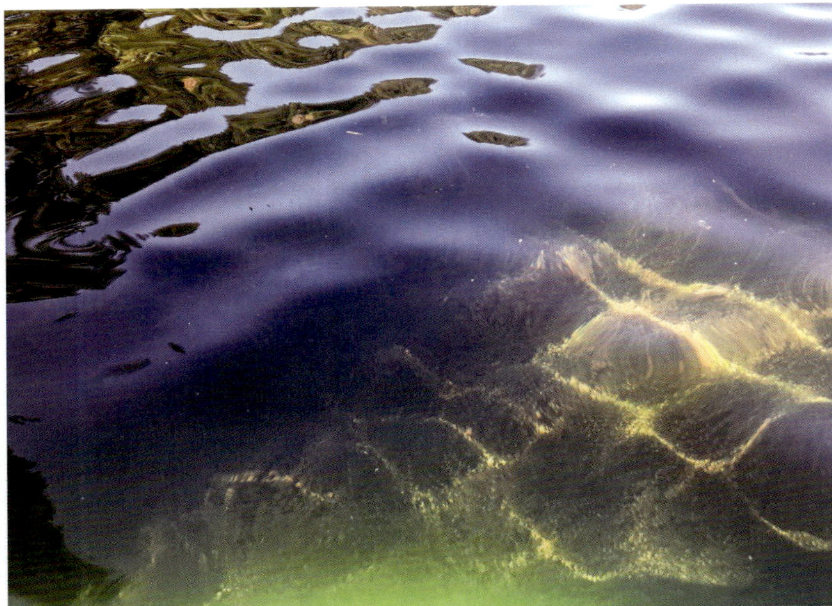

photo credit: Patricia O'Connor

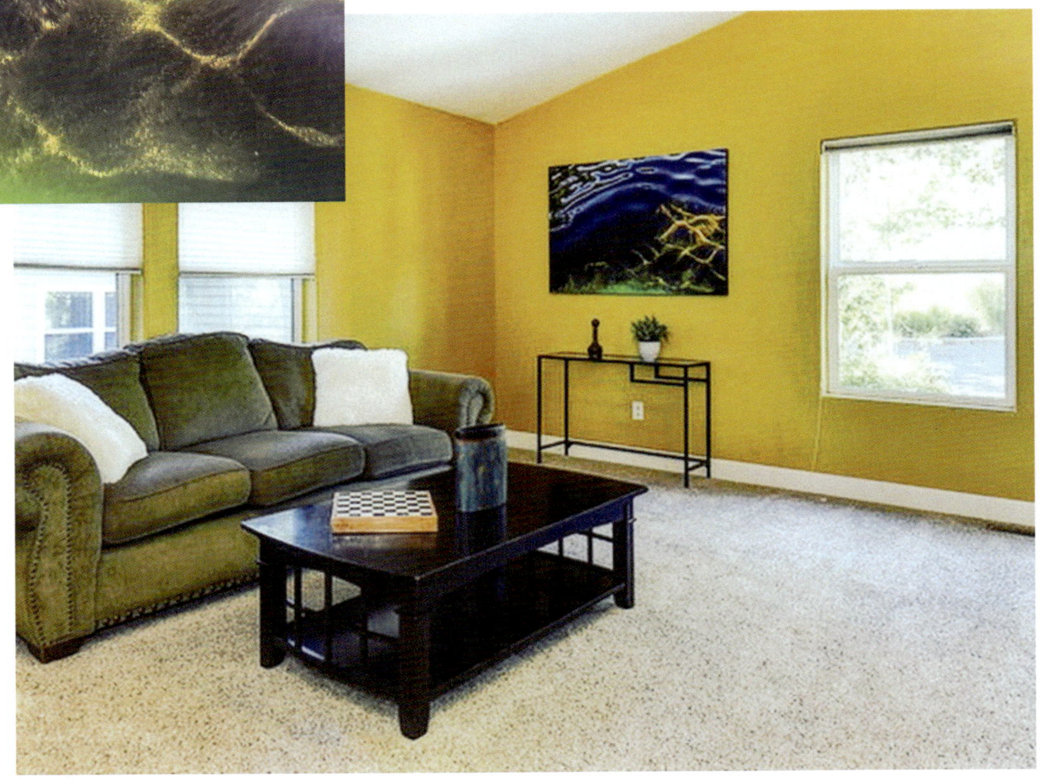

in situ

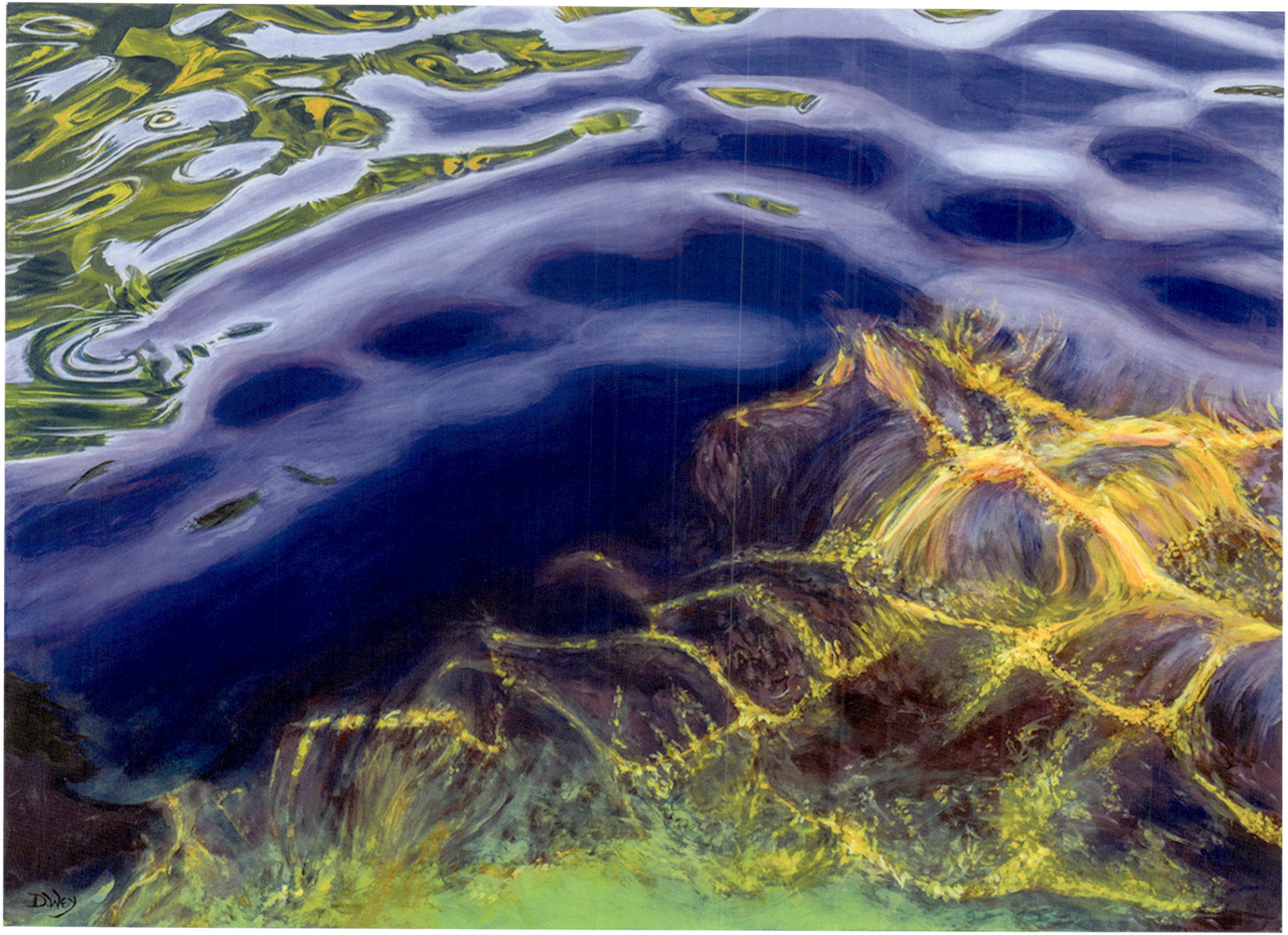

River Meditation II, #097, 36″ x 48″, acrylic on canvas, private collection

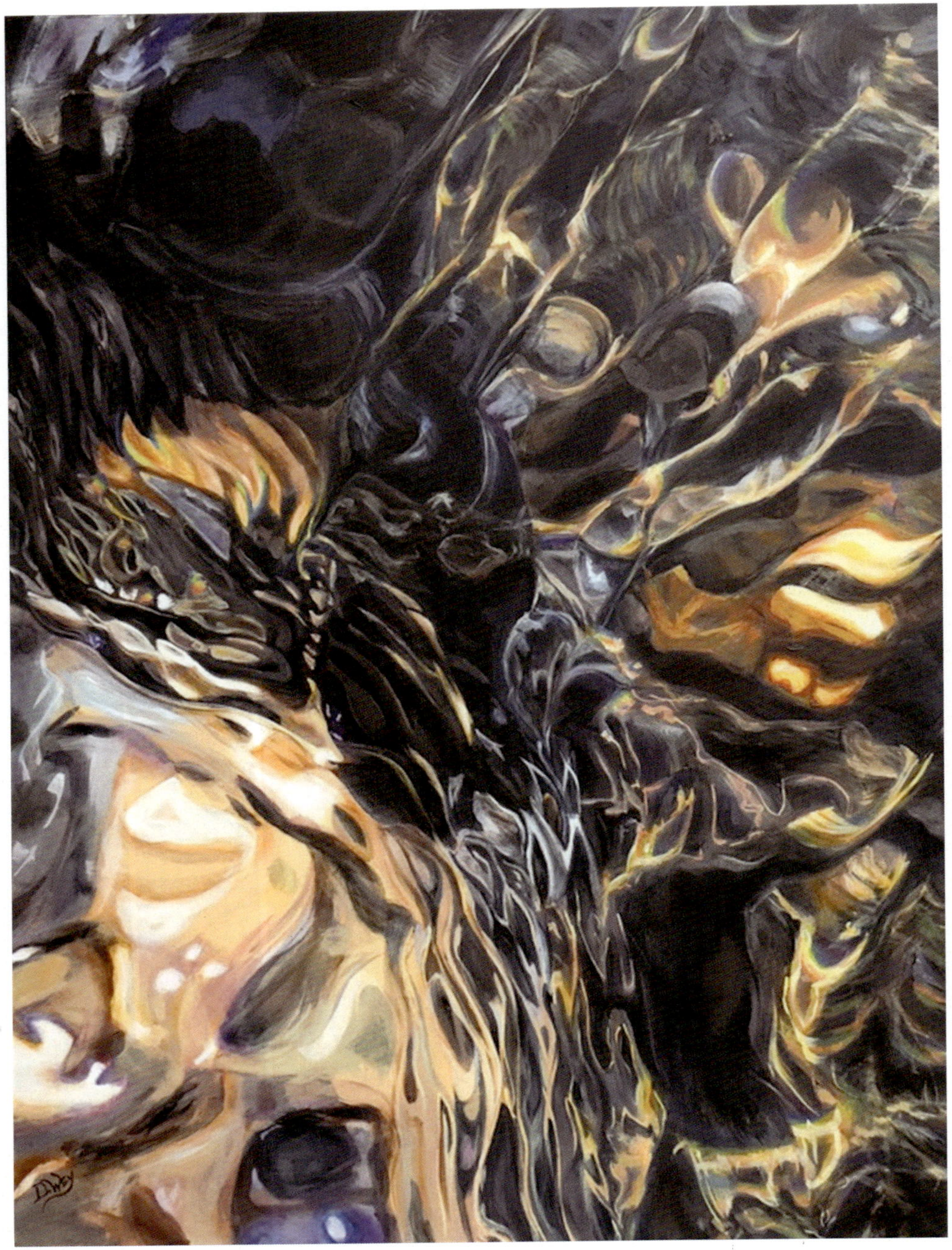

River Alchemy II, #091, 40″ x 30″, acrylic on canvas

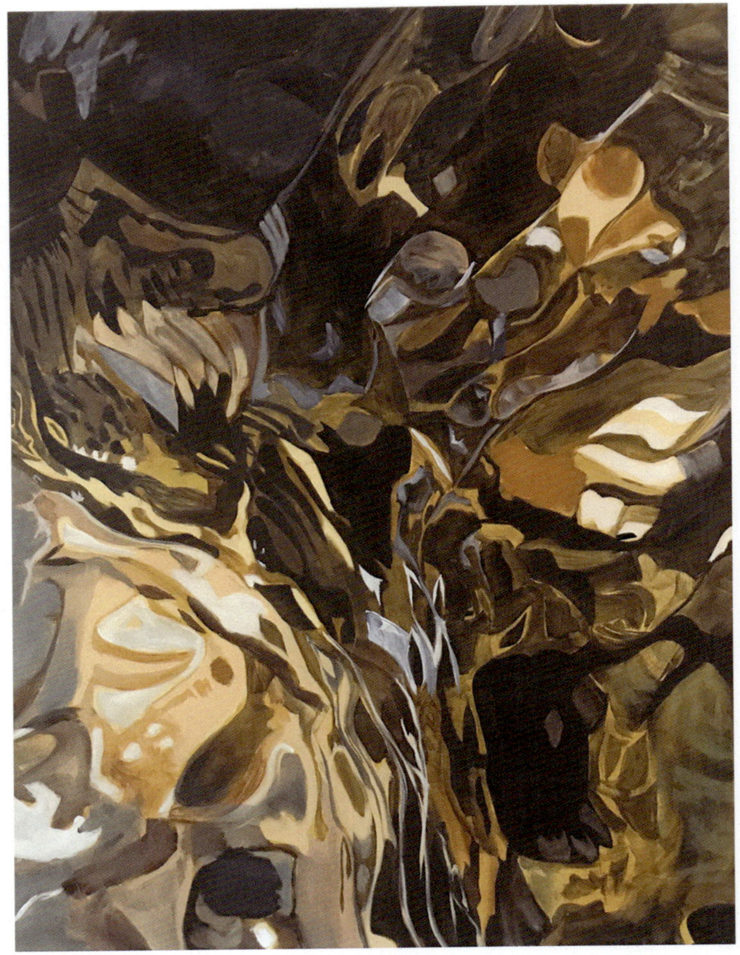

River Alchemy II in progress

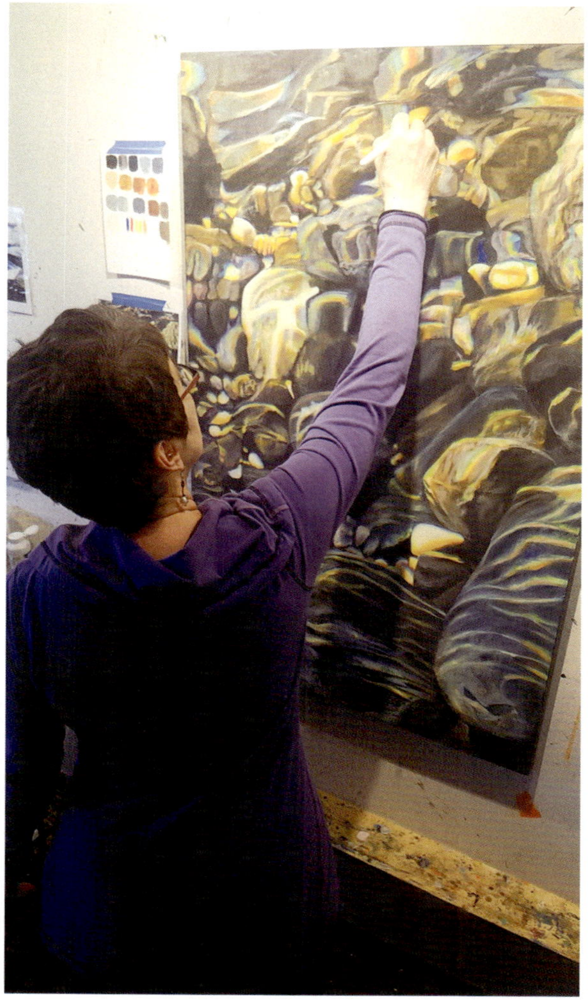

photo credit: Della Heywood

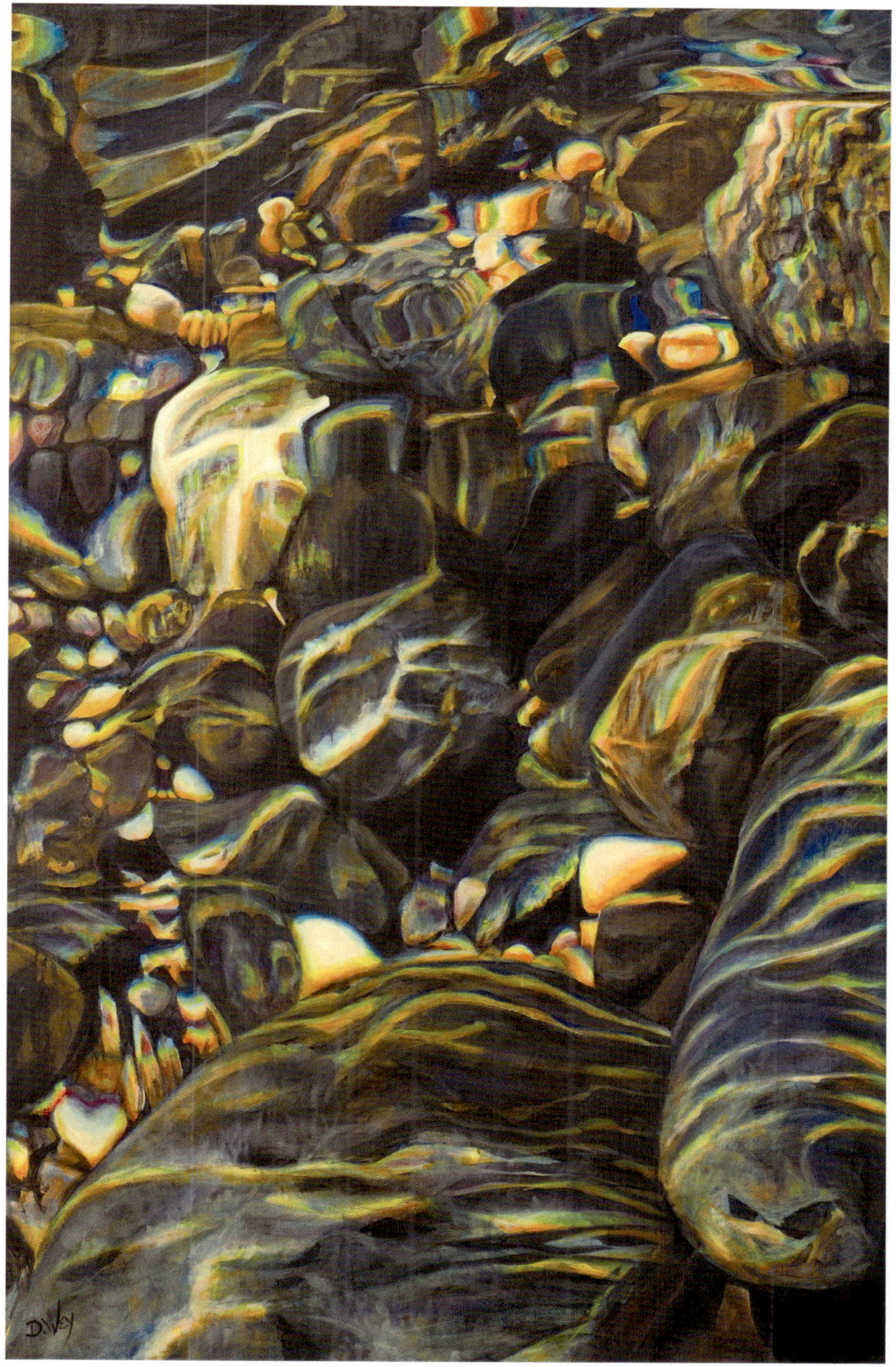

River Alchemy V, #103
30″ x 48″
acrylic on canvas

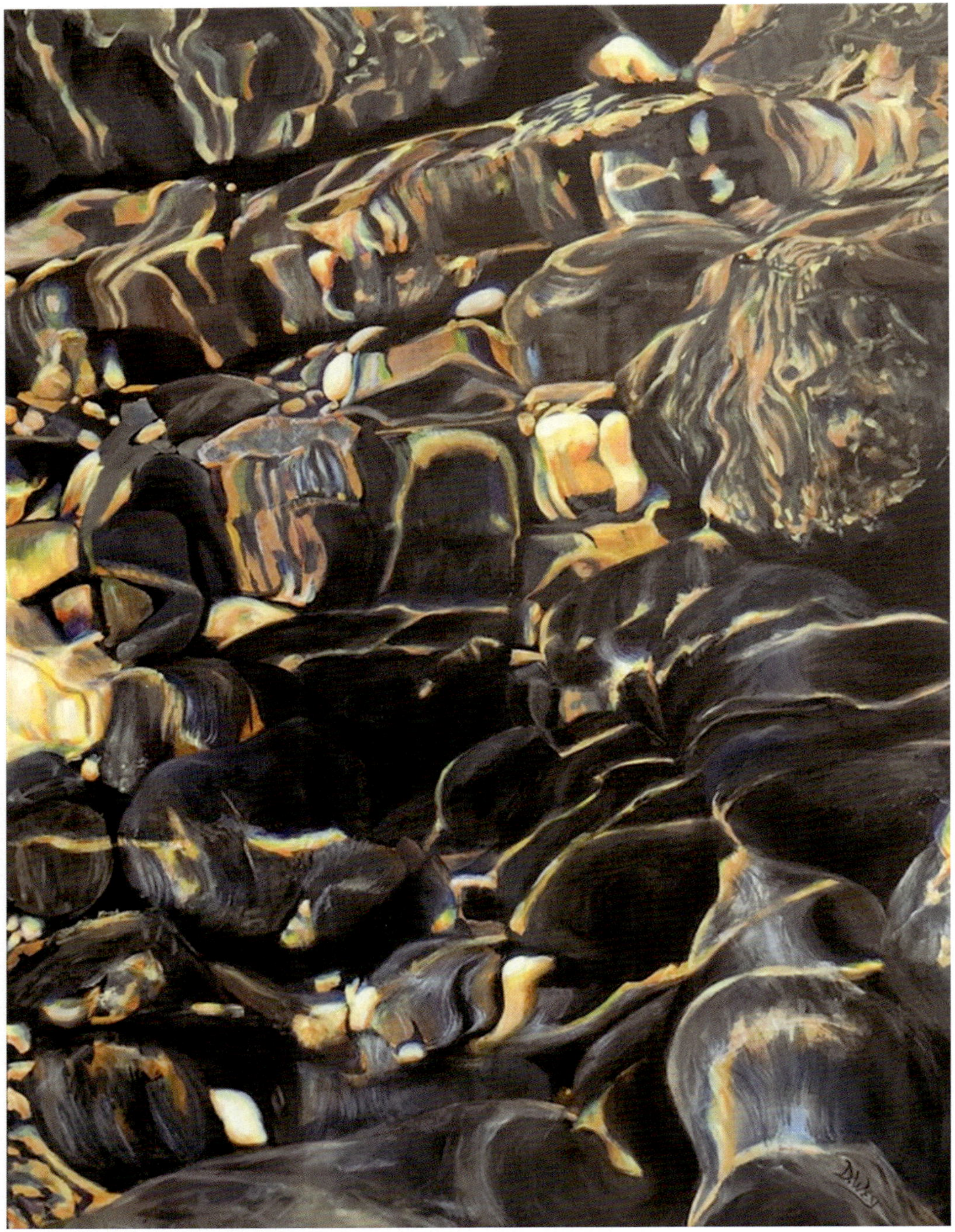

River Alchemy III, #092, 40″ x 30″, acrylic on canvas

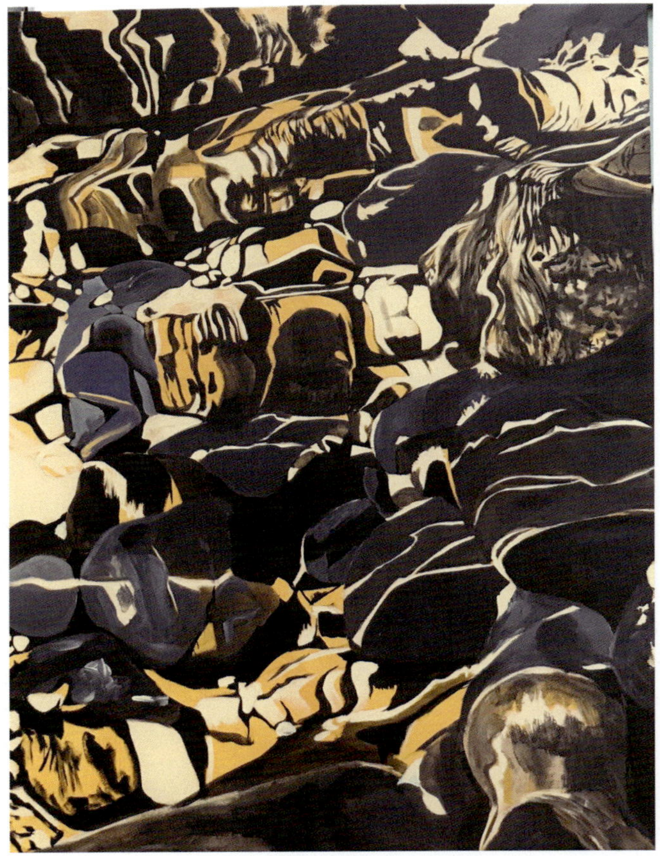

River Alchemy III in progress

This River Alchemy series came into being; these paintings are close-ups of river rocks under very shallow water with rainbow prisms showing the movement of light and flow of the river. The very act of drafting these patterns onto the canvas seemed to reveal the secret DNA of the meeting of the elements in that one moment in time. My job was not to interfere or even to understand but to facilitate a communication of sorts that seemed to want to happen. Painting is very intuitive.

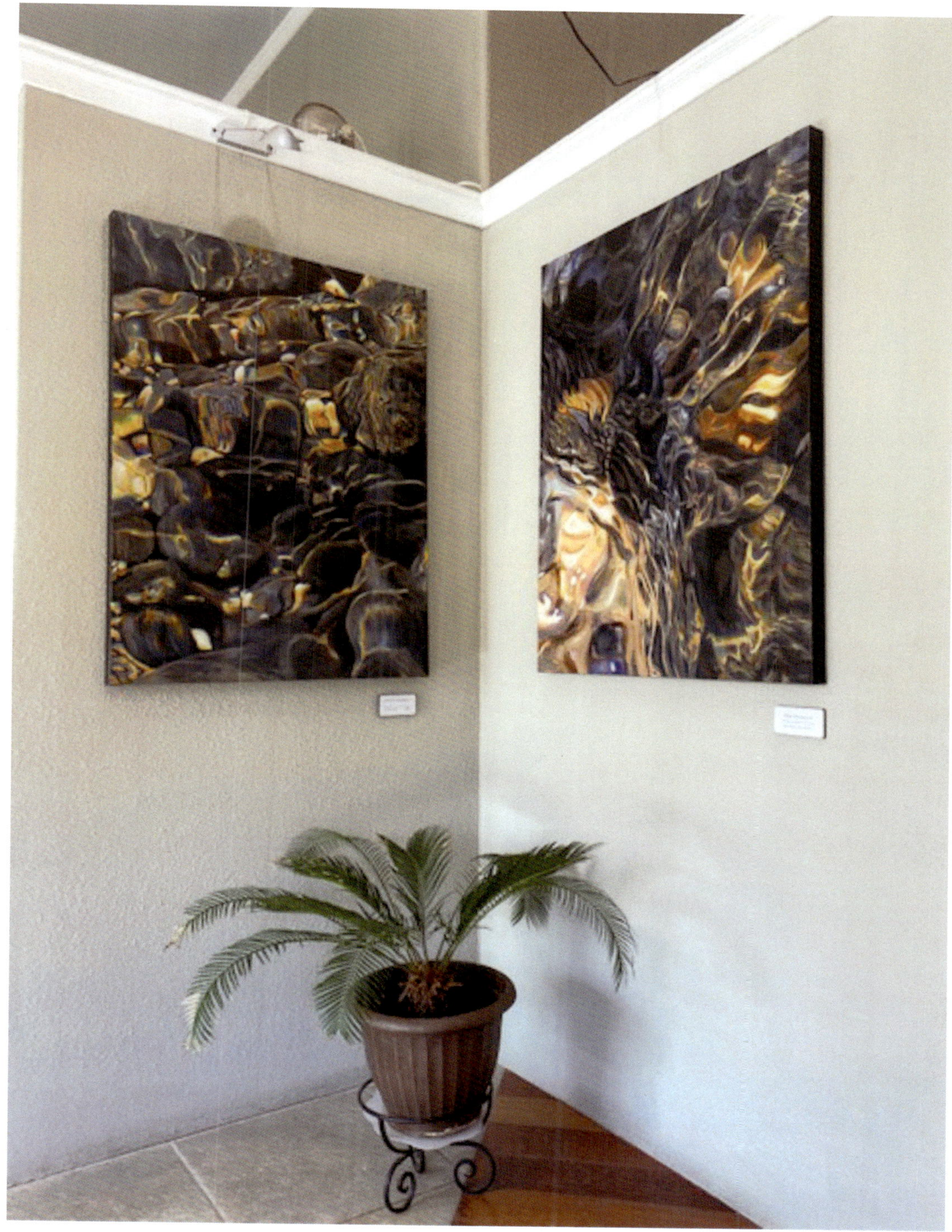

in situ

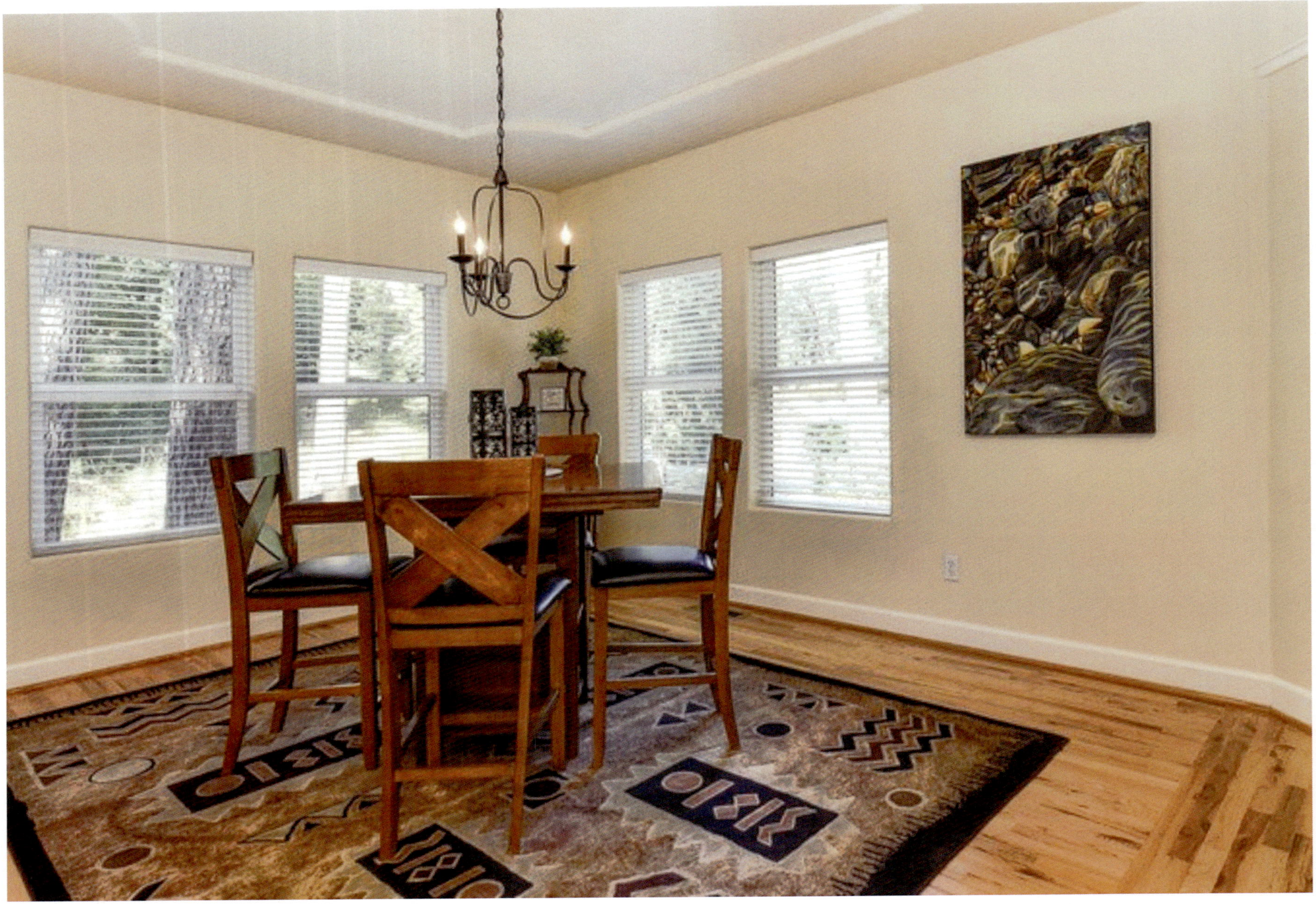

in situ

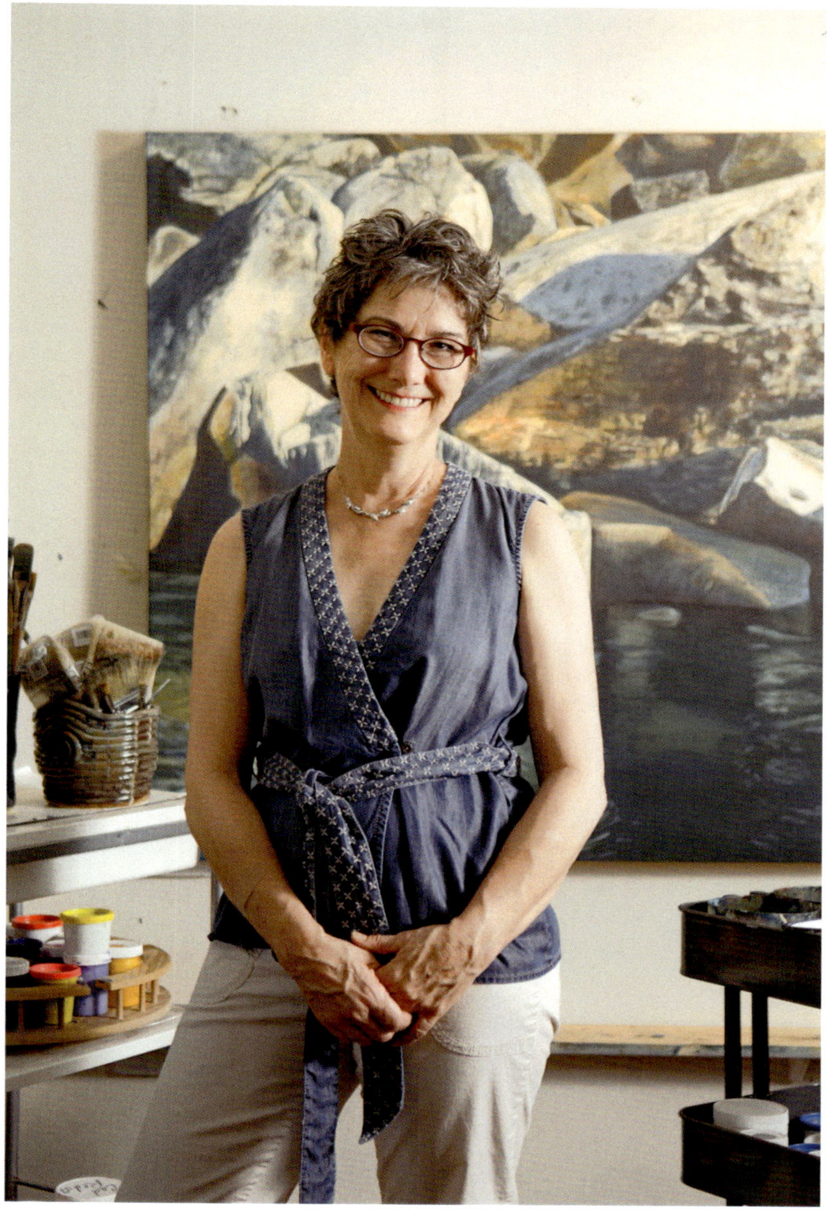

Denise in her studio
photo credit: Annabelle Schossig

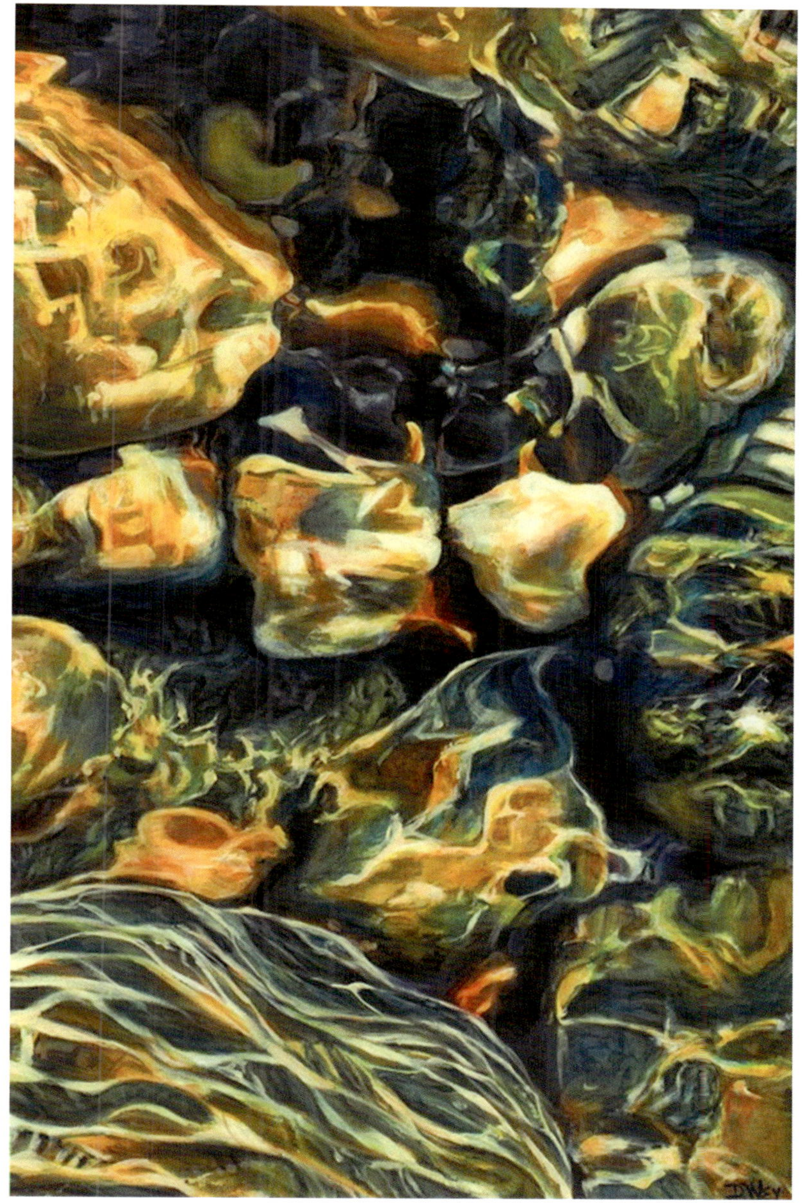

River Alchemy, #101
36″ x 24″, acrylic on canvas

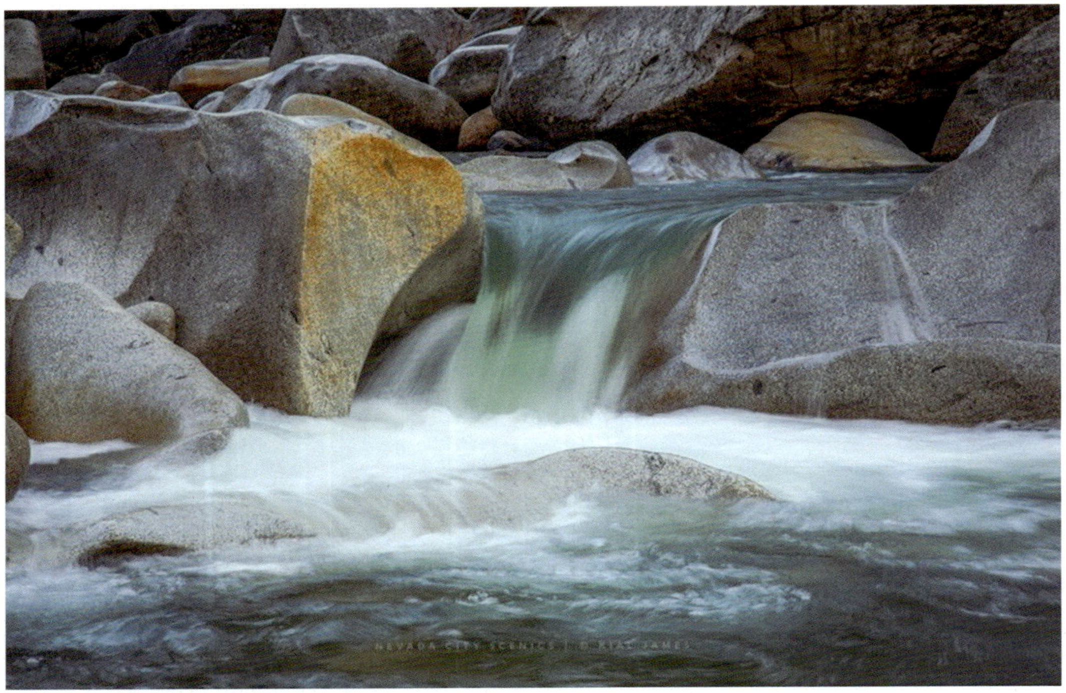

photo credit: Kial James Photography

A few large linen panels were bestowed on me this past year and I used one for this painting, "Breathe". These panels have a rather rough nubbly linen texture that is a dream to paint on.

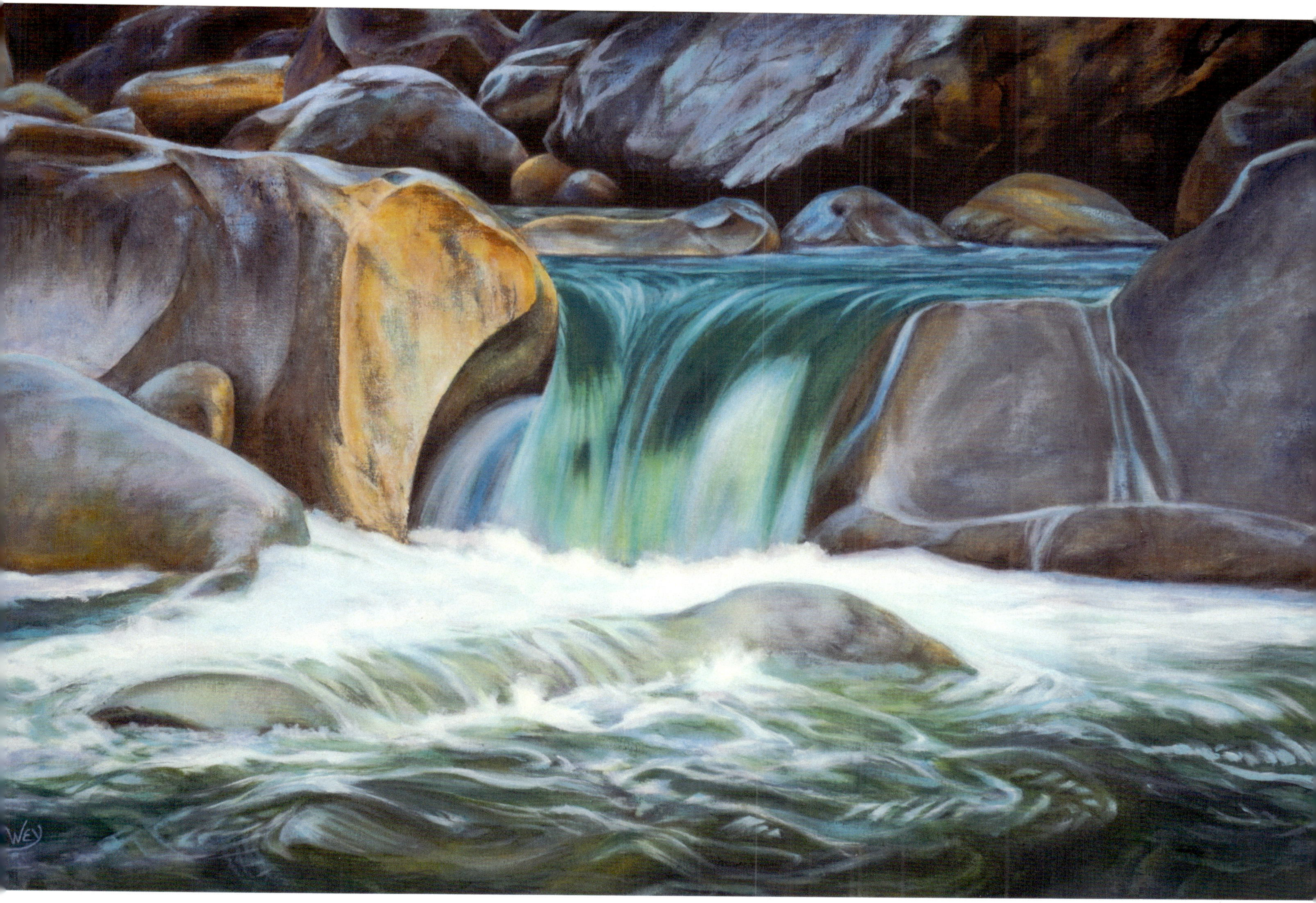

Breathe, #104, 48″ x 72″, acrylic or linen panel

AFTERWORD

Our breathtakingly beautiful river inspires adventures, paintings, prose and song for many of us. It is alive, vibrant and sacred and is truly the heart's blood of our community.

My original inspiration for this book was to contain all of my paintings of the last 22 years in one place, but turned into an experience of reflection about my artist journey. Working to put coherent concepts into written words opened windows for me. I even had a dream directly related to my paintings that contributed to a deeper understanding of why I do what I do.

The dream was centered around a "game'" that was taking place, where the secret goal was the transformative realization of the true self of each participant. To be successful, they must struggle to wade through personality and earthly baggage to reveal themselves with their true purpose and why they were here. I awoke to wonder about its meaning, and these dream fragments fell into place:

- Do what you love because Love energy heats the atoms and gets things circulating.
- Challenge yourself with Work that develops tools of awareness, attention and presence for sustained inner clarity and vision.
- Persist, for Will is the force that can reveal and move Purpose to manifest the results you seek.

Painting is my real work. I've chosen a path that matches my spirit's evolutionary yearning. My work may look like art and painting rivers. But my soul's purpose is to grow and evolve through this. What I'm really doing is learning to kindle purpose and will through the unrelenting focus of presence and attention. Love is the way through.

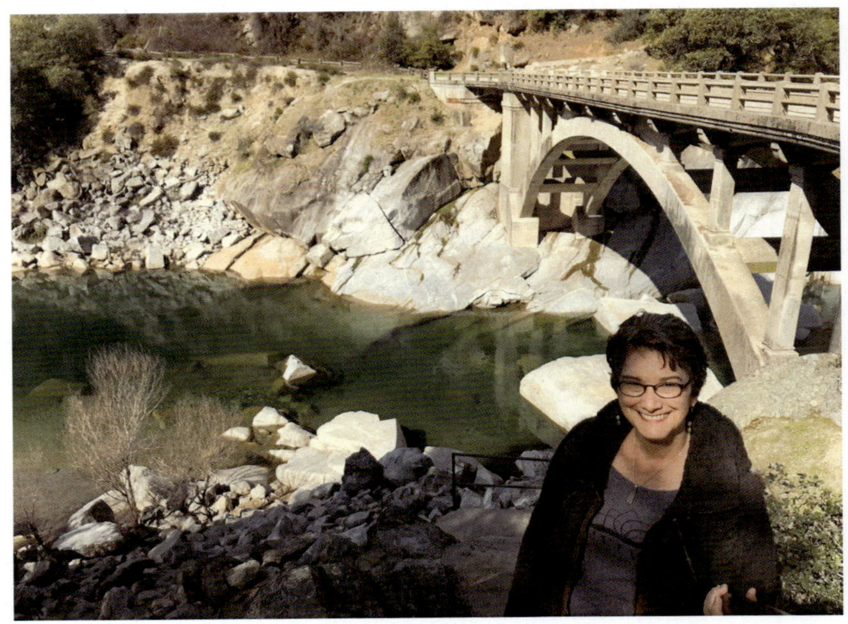

photo credit: Christena Wiebe

ACKNOWLEDGEMENTS:

In this space, I'd like to thank those who directly helped me bring this book into being:

E.J. Gold, thank you for your inspiration and making space for me to be more.

Lil McGill, thank you for your beautiful words and impeccable creativity guidance.

Della Heywood, thank you for your fine artistic eye and unending support on what matters.

Iven Lourie, thank you for your expertise in writing and editing and the enthusiasm you generate for other people's projects.

Gailyn Porter, thank you for your skill in layout and design and your kind generosity.

Flo Fahrenheit, thank you for your competent help with editing and for somehow managing to always show up at the right moment.

Chic Lotz, thank you for sharing the best part of your world with me.

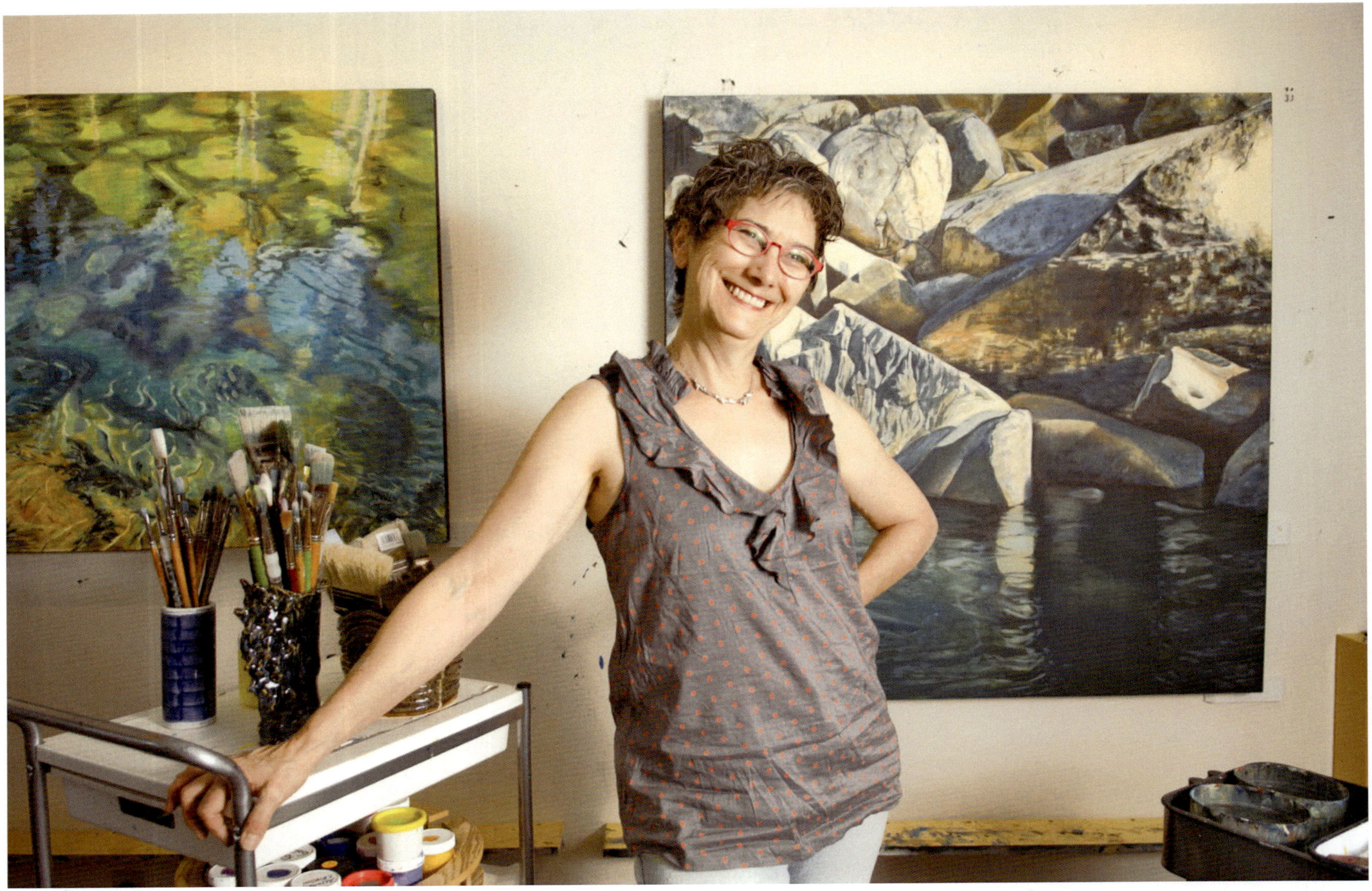

photo credit: Annabelle Schossig

ABOUT THE ARTIST AND HER WORK

Denise Wey is a painter and teaching-artist residing in Nevada County, a small arts community in the Sierra Nevada Foothills of Northern California. A fine artist most of her life, she has worked in many art mediums besides acrylic painting—fine art serigraphy, textiles, pottery—and also ran a successful jewelry design studio before moving to California in the late 80's.

Here, Denise has found her muse in the beautiful Yuba River which she has painted for over two decades. Her vibrant, large-format paintings grace many homes in the county and beyond, bringing the river indoors where it can be enjoyed every day.

Denise has a passion not only for painting, but also for teaching. Generations of children have blossomed as artists under her loving and enthusiastic guidance, and some have gone on to become professional artists themselves.

Many adults have been introduced to the joy of painting and drawing in Denise's classes. She continues to teach classes in person and online.

Denise invites commissions. Have your favorite river spot painted.
To view her portfolio, order prints of paintings found in this book or explore classes
please contact her at dwey@denisewey.com
or visit her website: WWW.DENISEWEY.COM